ESSENTIAL INTERVIEWING

A programmed approach to effective communication

ESSENTIAL INTERVIEWING

A programmed approach to effective communication

David R. Evans
The University of Western Ontario
Margaret T. Hearn
War Memorial Children's Hospital
London, Ontario
Max R. Uhlemann
The University of Victoria
Allen E. Ivey
The University of Massachusetts

Brooks/Cole Publishing Company
Monterey, California
A Division of Wadsworth, Inc.

Printed in the United States of America

10 9 8 7 6 5 4 3 2 1

Library of Congress Cataloging in Publication Data
Main entry under title:

Essential interviewing.

Includes index.
1. Interviewing. I. Evans, David Russell
BF637.15E87   158'.3   79-13719
ISBN 0-8185-0342-4

PHOTO CREDITS: p. 1 © *Emilio A. Mercado;* pp. 16, 108, 184, 226 © *Karen R. Preuss;* p. 38 © *Suzanne Arms;* p. 60 © *Peeter Vilms;* p. 85 © *Russell Abraham;* p. 135 © *Elizabeth Crews;* p. 160 © *Philip Jon Bailey;* p. 200 © *B. Kliewe.* All photographs courtesy of Jeroboam, Inc.

Project Development Editor: *Ray Kingman*
Production Editor: *Robert Rowland*
Interior and Cover Design: *Ruth Scott*
Typist: *Donna Sharp*

preface

This book grew out of the need for an economical and experiential method of training individuals in the essential skills of effective interpersonal communication. Although there are a number of training programs in communication skills, the majority of them are offered only within the context of a structured workshop. The material in this book was developed to present to a broad audience the essentials of good communication in an individualized, readily available manner. The skills examined here are central to effective interaction in a variety of face-to-face situations. Competent interviewers, regardless of orientation and degree of training, find these skills basic to their relationships with clients. Physicians, nurses, ministers, teachers, psychologists, counselors, and other professionals use these skills repeatedly. Paraprofessionals, from crisis workers to community volunteers, require these skills to function in their daily activities. Parents note improvements in their relationships with their children when they implement the skills discussed in this book. Marriage partners can utilize the material presented here in their endeavors to improve their relationships with one another. The information and exercises offered here can be applied to personnel interviews, business conferences, and the development of harmonious work relationships.

A group of core communication skills is essential to any interview, whether it takes place in counseling, nursing, social work, personnel work, or information gathering. This book defines these communication skills and demonstrates how they may be used effectively in a wide array of situations.

Essential Interviewing, with its emphasis on the development of particular skills, may be employed as a self-training medium or as the basic material for courses or workshops. The mastery of any skill is dependent on practice. Chapter 1 outlines the ways in which the skills examined in this book may be practiced and utilized. Chapters 2 through 6 focus on building rapport and seeking information—skills that are basic to all effective communication. Chapters 7 through 11 deal with specific skills that may help you in effecting change. The Additional Resources includes a list of books that can be used in conjunction with this text.

We wish to acknowledge the support and cooperation of the members of Contact, the hotline in London, Ontario, and the administration, staff development personnel, and nurses of St. Thomas Psychiatric Hospital. We also wish to acknowledge the assistance of our colleagues and students at the University of Western Ontario for their kindly criticism and support. We especially wish to thank Pat Kubowski and Brenda Bannerman for their assistance in gathering material for the chapters on self-disclosure and confrontation respectively, and Gerald L. Stone for his helpful comments concerning the chapter on structuring. Thanks also go to Louise Pace of Freed-Hardeman College, Fred C. Pearman of South Oklahoma City Junior College, Florence L. Phillips of Texas Tech University, Barbara Vance of Brigham Young University, and Ellen Wallach for their reviews of the original manuscript of this book. Finally, we wish to thank Sandy Leboldus, Dianne McCormack, and Helen Etherington for their assistance in the preparation of the manuscript.

David R. Evans
Margaret T. Hearn
Max R. Uhlemann
Allen E. Ivey

contents

Chapter 1
GETTING
SET

Rather than tell you what to do, we will ask you to participate actively by dealing with actual interview material, choosing the appropriate response, and practicing the essential dimensions of interviewing. You may expect to acquire a basic knowledge of the interviewing process, equip yourself with useful skills important in interviewing and in day-to-day interactions, and establish a foundation for further practice as you develop your own unique style of working with others.

Although the focus in this text is on the client, both interviewer and client grow in the process of effective interviewing. As you read and participate in the step-by-step process of this programmed text, you may encounter ideas and skills that you want to experiment with in your daily life—skills that can help you to understand others and yourself more completely. Moreover, as you develop competence in relating to others, you will find that the material presented here will help you to understand what skilled interviewers are doing and

1

will enable you to adopt the elements of their style that seem valuable to you.

An effective interviewer can make a tremendous difference in the life of another human being. Our intention here is to provide you with specific formulas and methods of relating that have been proven useful in a variety of situations. However, no one method or interviewing skill is appropriate in every situation or with every individual. Therefore, we return to *you*. You, as an interviewer, are the individual who can "make a difference" if you combine the ideas and skills presented here with your own personal knowledge and experience. Therefore, your task is to use this text as a tool—to challenge, evaluate, and shape the material in such a way that you maintain uniqueness, individuality, and a sense of personal genuineness in your relationships with others. Effective use of the tools of interviewing can enhance the development of another human being, whereas poor interviewing can be destructive. If the tools provided in this text become an end in themselves and you act as a slave to them, you cannot be an effective interviewer.

STEPS TOWARD CLARIFYING THE INTERVIEWING PROCESS

Counseling, psychotherapy, and interviewing are commonly seen as complex, almost mystical activities that have remained immune to systematic study and definition. However, several trends that have emerged in the last 30 years have made the art of interviewing more definable and specific. In this section, we present some major trends that have been especially influential in the development of more effective counselors, psychotherapists, and interviewers. First, we deal with client-centered counseling and the work of Carl Rogers. Next, we examine seemingly antagonistic behavioral approaches and the work of B. F. Skinner. In a final section, we discuss the impact of some of the new, popular forms of helping such as transactional analysis and gestalt therapy.

The most influential psychotherapist of modern times is Carl Rogers, whose *Counseling and Psychotherapy* (1942) brought a precision and clarity to the helping process that had never existed before. His "nondirective" approach placed special emphasis on listening carefully to the client and provided specific suggestions for helping others to change and grow. Over the years, Rogers has continued to enrich the helping profession with his innovations, writings, and faith in human potential. *On Becoming a Person* (1961) reflects a high point of interviewing analysis and discussion. Moreover, it must be pointed out that Rogers has continuously changed and modified his points of view. He provided strong impetus for the encounter-group movement and, more recently, has examined the issue of personal power in helping situations.

Thanks to Rogers, the concepts of warmth, empathy, and positive regard have become basic to the helping professions and have assumed an important place in the lives of humanistically oriented individuals in many fields. Rogers studied the existence or absence of these concepts, or core conditions of helping, by observing interviews through the then new medium of audiorecording. In 1957, he presented a three-step training program to teach the skills he considered important in constructive therapeutic intervention. First, he proposed that students listen to audiotapes of both experienced and inexperienced helpers. He assumed that this exercise would help the students to discriminate between good and bad interviewing methods in practice. Second, students observed experienced helpers conducting therapy sessions or participated directly as clients. In the third step of training, students conducted interviews with the direct supervision of an experienced helper.

Truax and Carkhuff (1967) have done much to operationalize the underlying dimensions of effective helping proposed by Rogers. They systematized Rogers' thinking and made his work more explicit. They also demonstrated that it was possible to teach helping skills more quickly and efficiently than had previously been thought. A wide array of research literature validates Rogers' constructs and the work of Truax and Carkhuff (see Truax & Mitchell, 1971; Truax, Wargo, & Silber, 1966; Vernis, 1970).

Rogers has continued to make his ideas more explicit. His three-step program in helper training is still important: it is useful to see and hear both the effective and ineffective helper and to examine the specific qualities that facilitate positive personal change and development. Although it may be possible to discriminate between ineffective and effective helping, Rogerian concepts don't identify the actual *behavior* of the counselor. The behavioral psychologists, inspired by the work of Skinner, have identified many specific verbal and nonverbal behaviors that induce systematic change. For example, in 1955, Greenspoon determined that it is possible to shape the behavior of a client in an interview by using head nods, "uh hums," and other signs of approval. Subsequent research demonstrated that, through such simple behavior on the part of the interviewer, clients could be conditioned to talk about whatever the interviewer reinforced.

It is possible that so-called nondirective or client-centered counselors actually reinforce certain types of client verbalizations in the interview. Needless to say, a comprehensive investigation of this issue is beyond the scope of the brief review presented here, but a vast array of studies, clinical cases, and theoretical writings have clearly identified the power of behavioral approaches in helping and the underlying operation of behavioral principles in the interview. Behavioralists have introduced a carefully developed, systematic approach to helping that is important regardless of one's theoretical school. Numerous reviews and theoretical discussions of the behavioral approach are readily available (see Bandura, 1969; Craighead, Kazdin, & Mahoney, 1976; Krumboltz & Thoresen, 1969; Rimm & Masters, 1974; Spence, Carson, & Thibaut, 1976).

Abundant evidence clearly indicates that helping can be made more explicit and that concepts of listening effectively are central in both client-centered and behavioral approaches. How can we determine, then, which approach is more effective, and how can we translate these basic concepts of effective helping into workable programs for training people to become more empathetic? Evidence suggests that both client-centered and behavioral approaches are effective. A recent review of the outcomes of nearly 400 psychotherapy and counseling research studies (Smith & Glass, 1977) reveals that more than one approach to personal change "works." The authors found indications that different clients could be effectively reached through different approaches. Therefore, under certain circumstances a behavioral approach is likely to be effective, whereas under other circumstances a cliented-centered approach may be the preferred avenue of treatment. This point is complicated by the fact that approaches as diverse as transactional analysis, psychoanalysis, gestalt therapy, and others are effective instruments of change in the lives of many individuals.

Although this brief review has focused on client-centered (Rogerian) and behavioral approaches, it is important to point out that there are many other effective and useful approaches to the art of helping. Transactional analysis, for example, draws from psychoanalytic psychology and uses certain aspects of both the Rogerian and behavioral approaches to the interview. The transactional helper is concerned with diagnosing the *pattern* of relationships rather than focusing solely on interpersonal relationships or primarily on external behavior. Transactional analysis is concerned with identifying individual behavior as "parent," "adult," or "child" and broadening the possibilities for action by using these concepts. A useful source for additional information on this approach to helping is James and Jongeward (1971). Gestalt psychology, another humanistic approach to helping, focuses on the "here and now" and has a large array of exercises and methods to enable people to break through "impasses" and "splits" (see Fagan & Shepherd, 1970).

There are many other prominent helping approaches in current use with varying claims of effectiveness. Given the wide array of competing theories, the beginning student as well as the advanced practitioner may become confused when trying to choose the "correct" approach—the approach that is best for each individual under particular conditions. Although professionals are not yet fully e-quipped to choose the most appropriate approach in every case, there are certain actions that can be taken to train individuals in the basic dimensions of helping. For example, Ivey and Authier (1978) discuss an evolving metatheory (or theory about theory) of the helping process. Research data and clinical experience strongly suggest that certain key dimensions of interviewing underlie all counseling and therapeutic approaches. Although a full theoretical model of helping is beyond the scope of this text, we wish to emphasize these three points about interviewing: (1) behaviors have been identified that are crucial to the interview regardless of theoretical orientation, (2) these behaviors can be taught to interviewer trainees, and (3) it is possible and desirable for interviewers to learn basic skills before developing their own theory and unique personal approach to communicating with others. The interviewer of the future needs basic skills and an array of theoretical approaches that can be integrated into a unique personal approach to effective interviewing.

We now turn to an examination of how specific skills of interviewing can be taught. At a later point, we discuss in detail the behaviors underlying effective interviewing.

THE SINGLE-SKILLS APPROACH TO INTERVIEWING TRAINING

One problem in interviewing analysis is that the beginner is often overwhelmed by information because of the complexity of the interviewing process. As Rogers (1957) has suggested, people seem to learn and remember best those things that are developed in a step-by-step fashion. The question is how to break down the complex interviewing process and determine which skills are most useful under varying circumstances.

Ivey, Normington, Miller, Morrill, and Hasse (1968), and Zimmer and Park (1967) evaluated counselor/client interaction independently and isolated several specific, observable behaviors that constitute effective interviewing. Ivey and his associates used observational analysis of videotape and developed logical categories, whereas Zimmer and Park employed a complex statistical approach for examining the verbal responses of counselors. The findings of the studies were identical, lending additional support to the idea that it is possible to delineate particular skills of interviewing. The videotape analysis resulted in more emphasis on nonverbal behaviors, but the verbal categories of the two research teams are extremely close.

Since it is possible to identify specific behaviors of interviewers, you may now be wondering (1) What behaviors have been identified as crucial to an interview? and (2) Can these behaviors be taught? We'll answer the second question first and then describe the behaviors identified thus far in an ensuing section.

The video analysis system is called *microcounseling* (Ivey, et al., 1968; Ivey, 1971; Ivey & Authier, 1978) because microportions of interviews are identified and classified. Microcounseling stresses teaching *single-skill* units of the interview one at a time, thus making it possible for the beginner to grasp concepts quickly. Although there are a number of variations of the basic microcounseling format, the standard paradigm consists of the following steps:

1. A five-minute audio or videotape interview, which is held between a trainee and a real or role-played client.
2. Training in a single skill, which includes:
   a. reading a manual that describes the skill to be taught,
   b. presentation of video or audiotaped examples of experts engaging in the skill, and
   c. self-observation by trainees who compare their own work to the manual and the taped presentations.
3. Taping of a second five-minute interview between the client and the trainee. The tape is reviewed with a supervisor to determine whether the trainee has met competency standards. The steps are repeated until mastery of the skill is demonstrated.

Over a period of time, the trainee learns many skills and practices integrating the array of skills into a natural interviewing style. Trainees are encouraged to use the skills in their own unique fashion.

The research base of microcounseling is extensive. Ivey and Authier (1978) and Kasdorf and Gustafson (1978) cite approximately 150 data-based studies indicating that identified skills can be taught to a wide array of people. Interviewing skills in the microcounseling model have been taught to medical students, nurses, clinical and counseling psychologists, social workers, community-service personnel, teachers, administrative personnel in industry, paraprofessional and community-action volunteers, and many lay people, including sales personnel, parents, and elementary school students. Research data comparing the microcounseling single-skills format with other approaches are encouraging. However, if individuals don't practice the skills on the job or in the home, the training will be lost. Evidence suggests that one must use communication skills if they are to be maintained, just as one must practice the piano, ballet, or tennis if these skills are to be maintained.

This programmed text is based partially on the microcounseling concept of single skills. Research evidence indicates that this material is a workable alternative to the full microcounseling model. Using the materials in this book, you can learn skills of interviewing that are useful in many settings. But again, unless you systematically practice and use these skills, the effort of learning them will be wasted. The emphasis in each section of this text is on the development of systematic ways in which you can take the ideas presented here and use them immediately. Cognitive learning or merely reading the material is not enough: these skills must become an integrated part of you. The skills presented here serve as an important base for establishing constructive interpersonal relationships as well as for sharing, information gathering, self-exploration, and positive personal change. Now let's look at the interviewing skills emphasized in this text.

BUILDING A STEP-BY-STEP MODEL OF INTERVIEWING SKILLS

Find a partner who is willing to be interviewed by you. If at all possible, audiotape the session or have a third person watch the interview and give you feedback. Here are your instructions for the interview.

Imagine you are to conduct an interview; however, you are to do the *worst* job possible; do as many things wrong as you can, and do them deliberately. Be creative and, above all, ineffective in the session. As a result of being ineffective, you can later define some positive aspects of interviewing. Spend about three minutes in this interview. Remember, do the worst job possible and exaggerate to make clear what you are doing. After you have completed the exercise, go back and list *specific* things that indicate a poor interviewing technique.

This procedure is similar to the first step of Carl Rogers' innovation in training, in which interviewers listen to high- and low-quality sessions. However, the exercise presented here involves you and asks you to identify in precise terms the *specific* things that are done incorrectly.

In one classroom exercise, the following list was drawn up by the students:

interrupted	maintained poor eye contact
interviewers talked all the time	paid no attention to emotions
listened poorly	contradicted the client
gave extensive advice	appeared bored at times
maintained sloppy posture	expressed no empathy
played with lighter	seemed phony
didn't seem interested	looked at floor frequently

In lists such as this, we see some of the many things that constitute inappropriate behavior on the part of an interviewer. Obviously, in order to be effective, you should aim to develop skills that counter these behaviors. However, correcting these all at once may prove to be too much for many beginning interviewers. A more appropriate approach is to select just a few behaviors, perhaps only one, master that, and then move on to others.

This book is a structured learning experience in eight basic skill areas that are crucial to interviewing of all types. An overview of these areas, with a brief summary of key dimensions of each, is provided in Table 1-1. Note that the first four skill areas—focusing and

TABLE 1-1   **An Overview of the Skills Covered in This Book**

1. *Focusing and following (Chapter 2).* You may expect to sharpen your general listening skills as well as your attending skills of eye contact, appropriate verbal and nonverbal following.
2. *Effective inquiry (Chapter 3).* You will learn to ask open and closed questions and to make minimal encouragements. You will also learn their usefulness in helping clients to express themselves fully.
3. *Reflecting feeling (Chapter 4).* The skill of reflection of feeling—the accurate sensing of the emotions of the client—will be discussed, and you will have the opportunity to learn and practice this skill.
4. *Reflecting content (Chapter 5).* Effective listening requires more than attending, questioning, and tuning in with emotions. It also requires the ability to *hear* and reflect clearly the verbal content of a client's statements.
5. *Integrating skills (Chapter 6).* This chapter reviews the preceding skills in an interview in which you will have an opportunity to see how well you have mastered the material thus far. At this point, we suggest that you conduct several practice interviews with real or role-played clients in which you use only the skills emphasized thus far in the book. You may be surprised at

Table 1-1 (continued)

how much you have learned and how effectively you can draw out another person.

6. *Communicating feeling and immediacy (Chapter 7).* There are times when it is important to share your own *immediate* feelings in the interview with the client. This chapter presents examples of appropriate and inappropriate communications of feeling and immediacy.

7. *Effective confrontation (Chapter 8).* Specifically, confrontation involves the identification of discrepancies or inconsistencies in a client's behavior. Before you confront a client, however, you must be able to identify inconsistencies and state them clearly without value judgments.

8. *Self-disclosure (Chapter 9).* At times, it is appropriate for an interviewer to self-disclose. However, this must be done without taking over an interview or leaving the client little room for self-exploration.

9. *Effective structuring (Chapter 10).* Structuring is the unique skill of enabling clients to examine issues, consider alternatives, and make their own decisions.

10. *Putting it all together—integrating the preceding skills (Chapter 11).* The challenge of this book is manifested most completely in this chapter. You will move through an interview, selecting from an array of potential responses. When you have mastered the material in the preceding chapters, integration of the skills and concepts will come naturally to you. However, mastery does not come by reading alone. This book will be successful only when you take the concepts out of each section and practice them in interviewing situations.

---

following, effective inquiry, reflecting feeling, and reflecting content —emphasize *listening* to the client. Interviewer trainees must realize that the client's problem need not (indeed, should not) be solved by the first two or three comments made by the interviewer. You may find that, in practice interviews, you ask one or two questions, obtain a sense of the client's problem, and suggest solutions ("Have you tried talking to your parents?" "Why not try . . .?" and so on). We urge your patience and careful attention to these four skill areas, for unless you can truly hear the client's concern there is little chance of effective change. The patient and careful clarification of the client's concerns and problems in detail is a characteristic that separates interviewing from the routine superficial advice that friends often give to one another. We strongly suggest that you shouldn't read the later sections of this book until you have mastered these basic introductory skills at a high level, as assessed in Chapter 6, and can effectively conduct an interview with a real or role-played client for at least five minutes without using action-oriented skills. When you have demonstrated that you can listen, you should move on to the complex skills presented in later chapters.

The second section of this book focuses on the effective use of four skill areas that require more activity on the part of the client— communicating feeling and immediacy, confronting, self-disclosing, and structuring. The precise meaning of these skills is presented in Table 1-1. It's important to realize that effective use of the initial skills presented here, in addition to mastery of the advanced skills, will lead to effective interviewing with the client.

In the final chapter, the text provides an opportunity for you to apply the skills you've learned as you act as an interviewer working with real client problems. You will have an opportunity to demonstrate that you can select appropriate skills from the array of possibilities presented throughout the book. In order to master these skills, however, you must be able to employ them effectively in real and role-played interviews. We suggest that you obtain an audiotape recorder and practice each skill with a friend until you are able to use the skill at will and note its positive impact in the interview.

We believe in a solid, step-by-step approach to mastery and competence in interviewing. We can provide guidance, but you must provide the expertise and work. Having presented the rationale and structure for this series of skills, we now examine the effectiveness of this step-by-step program.

RESEARCH ON ESSENTIAL INTERVIEWING PROGRAM

The programmed-text format followed here presents both positive and negative instances of interviewing behavior. You'll be presented with some information, an interviewing problem or issue, and you'll be asked to respond to a question. You will then be directed to the next frame, where your answer to the question is evaluated. If your answer is correct, we will explain why it is correct and ask you to continue. If your answer is incorrect, we will explain why it is wrong and ask you to return to the original frame to select another answer. You should not move ahead until you have mastered each step of the program.

The technique used in this book was developed by Crowder (1960), who demonstrated that mistakes can be considered opportunities to receive additional clarification on critical issues. Research has demonstrated that reward of accomplishment is important in programmed-learning formats. There is ample evidence that the programmed approach to learning is effective (see Hartley, 1974; Mackie, 1975; Stones, 1968; Taber, Glaser, & Schaefer, 1965).

Three studies have been conducted to evaluate the effectiveness of the initial training units in this book. Hearn (1976) taught interviewing skills using traditional microcounseling methods, a sensitivity-training group, and the programmed-text material alone. Results in follow-up taped posttraining interviews with role-played clients revealed significant changes in interviewing skills in both the microcounseling and programmed format. The sensitivity-training group was similar to a placebo-control group.

Uhlemann, Hearn, and Evans (1977) examined the effectiveness of portions of the programmed text with community-hotline volunteers and found significant improvements in interviewing skills. The programmed-learning group and the microcounseling group received equal time in training practice and feedback. The results of this study indicated that the two training procedures were equally effective in producing change. When cost effectiveness and time issues are considered, it is obvious that the programmed method is a viable alternative for teaching interviewing skills.

In the third study (Uhlemann, Evans, Stone, & Hearn, 1977), paraprofessional workers from a therapeutic community center were divided into three groups. One group read portions of the programmed text and participated in role-play practice and feedback. A second group read the entire programmed text, observed live modeling of each skill, and engaged in role-play practice with feedback. A third group received no training. The results of this study were encouraging for the two programmed-text groups. Little significant difference was found between the two training groups, although the workers who watched their trainers model the skills were more enthusiastic about training.

These three studies strongly suggest that the programmed-learning format is a viable alternative or supplement to the traditional microcounseling model of single-skills training. Moreover, the programmed-learning format is economical in terms of both equipment and time. Careful study of the data derived from the three studies also reveals that participants were more involved when text material was supplemented by experiential exercises. This information suggests that, although the material is strong enough to stand on its own as a means of teaching interviewing skills, training may be enriched by the addition of modeling and systematic role-play practice with feedback. The format, amount, and frequency of the supplemental-training activities are flexible and should be geared to the needs of the participants. The most important component in the process is active and involved participation.

CULTURAL ISSUES IN INTERVIEWING

Patterns of communication vary from culture to culture. The predominant mode of communication in American culture involves a reflective/listening approach when issues and concerns are discussed leisurely and in detail. Feelings and emotions are often stressed. There are normative patterns of verbal and nonverbal behavior. For example, Haase and Tepper (1972) state that an interviewer should lean toward a client and maintain eye contact and that client and interviewer should be at least an arm's length apart.

Don't assume that what is considered correct in one culture is appropriate with all people. Workshops on listening skills conducted in Alaska and the Canadian Northwest Territories have floundered on the critical issue of cultural differences. Eye contact among some Eskimos or Inuit is considered inappropriate and distracting. In the U.S., patterns of eye contact among Blacks sometimes differ from those of Whites. Individuals in the Middle East stand closer together when they talk than people in the United States and Canada; therefore, interviewing at what is considered normal distance in America would be uncomfortable for individuals from Egypt or Lebanon. The direct approach of staying on one topic and focusing on problems may be inappropriate for some Asian populations who may prefer more indirect, subtle approaches.

Recent examinations of beginning interviewers have revealed that White males tend to ask many questions, whereas White females use more reflective listening responses such as paraphrasing and reflection of feeling. Also, evidence indicates that Blacks tend to give more directions and advice than Whites (Berman, 1977). Members of different racial groups, religious groups, socioeconomic classes, regions of a nation, or parts of the world respond differently to interviewing.

You should be sensitive to individual and cultural differences when interviewing someone whose background differs from your own. Although the skills outlined in this book are based on solid research and experience, they must be used carefully with each individual you interview. All cultures use listening skills such as those presented here, but they use them in different ways. The interviewer's task is to learn how listening skills are used in different settings and make appropriate adjustments in order to communicate with others. Two particularly useful supplemental references on cross-cultural issues are Hall's *The Silent Language* (1959) and a special issue of the *Personnel and Guidance Journal* (1977).

SUMMARY

This is an action-oriented book that demands participation, involvement, and decisions on your part. Due to the format of programmed instruction, it may seem easy to passively accept our decisions concerning the correct answers. Although we believe we have justification for our answers as well as for using this particular structure, we know that no training program in interviewing can be successful unless you, the reader and participant, use it. Moreover, we hope that you use the material in your own unique fashion. In addition to reading the text and doing the exercises, it will be necessary for you to leave your room, the library, or the classroom and test the ideas and concepts presented here in your own daily life. In this way, interviewing can become alive and meaningful for you and others.

REFERENCE NOTES

1. Uhlemann, M. R., Hearn, M. T., & Evans, D. R. *Programmed learning in the microcounseling paradigm.* Paper presented at the meeting of the American Association of Suicidology, Boston, 1977.
2. Uhlemann, M. R., Evans, D. R., Stone, G. L., & Hearn, M. T. *Effective microcounseling as a function of modeled learning and teaching others.* Manuscript submitted for publication, 1977.

REFERENCES

Bandura, A. *Principles of behavior modification.* New York: Holt, Rinehart & Winston, 1969.

Carkhuff, R. R. *Helping and human relations* (2 vols.). New York: Holt, Rinehart & Winston, 1969.

Craighead, W. E., Kazdin, A. E., & Mahoney, M. J. *Behavior modification: Principles, issues, and applications.* Boston: Houghton Mifflin, 1976.

Crowder, N. A. Automatic tutoring by means of intrinsic programming. In A. A. Lumsdaine & R. Glaser (Eds.), *Teaching machines and programmed learning.* Washington, D.C.: National Education Association, 1960, pp. 286-298.

Fagan, J., & Shepherd, I. *Gestalt therapy now.* Palo Alto, Calif.: Science and Behavior Books, 1970.

Greenspoon, J. *American Journal of Psychology,* 1955, *68,* 409-416.

Hasse, R., & Tepper, D. Nonverbal components of empathic communication. *Journal of Counseling Psychology,* 1972, *19,* 417-424.

Hall, E. The silent language. New York: Doubleday, 1959.

Hartley, J. Programmed instruction 1954-1974: A review. *Programmed Learning & Educational Technology,* 1974, *11*(6), 278-291.

Hearn, M. T. Three modes of training counselors: A comparative study. Unpublished doctoral dissertation, The University of Western Ontario, London, Canada, 1976.

Ivey, A. E. *Microcounseling: Innovations in interviewing training.* Springfield, Ill.: C C Thomas, 1971.

Ivey, A. E., & Authier, J. *Microcounseling: Innovations in interviewing, counseling, psychotherapy and psychoeducation.* Springfield, Ill.: C C Thomas, 1978.

Ivey, A. E., & Gluckstern, N. B. *Basic attending skills: Leader manual.* Amherst, Mass.: Microcounseling Associates, 1974. (a)

Ivey, A. E., & Gluckstern, N. B. *Basic attending skills: Participant manual.* Amherst, Mass.: Microcounseling Associates, 1974. (b)

Ivey, A. E., & Gluckstern, N. B. *Basic Influencing skills: Leader manual.* Amherst, Mass.: Microcounseling Associates, 1976. (a)

Ivey, A. E., & Gluckstern, N. B. *Basic influencing skills: Participant manual.* Amherst, Mass.: Microcounseling Associates, 1976. (b)

Ivey, A. E., Normington, C. J., Miller, C. D., Morrill, W. H., & Haase, R. F. Microcounseling and attending behavior. *Journal of Counseling Psychology,* 1968, *15,* 1-12. (Monograph)

James, M., & Jongeward, D. *Born to win: Transactional analysis with gestalt experiments.* Reading, Mass.: Addison-Wesley, 1971.

Kasdorf, J., & Gustafson, K. Research related to microcounseling. In A. E. Ivey & J. Authier (Eds.), *Microcounseling: Innovations in interviewing, counseling, psychotherapy and psychoeducation.* Springfield, Ill.: C C Thomas, 1978.

Krumboltz, J. D., & Thoresen, C. E. *Behavioral counseling: Cases and techniques.* New York: Holt, Rinehart & Winston, 1969.

Mackie, A. Programmed learning: A developing technique. *Programmed Learning & Educational Technology,* 1975, *12* (4), 225-228.

Personnel and Guidance Journal, 1977, *55* (7), 381-425.

Rimm, D. C., & Masters, J. C. *Behavior therapy: Techniques and empirical findings.* New York: Academic Press, 1974.

Rogers, C. R. *Counseling and psychotherapy.* Boston: Houghton Mifflin, 1942.

Rogers, C. R. Training individuals in the therapeutic process. In C. Strother (Ed.), *Psychology and mental health.* Washington, D.C.: American Psychological Association, 1957.

Rogers, C. R. *On becoming a person.* Boston: Houghton Mifflin, 1961.

Skinner, B. F. *Science and human behavior.* New York: Macmillan, 1953.

Skinner, B. F. *Verbal behavior.* New York: Appleton-Century-Crofts, 1957.

Smith, M., & Glass, G. Meta-analysis of psychotherapy outcome studies. *American Psychologist,* 1977, *32,* 752-760.

Spence, J. T., Carson, R. C., & Thibaut, J. W. (Eds.), *Behavioral approaches to therapy.* Morristown, N.J.: General Learning Press, 1976.

Stones, E. Strategy and tactics in programmed instruction. *Programmed Learning and Educational Technology,* 1968, *5,* 122-128.

Taber, J., Glaser, R., & Schaefer, H. H. *Learning and programmed instruction.* Reading, Mass.: Addison-Wesley, 1965.

Truax, C. B., & Carkhuff, R. *Toward effective counseling and psychotherapy: Training and practice.* Chicago: Aldine, 1967.

Truax, C. B., & Mitchell, K. M. Research on certain therapist interpersonal skills. In A. E. Bergin & S. L. Garfield (Eds.), *Handbook of psychotherapy and behavior change.* New York: Wiley & Sons, 1971, pp. 299-344.

Truax, C. B., Wargo, D., & Silber, D. D. Effects of high accurate empathy and non-possessive warmth during group psychotherapy upon female institutionalized delinquents. *Journal of Abnormal Psychology,* 1966, *71,* 264-267.

Vernis, J. S. Therapeutic effectiveness of untrained volunteers with chronic patients. *Journal of Consulting and Clinical Psychology,* 1970, *34,* 152-155.

Zimmer, J. M., & Park, P. Factor analysis of counselor communications. *Journal of Counseling Psychology,* 1967, *14,* 198-203.

Chapter 2
FOCUSING
AND FOLLOWING

The material in this chapter is intended to help you master the skills of focusing and following. After you have completed this chapter, you should be able to:

1. Maintain appropriate eye contact during an interview.
2. Maintain natural, relaxed, and attentive posture during an interview.
3. Demonstrate, by means of your verbal responses, that you are focusing on and following what is being communicated by a client.
4. Manage appropriate silences during an interview.

The words *focusing* and *following* are used here to denote the basic skill of attending to what a client communicates. Focusing and following are basic to good interviewing and must be mastered before other skills can be learned and used effectively. There are three important component skills associated with focusing and following: eye contact, nonverbal behavior, and verbal following. We will consider each of these component skills and then examine the role of silence in interviewing.

As we pointed out in Chapter 1, there are cultural and racial differences in the use of eye contact, other nonverbal behavior, and silence. Because of the diversity of these differences, it is impossible to consider all of them in this chapter. When you deal with people whose cultural background differs greatly from your own, you should amend your behavior accordingly. Your nonverbal behavior should convey your interest and attention in an appropriate manner.

The program in this chapter is based on an interview between a nurse (male or female) and a client on a rehabilitation unit. The client is a married female patient who has recovered from major surgery. However, she has shown reluctance to leave the hospital and resume her normal daily activities. Proceed to 2.1 to begin this program.

2.1

Very few people in our society are effective listeners; most of us find it difficult to focus our attention on others and their comments. One of the component skills that constitutes focusing and following is appropriate eye contact.

Interviewer: Could you tell me what it is that's making it difficult for you to return to your home?

Client: Well, it's difficult to know where to start. I guess things just got to be too much for me. I seem to be tense all the time.

Choose the most appropriate response.

Interviewer: (Turn to the side and take notes.) Go to 2.2
Interviewer: (Because you might upset the client, avoid looking directly at her.) Go to 2.3
Interviewer: (Look directly at the client and, with your eyes, encourage her to continue talking.) Go to 2.4

2.2

Your Answer: (Turn to the side and take notes.)

Unless it is absolutely necessary, you should not take notes during an interview; it's best to take them after the interview, when you are more aware of key issues. Taking notes during an interview can distract and upset a client. To indicate that you are interested in what a client is saying, you need to maintain direct eye contact. Return to 2.1 and choose the response that indicates that you are following the client.

2.3

Your Answer: (Because you might upset the client, avoid looking directly at her.)

You're likely to upset the client by not looking at her. Direct eye contact will tell her that you're interested in what she is saying. Return to 2.1 and try again.

2.4

Your Answer: (Look directly at the client and, with your eyes, encourage her to continue talking.)

Correct. When you talk to someone, you should look at them. There is no need to stare; simply be aware of the fact that you are talking to another person. Proceed to 2.5.

2.5

The amount of eye contact you maintain is an obvious indication of your interest or disinterest in a client. Therefore, you should be aware of "eye-contact breaks." Frequent eye-contact breaks indicate your failure to focus on a client.

Interviewer: Could you tell me more about it?

Client: I was afraid to go outside the house. Just thinking about going out into the yard made me tense. I just couldn't do it.

Choose the most appropriate response.

Interviewer: (Maintain eye contact with the client and smile or nod as she talks.) Go to 2.6

Interviewer: (Look out the window while you listen to the client.) Go to 2.7

Interviewer: (Look around the room.) Go to 2.8

2.6

Your Answer: (Maintain eye contact with the client and smile or nod as she talks.)

Correct. By maintaining eye contact with the client, you indicate that you are focusing on her and following what she is telling you. Proceed to 2.9.

2.7

Your Answer: (Look out the window while you listen to the client.)
        Although you are listening to the client, you are not maintaining eye contact. The client may assume that you aren't listening. Direct eye contact indicates that you are interested in what she is saying. Return to 2.5 and try again.

2.8

Your Answer: (Look around the room.)
        This behavior will indicate that you aren't interested in what your client is saying. The first step in helping a client is to follow carefully what he or she is saying by listening and by maintaining eye contact. Return to 2.5 and try again.

2.9

        You should develop a natural style of eye contact with a client. You shouldn't stare or avoid a client's gaze. Use varied appropriate eye contact to indicate that you are following what a client is saying.

Interviewer: Uhmhmm.
Client: It's not that I don't want to go out. I do. But when I try to leave the house, I feel anxious and can't do it.
        Choose the most appropriate response.
Interviewer: (Avoid the client's anxious gaze.)   Go to 2.10
Interviewer: (Maintain varied, natural eye contact to show your interest.)   Go to 2.11
Interviewer: (Keep your eyes on the client's eyes at all times to show your interest.)   Go to 2.12

2.10

Your Answer: (Avoid the client's anxious gaze.)
        An interviewer should respond to a client's fears and help allay them. If you avoid a client's gaze, you'll probably add to his or her fears. Return to 2.9 and try again.

2.11

Your Answer: (Maintain varied, natural eye contact to show your interest.)

Correct. By maintaining varied and natural eye contact, you indicate your interest in what a client is saying. Proceed to 2.13.

2.12

Your Answer: (Keep your eyes on the client's eyes at all times to show your interest.)

An unwavering stare on the part of an interviewer can be very disconcerting to a client. The use of natural eye contact indicates that you are focusing on and are interested in what a client is saying. Return to 2.9 and try again.

2.13

As we indicated earlier, interviewing is not merely a verbal relationship. Some estimates suggest that 86% of our communication is nonverbal. To indicate that you are focusing on a client, assume a relaxed position and communicate that you are involved.

Interviewer: You try to go out, but you can't.

Client: Yes. I want to be able to go to work again and visit people, but I just can't do it.

Choose the most appropriate response.

Interviewer: (Sit in a relaxed position and lean toward the client.)
                                                              Go to 2.14

Interviewer: (Sit in an erect, professional manner.)   Go to 2.15

Interviewer: (Sit back, relax, and put your feet on the desk.)
                                                              Go to 2.16

2.14

Your Answer: (Sit in a relaxed position and lean toward the client.)

Correct. This is an appropriate way to sit during an interview, because it indicates that you are interested in what the client has to say. Proceed to 2.17.

2.15

Your Answer: (Sit in an erect, professional manner.)

If you appear to be rigid, the client will find it difficult to relax. If you assume a natural, relaxed position, both you and the client will feel free to relax. Return to 2.13 and try again.

2.16

Your Answer: (Sit back, relax, and put your feet on the desk.)

If you seem to be too relaxed, the client may feel that she is boring you, and she may become hesitant to discuss her difficulties with you. Your posture should indicate that you are at ease in her presence and that you are focusing on her problems. Return to 2.13 and try again.

2.17

As an interviewer, you should be aware of your tone of voice. Some vocal tones communicate caring and involvement, whereas others tend to alienate clients.

Client: It's so much worse when I try to go out. I get tense and can't do it, and then I get very depressed about it.

Choose the most appropriate response.

Interviewer: (In an abrupt tone of voice) Tell me how it all started.
Go to 2.18

Interviewer: (In a warm tone of voice) Tell me how it all started.
Go to 2.19

Interviewer: (In a bored tone of voice) Tell me how it all started.
Go to 2.20

2.18

Your Answer: (In an abrupt tone of voice) Tell me how it all started.

Your use of an abrupt tone of voice may give the client the impression that she is wasting your time and pressure her to proceed too quickly. Many clients are unable to proceed when they feel pressured. Your task is to help the client relate to you. Return to 2.17 and try again.

2.19

Your Answer: (In a warm tone of voice) Tell me how it all started.

Correct. You should always use a warm, expressive tone of voice when you conduct an interview, thereby helping the client to relax and concentrate on the problem under discussion. Proceed to 2.21.

2.20

Your Answer: (In a bored tone of voice) Tell me how it all started.

      If the client realizes you are bored, she is unlikely to reveal important information about herself. Your task is to communicate your interest in helping her. Return to 2.17 and try again.

2.21

      Interviewers often attempt to solve problems too quickly by offering sympathy and solutions before a client has had an opportunity to explain a problem in detail. You'll accomplish more with a client if you are a good listener and refrain from giving advice.

Client: I fainted in the bank about four years ago, and when I came to, a lot of people were standing over me.

      Choose the most appropriate response.

Interviewer: But that was four years ago. It shouldn't bother you now.   Go to 2.22

Interviewer: You should try to go back to the bank every day until your confidence is reestablished.   Go to 2.23

Interviewer: You must have felt quite uncomfortable when that happened.   Go to 2.24

2.22

Your Answer: But that was four years ago. It shouldn't bother you now.

      This response tends to play down the importance of the client's problem when she has only begun to tell you about it. Effective following behavior involves focusing on what a client says and feeding it back so the client will go on talking. Try to refrain from giving advice. Return to 2.21 and try again.

2.23

Your Answer: You should try to go back to the bank every day until your confidence is reestablished.

      In order to listen effectively, an interviewer must do more than provide answers and sympathy. Your task is to listen carefully, respond to the client, and focus on the topic being discussed. Return to 2.21 and try again.

2.24

Your Answer: You must have felt quite uncomfortable when that happened.

Correct. This response reflects back on how the client must have felt in the situation and indicates that you are following her. It also gives her a chance to continue telling you about her experiences. Proceed to 2.25.

2.25

As an interviewer, you should pick up on what has already been said rather than introduce a new topic. This isn't easy, but you will be well on the way to becoming a skillful interviewer when you can stay on topic.

Client: Yes. And I found it difficult the next time. In fact, I left before I had deposited my money. There were so many people.

Choose the most appropriate response.

Interviewer:	There were so many people.	Go to 2.26
Interviewer:	Which bank was it?	Go to 2.27
Interviewer:	What did your husband think?	Go to 2.28

2.26

Your Answer: There were so many people.

Correct. This response indicates that you were listening to what the client was saying and are interested in hearing more. Proceed to 2.29.

2.27

Your Answer: Which bank was it?

The name of the bank isn't really important information. The client has referred to her next visit to the bank and you have indicated your lack of attention to what she is saying by changing the topic. As an interviewer, you must listen carefully to the client and stay on topic. Return to 2.25 and try again.

2.28

Your Answer: What did your husband think?

        You have introduced a new topic—the client's husband. This information may be of interest to you but is irrelevant to the client at this point in the interview. Your task is to focus your attention on what the client is saying, and your response should reflect this attention. Return to 2.25 and try again.

2.29

        Remember to stay on topic. Don't jump from topic to topic or interrupt the client. Take your cues from what the client has said.

Client: Yes. All the people bothered me. Then I began to get upset in other places where there were lots of people.

        Choose the most appropriate response.

Interviewer: Excuse me for a moment. I have to find something. I hope you don't mind.   Go to 2.30

Interviewer: Could you tell me more about that?   Go to 2.31

Interviewer: (Interrupt her after she has said "all the people bothered me.") How many people were there? Go to 2.32

2.30

Your Answer: Excuse me for a moment. I have to find something. I hope you don't mind.

        You have interrupted the client, and, as a result, you may find it impossible to get back on topic during this session. The client may not be inclined to repeat herself for someone whose thoughts were obviously elsewhere. Your task is to follow intently what the client is saying. Return to 2.29 and try again.

2.31

Your Answer: Could you tell me more about that?

        Correct. This question allows the client to discuss her problems further. When you respond appropriately, the client will often go on to give you more information. Proceed to 2.33.

2.32

Your Answer: (Interrupt her after she has said "all the people bothered me.") How many people were there?

This interruption prevents the client from presenting her problem in the manner that suits her, and it indicates that you think that what she is relating to you is unimportant. You should refrain from interrupting the client. It is important that, as an interviewer, you attend to *all* the information the client communicates to you. Return to 2.29 and try again.

2.33

As an interviewer, you should attend to what the client has said and direct it back to her.

Client: Well, it soon became unbearable for me to go into stores or to get my hair cut—to do all the things I should do.

Choose the most appropriate response.

Interviewer:	Who cut your hair?	Go to 2.34
Interviewer:	How do you buy new clothes?	Go to 2.35
Interviewer:	All the usual things became unbearable.	Go to 2.36

2.34

Your Answer: Who cut your hair?

Because you have changed topics, the client will probably become confused. You should listen carefully to the client and direct what she has said back to her for further clarification. Return to 2.33 and try again.

2.35

Your Answer: How do you buy new clothes?

It is unlikely that this information will assist you in helping the client with her problem. You've changed the topic that the client was discussing by pursuing a topic about which you are curious. As an interviewer, you should pay careful attention to what the client says in order to pick up some aspect of her communication and direct it back to her. Return to 2.33 and try again.

2.36

Your Answer: All the usual things became unbearable.

Correct. Your response is on topic and invites the client to tell you more about her difficulties. Proceed to 2.37.

2.37

You shouldn't talk too much during an interview. The client has come to you with a problem and should do most of the talking. There is no need to talk about yourself or to give answers to the client. Your responsibility is to assist the client in finding her own answers.

Client: Yes. When I go out, my stomach gets upset. I get a headache, my throat is tight, and I can't breathe.

Choose the most appropriate response.

Interviewer: How do you think this relates to what happened in the bank? Go to 2.38

Interviewer: Well, I fainted in public once too, and I never have those problems. Go to 2.39

Interviewer: Well, I don't see any reason for you to feel that way. I don't think other people feel that way, so you shouldn't either. Go to 2.40

2.38

Your Answer: How do you think this relates to what happened in the bank?

Correct. With this response, you are asking the client to explain how her physical reactions in crowded situations relate to her initial fainting spell in the bank. Proceed to 2.41.

2.39

Your Answer: Well, I fainted in public once too, and I never have those problems.

This information doesn't help the client. She is aware of the fact that she doesn't react the way other people do; you are simply telling her that she doesn't react the way you do. Moreover, you've changed the topic and indicated that you are interested in discussing yourself rather than the client. Return to 2.37 and try again.

2.40

Your Answer: Well, I don't see any reason for you to feel that way. I don't think other people feel that way, so you shouldn't either.

This response denies the client the right to feel the way she does. Moreover, you are giving her advice that she can't follow and, by talking so much, preventing her from clarifying what she is trying to tell you. Return to 2.37 and choose the response that indicates that you are focusing on what the client is saying and are interested in helping her to find her own answers. Return to 2.37 and try again.

2.41

An interviewer's comments should reflect a client's need to clarify the problem, not an interviewer's need to support a client or satisfy curiosity.

Client: Well, I guess when I get into situations in which there are people, I'm always afraid I'll faint. And so I become tense. I'm all right here, though. I'm used to it.
          Choose the most appropriate response.

Interviewer: Have you told anyone else about this?   Go to 2.42
Interviewer: Can you clarify for me whether it is the people or the situations that cause you to be afraid?   Go to 2.43
Interviewer: Well now, we'll have to see what we can do about that. But don't worry any more.   Go to 2.44

2.42

Your Answer: Have you told anyone else about this?
      This response reflects curiosity rather than listening skills. With this response, you have changed the topic and neglected to help the client clarify her concerns. Return to 2.41 and try again.

2.43

Your Answer: Can you clarify for me whether it is the people or the situations that cause you to be afraid?
      Correct. This is an appropriate response, because it requests that the client clarify for both of you the cause of her fear of fainting. Proceed to 2.45.

2.44

Your Answer: Well now, we'll have to see what we can do about that. But don't worry any more.

This patronizing statement places all the responsibility for the client upon you. Unfortunately, it is seldom possible to solve a client's problem immediately, and therefore a well-intentioned response such as this can be misleading. Concentrated listening will enable you to attend to what the client tells you and will help her explore the topic she is pursuing. Return to 2.41 and try again.

2.45

If you find that you are momentarily unsure of what to say to the client, go back and ask a question or make a comment about a relevant topic that was discussed earlier in the interview.

Client: I don't know. I guess I'm afraid of both the people and the situations. Right now I stay away from both, so I can't really say. I don't know what else to say.

Choose the most appropriate response.

Interviewer: You were telling me earlier about not being able to go out to the bank. What happened then?   Go to 2.46

Interviewer: I think I might be able to decide.   Go to 2.47

Interviewer: (Remain silent and wait for the client to continue.)
Go to 2.48

2.46

Your Answer: You were telling me earlier about not being able to go out to the bank. What happened then?

Correct. When you reach a dead end with a discussion, a completely new topic may seem appealing. However, you should refer back to a topic the client discussed with you earlier in the interview— something that is of interest to her. This is good following behavior. Proceed to 2.49.

2.47

Your Answer: I think I might be able to decide.

This response directs the interview away from what the client is discussing. Pause for a moment, think back over what the client was discussing earlier, and reintroduce a point that you would have followed if you'd had the opportunity. Return to 2.45 and try again.

2.48

Your Answer: (Remain silent and wait for the client to continue.)

    The client has told you that she has reached an impasse. Your silence at this point may be appropriate, but in view of the client's inability to clarify the source of her problem as she presently views it, you are responsible for making the next statement. You should pause for a moment, think back over what the client has told you, and then reintroduce a relevant aspect of her difficulties into the discussion. Return to 2.45 and try again.

2.49

    In many cases, a client needs only a little encouragement to continue talking.

Client: Well, as I told you, I stopped going out. Then I found that I couldn't go out socially or visit with friends anymore.

    Choose the most appropriate response.

Interviewer: Did your husband complain?   Go to 2.50

Interviewer: It must have been difficult for everyone in your family to make excuses for you all the time.   Go to 2.51

Interviewer: And then . . .   Go to 2.52

2.50

Your Answer: Did your husband complain?

    You have changed the topic by introducing the client's husband into the discussion. Skillful interviewers stay on topic and allow their clients to introduce new topics into the discussion. Return to 2.49 and try again.

2.51

Your Answer: It must have been difficult for everyone in your family to make excuses for you all the time.

    You aren't following what the client is telling you. You have changed the topic, ignored the fact that the client is distressed, and mentioned the difficulty she may have caused her family. Your response should reflect your attention and give the client an opportunity to continue. Return to 2.49 and try again.

2.52

Your Answer: And then . . .

Correct. This minimal encouragement invites the client to go on with what she was telling you. Proceed to 2.53.

2.53

Effective interviewers stop to listen, and are occupied with their clients rather than with thoughts of what to say next.

Client: For a while, I couldn't go out socially unless I'd had a few drinks.

Choose the most appropriate response.

Interviewer:	Could you tell me more about that?	Go to 2.54
Interviewer:	What did you drink?	Go to 2.55
Interviewer:	Are you an alcoholic?	Go to 2.56

2.54

Your Answer: Could you tell me more about that?

Correct. This question allows the client to go on with what she was discussing. You are free to focus on what she is saying rather than introduce a new topic. Proceed to 2.57.

2.55

Your Answer: What did you drink?

You don't need this information in order to help the client. You should be concerned with the client and her problem, not with areas that are unimportant to what she is telling you. If this information is important to her, she will tell you later in the interview. Return to 2.53 and try again.

2.56

Your Answer: Are you an alcoholic?

You're overinterpreting what the client has told you. At this point, you don't have sufficient information to ask this question. Moreover, it's possible that the client will be insulted by this question. You should stay with what the client is saying. Preoccupation with your own thoughts can result in an interview in which you do all the work. Return to 2.53 and try again.

2.57

As an interviewer, you must attend not only to the verbal cues given by the client but to the nonverbal cues as well—glances, gestures, bodily reactions, tone of voice, and pauses.

Client: (Looking down at the floor.) Well, I started having just a few drinks.

Choose the most appropriate response.

Interviewer: I'm here to listen. I can't help you if you won't tell me everything.　　　　　　　　　Go to 2.58

Interviewer: Maybe we should talk about something else.
　　　　　　　　　Go to 2.59

Interviewer: You find it difficult to tell me about it.　Go to 2.60

2.58

Your Answer: I'm here to listen. I can't help you if you won't tell me everything.

The client is aware of your role and doesn't really need to be reminded of your position. You have changed the topic from the client to yourself and your role. You should respond to the verbal and nonverbal cues put out by the client. Return to 2.57 and try again.

2.59

Your Answer: Maybe we should talk about something else.

Although you have responded to the client's verbal and nonverbal cues whereby she indicated her difficulty in discussing her drinking, you've changed the topic. Return to 2.57 and try again.

2.60

Your Answer: You find it difficult to tell me about it.

Correct. This is a good response, because it indicates that you were attending to the client's gesture (looking down) and her pauses in speech. It is obviously difficult for her to talk to you about her drinking. By reflecting how she feels, you give her a chance to settle her feelings before going on with the discussion. Proceed to 2.61.

2.61

Allow the client to be silent if she wishes. Don't feel obligated to fill the silence. Sit back and give the client time to think.

Client: (Sits silently for a minute and appears to be thinking.)
Choose the most appropriate response.

Interviewer: What's the matter? Cat got your tongue?   Go to 2.62
Interviewer: How many drinks do you have during an average day?
Go to 2.63
Interviewer: (Sits attentively and waits for the client to continue.)
Go to 2.64

2.62

Your Answer: What's the matter? Cat got your tongue?

You have responded to the client's silence but not in a way that will make her realize that you understand her difficulty in talking about drinking. Allow the client to be silent. Clients often need time to work things out before they can continue in an interview. Return to 2.61 and try again.

2.63

Your Answer: How many drinks do you have during an average day?

The client is uncomfortable with what she is about to discuss, and she needs your acceptance and support while she is thinking out her response. Your efforts to pressure her into talking will have little effect if she is not ready to talk. Return to 2.61 and try again.

2.64

Your Answer: (Sits attentively and waits for the client to continue.)

Correct. Silence is appropriate when the client is thinking and trying to decide how to continue with something that is difficult to discuss. At this point, the client needs your acceptance and support. She will continue as soon as she is ready. Proceed to 2.65.

2.65

As an interviewer, you need to remember that silence is sometimes a positive form of communication. Some clients need time to think, and you are not there to think for them.

Client: It's hard to talk about it. I haven't told anyone before, but I guess I should. You see, I drink from the time I get up until my husband gets home.

Choose the most appropriate response.

Interviewer: Does your husband drink?   Go to 2.66

Interviewer: I guess it's not an easy thing to talk about

          Go to 2.67

Interviewer: Who pays for all the liquor? It must cost a lot of money.   Go to 2.68

2.66

Your Answer: Does your husband drink?

You've changed the topic. The client is telling you about her problem at the moment, not about any problem that her husband might have. Your task is to stay on topic and to stay in tune with what the client is discussing. Return to 2.65 and try again.

2.67

Your Answer: I guess it's not an easy thing to talk about.

Correct. Your response reflects the client's obvious difficulty in talking about her drinking and is supportive of her discussion of her problem. Moreover, this response indicates that you are in tune with her feelings and understand what her earlier silence meant. Proceed to 2.69.

2.68

Your Answer: Who pays for all the liquor? It must cost a lot of money.

This information may be important later in the interview, but at this point you should focus on what the client is telling you and help her to explore the dimensions of her difficulties. Return to 2.65 and try again.

2.69

As an interviewer, your job is to be attentive by maintaining appropriate eye contact and an easy relaxed posture, and by following verbally what the client is discussing.

Client: No. I know I drink a lot, but I can't stop. That's what I am most ashamed of—I just can't stop.

Choose the most appropriate response.

Interviewer:	You feel you're letting yourself down.	Go to 2.70
Interviewer:	Maybe you should join A.A.	Go to 2.71
Interviewer:	What about your mother. Did she drink?	
		Go to 2.72

2.70

Your Answer: You feel you're letting yourself down.

Correct. This response invites the client to discuss her feelings about her drinking. This invitation to discuss the problem is very important at this time. You are focusing and following carefully. Proceed to 2.73.

2.71

Your Answer: Maybe you should join A.A.

This advice is inappropriate, because, as the client has told you, she can't go out. To be an effective interviewer, you must attentively follow everything that your client tells you. Return to 2.69 and try again.

2.72

Your Answer: What about your mother. Did she drink?

This response indicates that you are not following what the client is saying. You've introduced a new topic—the client's mother. As an interviewer, your task is to stay on the topic the client is discussing and help her explore it. Return to 2.69 and try again.

2.73

Remember to stay on topic!

Client: Yes. I've never been like this before and I really want to get better, but I just don't know what to do.

Choose the most appropriate response.

Interviewer:	Most people are able to stop drinking.	Go to 2.74
Interviewer:	You seem unsure of what to do about your problem.	
		Go to 2.75
Interviewer:	Do you have trouble sleeping?	Go to 2.76

2.74

Your Answer: Most people are able to stop drinking.

This response indicates that you are not accepting or supportive of the client and her problem. Return to 2.73 and try again.

2.75

Your Answer: You seem unsure of what to do about your problem.
Correct. This response summarizes the client's previous comment and invites her to continue. The appropriate combination of following, pausing, and responding is one of the most difficult aspects of interviewing to learn. At this point, you are beginning to learn this difficult combination of behaviors. Proceed to 2.77.

2.76

Your Answer: Do you have trouble sleeping?
The client hasn't mentioned a problem with sleeping. You've changed the topic, indicating to the client that you aren't focusing on what she is saying. Return to 2.73 and try again.

2.77

Indicate whether each of the following statements is true or false.

1. Good interviewers maintain intent eye-to-eye contact at all times.
2. It is most important to offer solutions to a client's problem as soon as possible in the interview.
3. A competent interviewer is comfortable with brief reflective silences.
4. A relaxed, attentive posture communicates an interviewer's concern for a client.
5. When an interviewer feels temporarily lost during an interview, it is usually a good idea to focus the discussion on something the client has related earlier in the interview.
6. A competent interviewer is more attentive to verbal cues than to nonverbal cues.

ANSWERS

1. *False.* If you answered *true,* go to 2.1 and review.
2. *False.* If you answered *true,* go to 2.21 and review.
3. *True.* If you answered *false,* go to 2.61 and review.
4. *True.* If you answered *false,* go to 2.13 and review.
5. *True.* If you answered *false,* go to 2.45 and review.
6. *False.* If you answered *true,* go to 2.57 and review.

If three or more of your responses were incorrect, you should return to 2.1 and work through this chapter again.

POINTS
TO
REMEMBER
ABOUT
FOCUSING
AND
FOLLOWING

1. **EYE CONTACT**:
   a. Suggests that you are attending to what is being communicated.
   b. Should be natural and direct without constituting a stare.
   c. Should be comparatively constant—frequent breaks in eye contact suggest inattention.
2. **BODY POSTURE**:
   a. Should be natural, attentive, and relaxed, communicating interest.
   b. Gestures should be easy and natural.
3. **VERBAL RESPONSES**:
   a. Should be made in a warm and expressive tone, communicating involvement.
   b. Should follow from the client's comments.
   c. Should not change the topic or interrupt the client.
   d. Should relate to concerns expressed previously by your client when the topic being discussed is exhausted.
   e. Should be made with regard to both the verbal (content and tone) and the nonverbal (glances, gestures, and other physical reactions) behavior of the client.
4. **SILENCES**:
   a. May occur, since clients often need time to think.
   b. Are often a positive form of communication.
   c. Should not become excessive without an interviewer response.

Remember that your eye contact, body posture, and verbal behavior should be adjusted according to cultural, racial, and individual differences.

MULTIPLE-
CHOICE
TEST

In order to evaluate your mastery of the material in this chapter, you should answer the following multiple-choice questions. In each case, select the most appropriate response based on the content of this chapter. The correct answers are listed in the Appendix.

Begin here

1. Client (a college student): My grades have dropped from an A average to almost straight C's in the last two months, and I don't know what to do to bring them back up.

   a.   Interviewer: How long have you been in college?
   b.   Interviewer: It sounds as if your grades have really gone down and you don't know how to change that.
   c.   Interviewer: Has this ever happened to you before?

2.   Client.   My grades really have gone down. I don't seem to study like I used to.

   a.   Interviewer: On the average, how many hours do you study a day?
   b.   Interviewer: Where do you study?
   c.   Interviewer: Could you tell me how your study habits have changed?

3.   Client: Even though I put in hours studying, I don't seem to be able to concentrate.

   a.   Interviewer: (In a soft, supportive voice) Trouble concentrating.
   b.   Interviewer: (Taking notes) Trouble concentrating.
   c.   Interviewer: (Staring at the client) Trouble concentrating.

4.   Client: (Looking down with hands between knees) I have trouble concentrating because I keep thinking about the problems my parents are having at home.

   a.   Interviewer: Could you tell me a little about your home?
   b.   Interviewer: It seems difficult for you to talk about that.
   c.   Interviewer: What is your home town like?

5.   Client: It's difficult to talk about. My parents are thinking of separating after all these years.

   a.   Interviewer: That would make it difficult for you to study.
   b.   Interviewer: Why are they thinking of separating?
   c.   Interviewer: Have you done anything about their situation?

6.   Client: When I sit down to study, I read the material but I think about what's happening at home.

   a.   Interviewer: (Sit quietly and let the client think, but give the client your full attention.)
   b.   Interviewer: What do you think is happening at home?
   c.   Interviewer: You should be able to put that aside while you study.

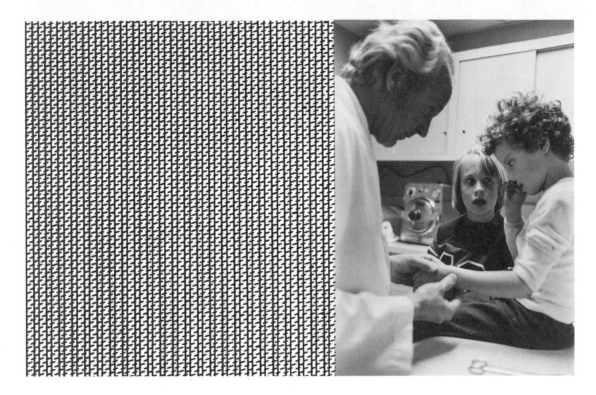

Chapter 3
EFFECTIVE INQUIRY

The material in this chapter is intended to help you master an effective style of inquiry that facilitates communication. Effective inquiry requires a knowledge of open inquiry, closed inquiry, and minimal encouragement. After you have completed this chapter, you should be able to do the following:

1. Formulate and make open inquiries.
2. Decide whether open inquiry is appropriate in a given situation.
3. Formulate and make closed inquiries.
4. Decide whether closed inquiry is appropriate in a given situation.
5. Identify the forms of inquiry that should be avoided.
6. Make minimal encouragements.
7. Decide whether minimal encouragement is appropriate in a given situation.

In this chapter, open and closed inquiries are defined, the various forms of open inquiry are considered, the comparative importance of open and closed inquiries in interviewing is examined, and situations are studied in which open and closed inquiries are appropriate. Following a discussion of the forms of inquiry that should be avoided, there is an examination of the use of minimal encouragements.

The program in this chapter focuses on portions of two interviews conducted by a marriage counselor. The client is a man who has come to discuss his stressful marriage. Proceed to 3.1 to begin this program.

3.1

A client comes to an interview to enter into a discussion. The task of the interviewer is to facilitate discussion by providing limited structure through the use of open inquiry.

An open inquiry, often referred to as an open-ended question, usually requires an extensive response rather than a "yes," "no," or a brief factual answer. In contrast, a closed inquiry, or closed-ended question, can be answered with "yes," "no," or a simple fact.

Client:	I'm having problems with my marriage.
	Choose the most appropriate response.
Interviewer:	How long have you been married?　　　Go to 3.2
Interviewer:	Could you tell me a little more about these problems?
	Go to 3.3
Interviewer:	Are you still living with your wife?　　Go to 3.4

3.2

Your Answer:　How long have you been married?

This closed inquiry invites a brief, factual answer and interferes with the client's discussion of his current concern. An open inquiry provides a less restrictive structure and encourages discussion. Return to 3.1 and try again.

3.3

Your Answer:　Could you tell me a little bit more about these problems?

Correct. This is an open inquiry that encourages the client to continue the discussion. Proceed to 3.5.

3.4

Your Answer: Are you still living with your wife?

This closed inquiry demands a "yes" or "no" answer and interferes with the client's discussion of his problem. An open inquiry is preferable at this point. Return to 3.1 and try again.

3.5

Before you can make effective inquiries, you have to listen carefully to what the client says. Development of this listening skill depends on your ability to focus and follow.

Client: My marriage is no good anymore. We're always fighting and quarreling. We don't even talk to each other very much anymore. I don't enjoy it.

Choose the most appropriate response.

Interviewer: What do you argue about?   Go to 3.6
Interviewer: How do you think you could change your behavior?
                                                       Go to 3.7
Interviewer: What was your home like when you were a child?
                                                       Go to 3.8

3.6

Your Answer: What do you argue about?

Correct. This is an open inquiry that allows you to attend to what the client is discussing. When you ask open-ended questions, the client will be inclined to discuss himself and his problems further. Proceed to 3.9.

3.7

Your Answer: How do you think you could change your behavior?

This is an open inquiry, but it's premature. You don't know enough about the client to begin seeking solutions to his problem. Moreover, you've shifted the focus from his concerns to yours. Return to 3.5 and try again.

3.8

Your Answer: What was your home like when you were a child?

This is an open inquiry, but it is off the topic the client is discussing. You'll be of more help to the client if you stay on the topic. Return to 3.5 and try again.

3.9

There are four commonly used methods of introducing an open inquiry. Questions that begin with *what* are frequently used to elicit factual data.

Client: I guess we fight about a lot of things, but the major thing we fight about is that I'm never home.

Choose the response that enables you to collect factual information about the client's problem.

Interviewer: How do you feel about your situation?   Go to 3.10
Interviewer: What does your wife do while you're away?
                                                Go to 3.11
Interviewer: What keeps you away from home?   Go to 3.12

3.10

Your Answer: How do you feel about your situation?

This is a good open inquiry, but it will not lead to the factual information you were requested to obtain. Return to 3.9 and try again.

3.11

Your Answer: What does your wife do while you're away?

This open inquiry is off topic and will not lead to factual information about the client's problem. Return to 3.9 and try again.

3.12

Your Answer: What keeps you away from home?

Correct. This open inquiry enables you to gather factual information concerning the client's problem. Proceed to 3.13.

3.13

Open inquiries that begin with the word *how* are often used to encourage a client to give a personal or subjective view of a situation. Therefore, these inquiries are considered people oriented rather than fact oriented.

Client: My wife is always worried about money, and I have to hold down two jobs to keep up with our bills. That means I work from seven in the morning until ten at night.

     Choose the response that enables you to focus the interview on the client's personal view of his situation.

Interviewer:	What kind of bills do you have?	Go to 3.14
Interviewer:	What's so terrible about having two jobs?	Go to 3.15
Interviewer:	How do you feel about that?	Go to 3.16

3.14

Your Answer: What kind of bills do you have?

     This is an open inquiry that will enable you to obtain primarily factual information. You should choose an open inquiry that is people oriented—one that focuses on the client and his reaction to his situation. Return to 3.13 and try again.

3.15

Your Answer: What's so terrible about having two jobs?

     This is a leading question: it implies that the client should accept your values. Moreover, this response doesn't encourage the client to consider his personal reaction to his situation. Return to 3.13 and try again.

3.16

Your Answer: How do you feel about that?

     Correct. This open inquiry places the focus of the interview on the client and his feelings. This response is people oriented rather than fact oriented. Proceed to 3.17.

3.17

     Interviewers frequently begin open inquiries with the words *could, could you,* or *can you.* Such inquiries stimulate detailed responses. This type of open inquiry offers a client flexibility in formulating responses and, therefore, responsibility for contributing to the discussion.

Client: I'm pretty angry. I work all the time, and then when I *am* home, I get told about not being home.

Choose the response that offers the client the greatest opportunity to contribute to the interview.

Interviewer: Could you describe one such occasion for me?

Go to 3.18

Interviewer: What do you do about your anger? Go to 3.19

Interviewer: Is that a valid reason to become angry? Go to 3.20

3.18

Your Answer: Could you describe one such occasion for me?

Correct. This open inquiry allows the client to select and describe an incident he wishes to discuss with you. Proceed to 3.21.

3.19

Your Answer: What do you do about your anger?

This is an open inquiry that directs the client to focus on a specific topic. Open inquiries that begin with the words *could* or *can* usually have a more general focus. Return to 3.17 and try again.

3.20

Your Answer: Is that a valid reason to become angry?

This judgmental and leading inquiry severely limits the client's ability to contribute to the discussion. You've insisted that he agree with your point of view. Return to 3.17 and try again.

3.21

The final type of open inquiry to be discussed in this chapter begins with the word *why*. Many skilled interviewers tend to avoid this type of inquiry, because it can make clients feel defensive.

Client: Well, last night, as soon as I was in the door, my wife started complaining. I was tired and didn't really want to hear her complaints. After all, I have complaints too.

Choose the most appropriate response.

Interviewer: Why did you react that way? Go to 3.22

Interviewer: Could you help me to understand what it is about her complaints that upsets you? Go to 3.23

Interviewer: Do you know why you didn't want to hear her complaints? Go to 3.24

3.22

Your Answer: Why did you react that way?

This open inquiry may seem to imply that the client should not have reacted the way he did and, as a result, may cause him to feel defensive. Return to 3.21 and try again.

3.23

Your Answer: Could you help me to understand what it is about her complaints that upsets you?

Correct. This open inquiry permits the client to discuss his problem without becoming defensive. Proceed to 3.25.

3.24

Your Answer: Do you know why you didn't want to hear her complaints?

This closed inquiry suggests that you disapprove of the client's feelings. As a result, he may become defensive and withdraw from his interaction with you. Return to 3.21 and try again.

3.25

In skilled interviewing, open inquiries are generally more important than closed inquiries. Open inquiries offer a client opportunities to introduce relevant topics, whereas closed inquiries offer limited opportunities to do so. Generally, closed inquiries focus on information that is of interest to the interviewer.

Client: It's probably her timing. First, it happens night after night; and second, the fact is, she never gives me time to relax before she starts.

Choose the most appropriate response.

Interviewer: You don't think she has the right to do that?

Go to 3.26

Interviewer: Would she stop if you did what she asked?

Go to 3.27

Interviewer: What do you feel like doing when she starts to complain?   Go to 3.28

3.26

Your Answer: You don't think she has the right to do that?

This is a closed inquiry. You've indicated your lack of interest in what the client has said by directing him away from his line of thought to ask him something that is of interest to you. Remember, when you make an open comment, the client has an opportunity to introduce and explore relevant concerns. Return to 3.25 and try again.

3.27

Your Answer: Would she stop if you did what she asked?

This closed inquiry demonstrates a lack of interest in the client and changes the topic he was pursuing. An open comment allows a client to explore his or her concerns with the support of an interviewer. Return to 3.25 and try again.

3.28

Your Answer: What do you feel like doing when she starts to complain?

Correct. This is an open inquiry that allows the client to introduce and discuss relevant information. Proceed to 3.29.

3.29

During an interview, inquiries should provide information for an interviewer and assist a client in exploring and clarifying his or her concerns. Open inquiries fulfill both of these functions, whereas closed inquiries tend to fulfill only the first.

Client: I have two reactions, really. Either I feel like yelling at her and telling her she's not the only one who feels tired and fed up, or I feel like turning around and walking right out of the house.

Choose the most appropriate response.

Interviewer: Could you help me to understand what's going on inside you when you feel this way?   Go to 3.30

Interviewer: When you yell at her, does she yell back?   Go to 3.31

Interviewer: Have you ever walked out?   Go to 3.32

3.30

Your Answer: Could you help me to understand what's going on inside you when you feel this way?
     Correct. This is an open inquiry that is centered on the concerns
of the client. This response will enable you to gather information and
help the client explore and clarify his problems. Proceed to 3.33.

3.31

Your Answer: When you yell at her, does she yell back?
     This is a closed inquiry that can be answered by "yes" or "no."
As a result, it produces little information and prevents the client
from exploring and clarifying his situation. Return to 3.29 and try
again.

3.32

Your Answer: Have you ever walked out?
     This is a closed inquiry that provides information only to the
interviewer. Your questions should be designed to gather information
and help the client explore and clarify his problems. Return to 3.29
and try again.

3.33

     Clients find interviews more enjoyable and satisfying when
they're permitted to discuss their problems in their own way. For
this reason, the use of open inquiries tends to put clients at ease,
whereas the repeated use of closed inquiries often upsets and irritates
them.

Client: My stomach gets all tied up in knots, and my hands
clench. I even grit my teeth together.
     Choose the most appropriate response.

Interviewer: Have you ever felt so tightened up inside that you've
become physically ill?   Go to 3.34
Interviewer: Have you ever hit your wife?   Go to 3.35
Interviewer: I wonder how you understand the way you're reacting?   Go to 3.36

3.34

Your Answer: Have you ever felt so tightened up inside that you've become physically ill?

This is a closed inquiry that may distract and irritate the client. You should attempt to acquire this information by using an inquiry that will put the client at ease and permit him to communicate more openly. Return to 3.33 and try again.

3.35

Your Answer: Have you ever hit your wife?

This statement is a closed inquiry. Although it may be important that you have this information at a later stage, this question interrupts the client's discussion. Interruptions such as this often irritate clients. Return to 3.33 and try again.

3.36

Your Answer: I wonder how you understand the way you're reacting?

Correct. This is an open inquiry that permits the client to continue discussing his problem with you. As a result, he will probably feel at ease, become more involved, and gain satisfaction from the interview. Proceed to 3.37.

3.37

Open inquiries are useful in a number of interviewing situations. For example, they can be employed when you want a client to elaborate on a point.

Client: I often feel that nobody—not my wife, anyway—really cares about me at all or about how hard it is for me to have to work all the time. They think all I'm good for is bringing home the money. I wish my wife would look at my situation differently.

Choose the most appropriate response.

Interviewer: Could you tell me more about that?　　　Go to 3.38
Interviewer: Is the money you bring home enough to justify all the work you do?　　　Go to 3.39

Interviewer: Who are the others who don't really care about you?

Go to 3.40

3.38

Your Answer: Could you tell me more about that?

    Correct. This is an open inquiry that allows you to help the client elaborate on the point he has just made—the fact that he wants his wife to view his situation differently. Proceed to 3.41.

3.39

Your Answer: Is the money you bring home enough to justify all the work you do?

    Your statement is a closed inquiry that requires only a "yes" or "no" answer. At this point in the interview, an open inquiry will help the client to elaborate on his previous comment. Return to 3.37 and try again.

3.40

Your Answer: Who are the others who don't really care about you?

    This is a closed inquiry that will elicit limited factual information. This question won't encourage the client to elaborate on the point he has just made concerning his wife's attitude. Return to 3.37 and try again.

3.41

    An open inquiry can be used to elicit concrete *examples* of *specific* behavior that help an interviewer understand what a client is describing.

Client: I would at least like to feel that all the work I do is appreciated and that my wife realizes how much effort I put into helping.

    Choose the most appropriate response.

Interviewer: But you and your wife have good times, don't you?

Go to 3.42

Interviewer: Why doesn't your wife appreciate you and all the work you do?   Go to 3.43

Interviewer: What sort of things would make you feel appreciated?

Go to 3.44

3.42

Your Answer: But you and your wife have good times, don't you?

    This is a closed inquiry for which you have suggested a specific answer. This response doesn't permit the client to describe his behavior. The use of an open inquiry in this instance is more likely to enable you to obtain specific information about the client's needs. Return to 3.41 and try again.

3.43

Your Answer: Why doesn't your wife appreciate you and all the work you do?

    This is an open inquiry, but it isn't the most appropriate response. Open comments that begin with the word *why* often irritate clients and make them feel defensive. Appropriate open inquiries allow clients to express their views and feelings openly. Return to 3.41 and try again.

3.44

Your Answer: What sort of things would make you feel appreciated?

    Correct. This is an open inquiry that will enable you to obtain specific examples of the client's needs in his present situation.

    This interview continues with an open discussion of the client's situation. At its conclusion, the interviewer and the client agree to meet again before any decision is made regarding the appropriateness of counseling sessions. Proceed to 3.45 to begin the second interview.

3.45

    Open inquiries are very useful as a method of initiating an interview.

    (The client looks inquiringly at the interviewer and waits for the interview to begin.)

    Choose the most appropriate response.

Interviewer: Were things a little better for you last week?
        Go to 3.46

Interviewer: What would you like to talk about today? Go to 3.47

Interviewer: How was your wife last week?   Go to 3.48

3.46

Your Answer: Were things a little better for you last week?

This is a closed inquiry that doesn't encourage the client to tell you about his problem. An open inquiry, on the other hand, would give him an opportunity to discuss his problem. Return to 3.45 and try again.

3.47

Your Answer: What would you like to talk about today?

Correct. This is an open inquiry that encourages the client to discuss his problem. By responding in this manner, you permit him to take up the discussion where it is most relevant to him. Proceed to 3.49.

3.48

Your Answer: How was your wife last week?

Although this is an open inquiry, it focuses on the client's wife rather than on the client. It's important to focus the interview on the client. Return to 3.45 and try again.

3.49

The emphasis in this segment has been on open inquiries; however, closed inquiries are sometimes useful in gaining precise information. They are also helpful in focusing a client on a specific point. The effective interviewer uses both closed and open inquiries but uses open inquiries whenever possible.

Client: I just can't stand living at home anymore. One night last week I got in the car and felt like smashing it into a pole and ending it all.

Choose the most appropriate response.

Interviewer: What do you plan to do about your situation?
Go to 3.50

Interviewer: Why don't you leave home? Go to 3.51

Interviewer: Did you actually try to kill yourself? Go to 3.52

3.50

Your Answer: What do you plan to do about your situation?

The client mentioned two important facts. Because of the gravity of his suggestion of suicide, it is important that you determine how seriously he is considering suicide. A closed inquiry at this point can help you achieve this objective quickly. If the client is sincere in his desire to end his life, it is essential that you focus on his potential suicide. If the client is not seriously considering suicide, then more will be gained by focusing on his desire to leave home. In either case, you should revert to the use of an open interviewing style. Return to 3.49 and try again.

3.51

Your Answer: Why don't you leave home?

This is an open inquiry, but, because it sounds like advice, it may cause the client to feel defensive. It's important that you determine whether the client's mention of suicide or his desire to leave home should be the focus of further inquiry. Your response indicates that you have made this decision before obtaining further information from the client. A closed inquiry at this point would allow the client to give you the required information. Return to 3.49 and try again.

3.52

Your Answer: Did you actually try to kill yourself?

Correct. This closed inquiry helps you to evaluate the degree of risk associated with the client's present state. If his answer is "yes," his potential suicide should be discussed. If his answer is "no," it would be appropriate to discuss his desire to leave home. In either case, you should continue to use open inquiries. Proceed to 3.53.

3.53

Although closed inquiries can be useful in an interview, you shouldn't ask one closed question after another. You should be prepared to follow a closed question with a response that allows greater participation on the part of the client.

Client: No, not really. I could never kill myself.

         Choose the most appropriate response.

Interviewer: Could you tell me more about your desire to leave home?   Go to 3.54

Interviewer: You didn't hurt yourself, then?   Go to 3.55

Interviewer: You weren't really serious, then, were you?

         Go to 3.56

3.54

Your Answer: Could you tell me more about your desire to leave home?

         Correct. This open inquiry permits the client to discuss his current situation freely. Proceed to 3.57.

3.55

Your Answer: You didn't hurt yourself, then?

         This closed inquiry suggests that you are dissatisfied with the client's response or that you don't believe him. Following the previous closed inquiry, this question may give the client the feeling that he is under cross-examination. Return to 3.53 and try again.

3.56

Your Answer: You weren't really serious then, were you?

         This assumption on your part doesn't encourage the client to discuss his present stressful situation. Your previous response was a closed question; a more open response is required if the client is to participate again in the discussion. Return to 3.53 and try again.

3.57

         Effective use of open and closed inquiry can result in interviews that are meaningful for both participants. It is possible, however, to misuse this skill during an interview. It's important that you ask only one question at a time. Clients quickly become confused when interviewers ask several questions at the same time.

Client: As far as I'm concerned, there's nothing I can do to make our marriage work, so I guess I'd be better off, out of it. But then, I should stay.

         Choose the most appropriate response.

Interviewer: What makes you feel that you should stay? How
would you get along if you left?   Go to 3.58
Interviewer: What makes you feel that you should stay?

Go to 3.59
Interviewer: How would you get along if you left? Would you rent
an apartment or move in with a friend?   Go to 3.60

3.58

Your Answer: What makes you feel that you should stay? How
would you get along if you left?

Your initial open inquiry is appropriate, but its impact is lost
when you follow it with a second question. Double and multiple
questions confuse clients. Return to 3.57 and try again.

3.59

Your Answer: What makes you feel that you should stay?

Correct. A single, open inquiry facilitates further exploration of
the problem by the client. Proceed to 3.61.

3.60

Your Answer: How would you get along if you left? Would you rent
an apartment or move in with a friend?

Often, an open inquiry loses its potential because of the addition of a closed inquiry. You should refrain from asking multiple
questions. Return to 3.57 and try again.

3.61

When your questions focus on the client's discussion, you avoid
leading questions that impose your ideas and assumptions on the
client.

As an interviewer, you shouldn't ask too many consecutive
questions; this can produce an atmosphere of cross-examination, particularly when the questions are closed ended.

Client: Well, if we could get our money problems sorted out,
I'm sure my wife and I could get along fine. Before
we had money problems, we had good times.

Choose the most appropriate response.
Interviewer: What about getting a consolidated loan?   Go to 3.62

Interviewer:	Could you tell me more about your money problems?
	Go to 3.63
Interviewer:	Did you have to acquire so many debts? Go to 3.64

3.62

Your Answer: What about getting a consolidated loan?

Leading questions such as this are inappropriate at any time during an interview. This question assumes that there is a single solution to the client's problem. Return to 3.61 and try again.

3.63

Your Answer: Could you tell me more about your money problems?

Correct. This open inquiry facilitates discussion of a central difficulty in the client's present situation. Proceed to 3.65.

3.64

Your Answer: Did you have to acquire so many debts?

Repeated use of closed inquiries is likely to result in irritation and defensiveness on the part of the client and create a climate that is not conducive to an open discussion of his situation. Return to 3.61 and try again.

3.65

Minimal encouragements indicate to others that you're interested in what they're saying. Once you've made an inquiry (or used any other interviewing skill), you should encourage the client to continue talking by using minimal encouragements. A minimal encouragement is a prompt that indicates that you're listening to what the client is saying and that you want him or her to continue.

Client: We just can't make ends meet. I didn't tell you last week—I couldn't—that I was married before, and I have to make maintenance payments. After I make those payments, we just don't have enough money to live on. That brings me to another problem. I never have time to be with my children, and . . . and . . . .

Choose the most appropriate response.

Interviewer: How many children do you have?   Go to 3.66

| Interviewer: | Do you enjoy your children? | Go to 3.67 |
| Interviewer: | Mm . . . hmm. | Go to 3.68 |

3.66

Your Answer: How many children do you have?

     The client is telling you about his interactions with his children. He has stopped briefly to gather his thoughts. At this point, a minimal encouragement will indicate that you are interested in what he is saying and would like him to continue. Return to 3.65 and try again.

3.67

Your Answer: Do you enjoy your children?

     This inquiry changes the topic and therefore is not an appropriate response. The client is telling you about his interactions with his children. He has stopped briefly to gather his thoughts. At this point, a minimal encouragement will indicate that you are interested in what he is saying and would like him to continue. Return to 3.65 and try again.

3.68

Your Answer: Mm . . . hmm.

     Correct. This minimal encouragement indicates that you are interested in what the client is saying and would like him to continue. Proceed to 3.69.

3.69

     The repetition of one or two key words of a conversation constitutes one type of minimal encouragement. Other examples of minimal encouragements are: *oh, so, then, umm, hmmm, uhhuh, sure, right,* and *go on.*

Client: I really would like to . . . well, to have the time to do things with my children.

     Choose the most appropriate response.

Interviewer:	Would they want that?	Go to 3.70
Interviewer:	Go on.	Go to 3.71
Interviewer:	Do you have boys or girls?	Go to 3.72

3.70

Your Answer: Would they want that?

This closed inquiry takes the client's attention away from what he was telling you and directs it to a topic that interests you. At this point, a brief, minimal encouragement will invite the client to relate his concerns. Return to 3.69 and try again.

3.71

Your Answer: Go on.

Correct. This minimal encouragement indicates to the client that you are interested and concerned about what he is saying and would like him to continue. Proceed to 3.73.

3.72

Your Answer: Do you have boys or girls?

This response changes the topic and interrupts the client. At this point, a brief, minimal encouragement will invite the client to relate his concerns. Return to 3.69 and try again.

3.73

The following is a list of closed inquiries. On a separate sheet, change each of these closed inquiries into an open inquiry. Try to use a variety of open inquiries. Compare your responses with the examples that follow this list.

1. Aren't your parents helping you?
2. Do you always argue?
3. Do you try to help?
4. Surely you love your husband?
5. Is it true that you want to leave home?
6. Do you enjoy being with that sort of person?
7. You've never married?
8. Have you stopped fighting with your wife?
9. Shouldn't you consider what your family thinks?
10. Do you want to do something about your problems?

The following open inquiries would encourage a client to discuss a situation or problem in great detail.

1. a. Could you tell me how your parents are reacting to your problem?
    b. What kind of support are your parents giving you?
2. a. Could you explain more clearly how you interact?
    b. How do you respond to these situations?
3. a. How do you help?
    b. What do you see as your role?
4. a. What are your feelings about your husband?
    b. Could you tell me about your relationship with your husband?
5. a. How do you feel about leaving home?
    b. Could you clarify for me how you stand on the issue of leaving home?
6. a. What are your feelings about being with that sort of person?
    b. How do you react to being with that sort of person?
7. a. Could you help me to understand your feelings toward marriage?
    b. How do you feel about your present marital status?
8. a. Could you describe the current situation between you and your wife?
    b. How are you and your wife getting along at present?
9. a. To what degree are you willing to consider your family in this situation?
    b. How important to you are your family's reactions?
10. a. How interested are you in changing your behavior?
    b. To what extent are you willing to work toward changing your behavior?

If you had difficulty providing open inquiries for three or more of the closed inquiries, you should work through this chapter again.

---

1. **CONCERNING OPEN INQUIRIES**:
    a. Ask a question that cannot be answered with "yes," "no," or a simple fact.
    b. Ask a question that is on topic.
    c. "What" questions are frequently fact oriented.
    d. "How" questions are frequently people oriented.
    e. "Could" and "Can" questions provide greatest flexibility for response.

    f.   "Why" questions often provoke defensive feelings and are not recommended.

2. **MAKE OPEN INQUIRIES TO:**
   a. Give clients greater opportunity to discuss topics relevant to them.
   b. Gather information and help clients explore and clarify their concerns.
   c. Put clients at ease.
   d. Begin an interview.
   e. Facilitate elaboration of a point.
   f. Elicit specific examples of general situations.

3. **WHEN MAKING CLOSED INQUIRIES:**
   a. Ask questions that can be answered with "yes," "no," or a simple fact.
   b. Ask questions that are on topic.

4. **MAKE CLOSED INQUIRIES:**
   a. Generally, as infrequently as possible.
   b. Specifically, when you need information that is important to the progress of the interview.

5. **FORMS OF INQUIRY TO BE AVOIDED:**
   a. Multiple questions in a single response.
   b. Leading questions.
   c. Cross-examinations.

6. **WHEN MAKING MINIMAL ENCOURAGEMENTS:**
   a. Use prompts such as "and then," "umm hmm," and "right."
   b. Repeat a few key words from a client's previous statement.

7. **MAKE MINIMAL ENCOURAGEMENTS TO:**
   a. Encourage a client to continue.
   b. Indicate that you are focusing and following.

MULTIPLE-CHOICE TEST

In order to evaluate your mastery of the material in this chapter, you should answer the following multiple-choice questions. In each case, select the most appropriate response based on the content of this chapter. The correct answers are listed in the Appendix.

1. Client (a 16-year-old female): I was sent to your office because a bottle of alcohol was found in my locker.

   a. Interviewer: You seem really upset.
   b. Interviewer: Could you tell me more about what has happened?
   c. Interviewer: Why did you have the alcohol in your locker?

2. Client: A friend of mine asked me to keep the bottle in my locker. I agreed to do it, but I wish I hadn't.

   a. Interviewer: Did you really want to keep the bottle?
   b. Interviewer: What did you want to do when your friend asked you to keep the bottle?
   c. Interviewer: Have you done this before?

3. Client: I didn't want to keep it, but if I hadn't, my friends would have thought I was "chicken."

   a. Interviewer: Who asked you to keep the bottle?
   b. Interviewer: Are you that concerned about what your friends think of you?
   c. Interviewer: What do you mean by "chicken"?

4. Client: My friends would think that I was afraid of getting caught.

   a. Interviewer: How do you feel now that you have been caught?
   b. Interviewer: Do you always do what your friends want you to do?
   c. Interviewer: What do you suppose your friends think now?

5. Client: I feel awful.

   a. Interviewer: So . . .
   b. Interviewer: Could you help me to understand what you mean by "awful"?
   c. Interviewer: Are you really disappointed in yourself?

6. Client: I feel so embarrassed, because everyone, including my parents, is going to find out what I did.

   a. Interviewer: Are your parents going to be angry with you?
   b. Interviewer: It's not that bad, is it?
   c. Interviewer: How do you expect your parents to react?

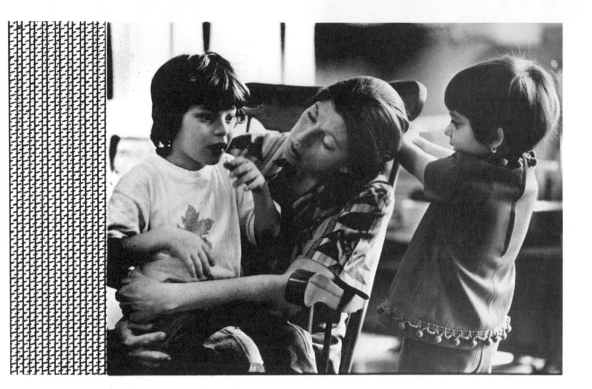

Chapter 4
REFLECTING FEELING

The material in this chapter is intended to help you master the skill of reflecting feeling. After completing this chapter, you should be able to do the following:

1. Identify the feelings a client conveys to you by selecting those words that best describe them.
2. Reflect a client's feelings with fitting words.
3. State the rationale for reflecting feeling.
4. Decide whether reflection of feeling is appropriate in a given situation.

The first part of this chapter deals with relatively simple emotions in order to help you develop the ability to identify and reflect feelings. In actual practice, however, individuals rarely convey simple emotions when they communicate. Most people demonstrate a number of emotions when they interact with one another. Therefore, the latter part of this chapter is devoted to the identification and reflection of "mixed" emotions. When identifying the emotions of others, it's important to attend not only to what they are saying, but also to how they say it. The posture, voice tone, and mannerisms of individuals often provide important information about their emotions. Each of the following frames is complete in itself—that is, each depicts a different client. Proceed to 4.1 to begin this program.

4.1

Client

In order to reflect feeling, you must be able to identify the emotions a client is experiencing. This first series of frames is designed to help you develop the ability to identify emotions.

(describing his relationship with his employer): I try and I try, but I hardly ever seem to succeed. Every time I try to do what he wants, it doesn't work out. When I try to do things the way I think they should be done, he doesn't like that either. I just don't know what to do.

Choose the word that best represents the client's feelings.

Guilty	Go to 4.2
Angry	Go to 4.3
Frustrated	Go to 4.4

4.2

Your Answer: Guilty

The client's response indicates that he is trying and has tried to do something about his situation. He would be likely to feel guilty only if he hadn't tried to do something about his problem. Return to 4.1 and try again.

4.3

Your Answer: Angry

The client may be angry, but you need more information to substantiate this conclusion. To identify feelings accurately, you must attend closely to the client. Return to 4.1 and try again.

4.4

Your Answer: Frustrated

Correct. The client is trying to reach his goal, but his attempts have failed, and he feels frustrated. Proceed to 4.5.

4.5

Client (whose car was recently damaged in an accident): I'd like to take something and wrap it around his head— anything to get even with that bastard.

Choose the word that best describes the client's feelings.

Depressed   Go to 4.6
Revengeful   Go to 4.7
Annoyed   Go to 4.8

4.6

Your Answer: Depressed

The client is feeling hostile—not depressed. Return to 4.5 and try again.

4.7

Your Answer: Revengeful

Correct. Although the first part of the client's statement communicates anger, the second part communicates a desire to get even. Proceed to 4.9.

4.8

Your Answer: Annoyed

The client is undoubtedly annoyed; however, the language being used suggests feelings that are far stronger than mere annoyance. This response is an understatement of the client's feelings. Return to 4.5 and try again.

4.9

Client (discussing a close friend): It bothers me, and I really worry about him. I want to help, but I just can't get through to him.

Choose the emotion that best represents the client's feelings.

Resigned	Go to 4.10
Frustrated	Go to 4.11
Concerned	Go to 4.12

4.10

Your Answer: Resigned

When attempting to identify feelings, you must attend to the client's entire message. The client has expressed a desire to help, which doesn't indicate an attitude of resignation. Return to 4.9 and try again.

4.11

Your Answer: Frustrated

Although the client may be frustrated, the feelings being revealed can be more accurately identified. Return to 4.9 and try again.

4.12

Your Answer: Concerned

Correct. "I want to help . . ." suggests concern. Proceed to 4.13.

4.13

Client   (discussing her recent remarriage): There is just one feeling I have when I look at him; I'm not sure I can find the word. I feel good inside—sort of glowing—like I used to when I woke up on Christmas morning.

Choose the emotion that best represents the client's feelings.

Happy	Go to 4.14
Surprised	Go to 4.15
Appreciated	Go to 4.16

4.14

Your Answer: Happy

Correct. It's as important to identify positive emotions as it is to identify negative ones. The example the client gives of how she feels suggests a strong positive emotion. Proceed to 4.17.

4.15

Your Answer: Surprised

The client hasn't said her feelings surprise her; she has told you how good and glowing she feels inside. Return to 4.13 and try again.

4.16

Your Answer: Appreciated

The client may feel appreciated, but she hasn't mentioned this feeling. She focuses on her own internal feelings rather than on her feelings about her relationship with her husband. Return to 4.13 and try again.

4.17

Client   (whose wife and children have recently left him): I feel deserted. There's nowhere to turn—just nowhere. I feel so left out. I'm sure no one cares whether I live or die.

Choose the emotion that best represents the client's feelings.

Depressed	Go to 4.18
Apprehensive	Go to 4.19
Afraid	Go to 4.20

4.18

Your Answer: Depressed

Correct. The first part of the client's statement indicates loneliness. The second part indicates that he believes no one cares whether he lives or dies—an indication of depression. Proceed to 4.21.

4.19

Your Answer: Apprehensive

The client may be apprehensive; however, his words indicate that the emotion he is feeling is stronger than apprehension. Return to 4.17 and try again.

4.20

Your Answer: Afraid

It is likely that the client is frightened by his situation; however, his last comment indicates that his reaction constitutes more than fear. Return to 4.17 and try again.

4.21

In the previous series of frames, you learned how to identify feelings. One of the most important aspects of helping others is the ability to reflect their feelings. The following frames are intended to help you learn how to form appropriate reflections of feelings.

Client (describing her husband's reaction to her decision to find a job): He laughed at me. My own husband just sat there and laughed at me. I felt like such a fool—so put down.

Choose the response that best reflects the client's feelings.

Interviewer:	Why didn't you tell him to stop?	Go to 4.22
Interviewer:	You felt humiliated.	Go to 4.23
Interviewer:	You felt angry.	Go to 4.24

4.22

Your Answer: Why didn't you tell him to stop?

This is an open inquiry rather than a reflection of feeling. Return to 4.21 and try again.

4.23

Your Answer: You felt humiliated.

Correct. This is an accurate reflection of the client's description of her feelings. It's often helpful to imagine yourself in the situation the client describes (you would probably feel humiliated if someone laughed at you). Proceed to 4.25.

4.24

Your Answer: You felt angry.

You should avoid overinterpretation of the client's feelings. This response assumes too much. The situation the client had described may have produced anger, hurt, or even depression; you need more information to accurately label her feelings. Return to 4.21 and try again.

4.25

When reflecting feeling, you should notice the affective words used in an interview and reflect them, or some variation of them, back to the client without repeating the client's words.

Client (describing difficulties at work): I try, honestly, but I don't get anywhere. Working hard doesn't seem to make any difference; I'm still behind.

Choose the response that best reflects the client's feelings.

Interviewer: I guess you're depressed.   Go to 4.26
Interviewer: I guess you must feel that working hard doesn't get you anywhere.   Go to 4.27
Interviewer: I guess you must be discouraged.   Go to 4.28

4.26

Your Answer: I guess you're depressed.

This response is a reflection of feeling, but it is too heavily loaded. The client has not indicated that she is depressed, only that she is discouraged. A response that is too strong may threaten or irritate the client. Return to 4.25 and try again.

4.27

Your Answer: I guess you must feel that working hard doesn't get you anywhere.

In making this response, you rely too heavily on the client's words. When you take a client's words out of context and repeat them, you sometimes change their meaning. Return to 4.25 and try again.

4.28

Your Answer: I guess you feel discouraged.

Correct. This is an accurate reflection of feeling in which you identify the affect associated with the client's comments and reflect that affect appropriately. Proceed to 4.29.

4.29

The ability to reflect feeling is useful at most points in an interview and in response to a variety of statements. The following statement is made in the early stages of an interview.

Client (a former drug addict discussing his rehabilitation): What can I do? I have no money, no skills, and no one to help me. I should do something, but I don't know what.

Choose the most appropriate response.

Interviewer: You sound bewildered at the moment.   Go to 4.30
Interviewer: You sound as though you've given up hope.
                                                      Go to 4.31
Interviewer: All of that must be frightening to you.   Go to 4.32

4.30

Your Answer: You sound bewildered at the moment.

Correct. Your answer indicates that you've accurately identified the client's feelings. Proceed to 4.33.

4.31

Your Answer: You sound as though you've given up hope.

This response indicates that you've focused on only part of what the client has said. By stating that he "should do something," he has shown that he has some desire to alter his situation. Return to 4.29 and try again.

4.32

Your Answer: All of that must be frightening to you.

This response is an overstatement of the emotion expressed by the client. He has said that he has no money or skills and that he doesn't know what to do; however, he has not indicated that he's frightened about his situation. Your inaccurate reflection may puzzle or even irritate the client. Return to 4.29 and try again.

4.33

It is appropriate to reflect clients' feelings at any time, regardless of the nature of those feelings (positive, negative, or ambivalent), and regardless of the direction of their expression (toward themselves, the interviewer, or the interviewing situation).

Client: There was a time when I felt depressed, but now, thanks to you, I don't feel that way anymore.

Choose the response that best reflects the client's feelings.

Interviewer: We still have a long way to go.   Go to 4.34

Interviewer: You feel that you've come a long way, and you're thankful for that.   Go to 4.35

Interviewer: You feel that I've helped you a great deal, but you did the work.   Go to 4.36

4.34

Your Answer: We still have a long way to go.

This response isn't a reflection of feeling: it's a piece of advice that is unlikely to be of benefit to you or the client. Return to 4.33 and try again.

4.35

Your Answer: You feel that you've come a long way, and you're thankful for that.

Correct. It's always appropriate to reflect feelings, even when they are directed toward you, the interviewer. Reflection of such feelings will help the client to clarify your relationship. Proceed to 4.37.

4.36

Your Answer: You feel that I've helped you a great deal, but you did the work.

This reflection of feeling detracts from the statement the client has made. By making this response, you deny the client the right to express his or her feelings. Return to 4.33 and try again.

4.37

Clients are occasionally out of touch with their feelings or are unable to discuss them. When their feelings are reflected back to them, however, they become more aware of them and are able to evaluate their appropriateness.

Client (describing the discovery of an accident in his home):

I turned on the light and saw him lying on the floor. There was blood everywhere. It was unbelievable.

Choose the response that best reflects the client's feelings.

Interviewer:	What on earth did you do?	Go to 4.38
Interviewer:	You must have been paralyzed.	Go to 4.39
Interviewer:	You must have been shocked.	Go to 4.40

4.38

Your Answer: What on earth did you do?

This is an open inquiry that will elicit factual information. At this point in the interview, however, your task is to help the client become aware of and accept the feelings that the incident aroused. Return to 4.37 and try again.

4.39

Your Answer: You must have been paralyzed.

By using the word *paralyzed,* you infer a feeling that is not implied in the client's statement. Return to 4.37 and try again.

4.40

Your Answer: You must have been shocked.

Correct. Your response allows the client to consider how he feels and indicates that his feelings and reactions were appropriate under the circumstances. Proceed to 4.41.

4.41

Reflecting feeling may be defined as responding to the underlying *feeling* or *emotional* aspect of a client's statement while ignoring its cognitive aspects or content.

Client (describing a co-worker): You should see him. He is really something! Good looking! And I've got a date with him.

Choose the response that best reflects the client's feelings.

Interviewer:	You're very excited about that!	Go to 4.42
Interviewer:	Don't get your hopes up; it's only a date.	Go to 4.43
Interviewer:	So you have a date with him.	Go to 4.44

4.42

Your Answer: You're very excited about that!

       Correct. Your response ignores the cognitive aspects of what the client has said and reflects her feelings—her excitement. Proceed to 4.45.

4.43

Your Answer: Don't get your hopes up; it's only a date.

       This response is a piece of advice, not a reflection of feeling. You have ignored the feelings of the client and concentrated on the cognitive aspect of what she has said—her date and its meaning. Return to 4.41 and try again.

4.44

Your Answer: So you have a date with him.

       This response is a reflection of content—a repetition of a portion of what the client said. Although this response can be appropriate, it is not the response requested of you here. Return to 4.41 and try again.

4.45

       What the client says represents the content portion of a message. You should also be aware of *how* the client conveys a message. For example, the client may speak more quickly when communicating enthusiasm, more slowly when communicating discouragement, and so on.

Client (with her head down, speaking in a low tone of voice):
I was going to go skiing, but my mother is coming to stay with me.

       Choose the response that best reflects the client's feelings.

Interviewer:	It sounds as though that will be just as enjoyable.	Go to 4.46
Interviewer:	You seem unhappy about that.	Go to 4.47
Interviewer:	You must be looking forward to her arrival.	Go to 4.48

4.46

Your Answer: It sounds as though that will be just as enjoyable.

You haven't attended to *how* the client delivered her previous response. Her head was down and she spoke in a low tone of voice. It is unlikely that her behavior indicated that she was happy about what she was telling you. Return to 4.45 and try again.

4.47

Your Answer: You seem unhappy about that.

Correct. By noting her posture and tone of voice, you have accurately identified the client's feelings. Proceed to 4.49.

4.48

Your Answer: You must be looking forward to her arrival.

The client has made no mention of looking forward to her mother's arrival. This is *your* interpretation, not an accurate reflection of the client's feelings. Return to 4.45, and attend carefully to *how* the client delivers her message.

4.49

Discussing feelings is often an important prerequisite to solving problems. By selectively attending to and reflecting feelings, the interviewer helps the client to talk about them.

Client: I passed the test! I passed! I even got a good mark!

Choose the response that best reflects the client's feelings.

Interviewer: You feel like you're on top of the world.   Go to 4.50

Interviewer: You feel quite relieved to know you passed.

Go to 4.51

Interviewer: So, you got a good grade on your test.   Go to 4.52

4.50

Your Answer: You feel like you're on top of the world.

Correct. Your response focuses on how the client feels, not on what is being said. Proceed to 4.53.

4.51

Your Answer: You feel quite relieved to know you passed.

This response fails to reflect the client's exhilaration. Moreover, you've assumed a feeling of relief, which may not be present. Return to 4.49 and try again.

4.52

Your Answer: So, you got a good grade on your test.

This response helps the client to talk about grades and this particular test, but it doesn't help the discussion of *feelings*. You have ignored the emotional aspects of the response. Return to 4.49 and try again.

4.53

When you reflect feelings, you indicate that you can accurately sense the world as the client feels and perceives it; as a result, you build a good relationship with the client.

Client: I'm glad I finally told you about it. You seem to understand. You seem to understand everything I tell you.

Choose the response that best reflects the client's feelings.

Interviewer: You sound happy about that.   Go to 4.54
Interviewer: You should have told someone about this years ago.
      Go to 4.55
Interviewer: It's a relief to be able to talk about it, isn't it?
      Go to 4.56

4.54

Your Answer: You sound happy about that.

This is a reflection of feeling, but a poor one. You've merely parroted the client's statement. When you reflect feeling, it is important to identify the essence of the underlying feeling. Return to 4.53 and try again.

4.55

Your Answer: You should have told someone about this years ago.

This response ignores what the client has told you. Your advice is of no use to the client and will probably hinder the development of your relationship. Return to 4.53 and try again.

4.56

Your Answer: It's a relief to be able to talk about it, isn't it?

Correct. You've indicated that you know how the client feels now that he has finally told you something he has been reticent to tell you before. Proceed to 4.57.

4.57

An important aspect of reflecting feeling is the ability to clearly summarize the emotional aspects of clients' messages, thus enabling them to understand and deal with their own emotions.

Client (discussing her aging father): I'm so worried about him. He's working too hard. I don't know what to do to slow him down.

Choose the response that best reflects the client's feelings.

Interviewer: You sound very worried about what your father will do to himself by working too hard. You want to help him, but you don't know what to do. You're frustrated by all of this—maybe even a little angry.

Go to 4.58

Interviewer: You're anxious, and you're concerned about what can be done for your father. Go to 4.59

Interviewer: You sound worried. If I were you, I'd go and have a talk with the family doctor or maybe your minister.

Go to 4.60

4.58

Your Answer: You sound very worried about what your father will do to himself by working too hard. You want to help him, but you don't know what to do. You're frustrated by all of this—maybe even a little angry.

A reflection of feeling should be clear, concise, accurate. This reflection of feeling is confused, lengthy, and inaccurate. The client hasn't given an indication of frustration or anger. Return to 4.57 and try again.

4.59

Your Answer: You're anxious and you're concerned about what can be done for your father.

  Correct. Your clear, concise summary will help the client to identify and cope with her feelings. Proceed to 4.61.

4.60

Your Answer: You sound worried. If I were you, I'd go and have a talk with the family doctor or maybe your minister.

  The client would have resolved her problem if the solution were this simple. She needs to explore her problem in order to reach a solution, and you can help her in this exploration by reflecting her feelings. Return to 4.57 and try again.

4.61

  Although a client's comments often refer to past, present, and future events, interviewers are most productive when they reflect and explore feelings that represent a client's current emotional state.

Client (separated from her husband three months ago): When he first told me that he was going to leave me, I was very angry, but now I'm managing by myself without his help.

  Choose the response that best reflects the client's feelings.

Interviewer: In the future, you'll be glad it worked out this way.

              Go to 4.62

Interviewer: You were really angry when he first told you.

              Go to 4.63

Interviewer: You're really proud that you have managed by yourself.   Go to 4.64

4.62

Your Answer: In the future, you'll be glad it worked out this way.

  There is no basis for this assumption in what the client has told you (although it may be true). Moreover, reflections of feeling are most productive when they focus on a client's current emotional state. Return to 4.61 and try again.

4.63

Your Answer: You were really angry when he first told you.

This response is a reflection of past feeling. You have attended only to one part of the client's response, not to her current feelings. Return to 4.61 and try again.

4.64

Your Answer: You're really proud that you have managed by yourself.

Correct. You've accurately reflected the client's current feelings. This reflection will help her to explore her feelings. Proceed to 4.65.

4.65

It is important to reflect and explore emotions that pertain to the immediate interview.

Client: My father was a counselor. Boy, did I ever hate him. I'm sure all counselors are alike.

Choose the response that best reflects the client's feelings.

Interviewer: I get the feeling you don't like counselors, including me.   Go to 4.66

Interviewer: You must have hated your father very much.   Go to 4.67

Interviewer: You shouldn't feel that all counselors are bad.   Go to 4.68

4.66

Your Answer: I get the feeling you don't like counselors, including me.

Correct. The client has implied that he hates all counselors, including you. With this response, you are asking him to explore his feelings about you. It is important that the client understands his feelings about you before he goes on to discuss other matters. Proceed to 4.69.

4.67

Your Answer: You must have hated your father very much.

You've reflected the client's feelings, but you've missed the point of what he told you about counselors, of whom *you* are one.

You need to respond to the emotions the client expresses toward you before you can help him understand his feelings. Return to 4.65 and try again.

4.68

Your Answer: You shouldn't feel that all counselors are bad.

This response denies the client the right to express, explore, and resolve his feelings. Return to 4.65 and try again.

4.69

Clients usually express mixed feelings, rather than basic feelings, during interviews. One of the responsibilities of an interviewer is to help clients sort out their mixed feelings.

Client (discussing her estranged husband): I hope Joe will pay child support. He was no good, but he did provide. I worry about what we will do if he doesn't.

Choose the response that best reflects the client's feelings.

Interviewer: It sounds as though you depend on Joe to come through. Go to 4.70

Interviewer: You hope that you'll have some financial support, but you're anxious, because you're not sure that Joe will come through. Go to 4.71

Interviewer: I guess you're anxious about being left without any financial support. Go to 4.72

4.70

Your Answer: It sounds as though you depend on Joe to come through.

This response reflects only one aspect of the client's feelings. She is displaying mixed emotions, and you should help her sort out these emotions. Return to 4.69 and try again.

4.71

Your Answer: You hope that you'll have some financial support, but you're anxious, because you're not sure that Joe will come through.

Correct. You've identified the client's mixed emotions, thereby helping her to talk about her feelings rather than focus on only one feeling. Proceed to 4.73.

4.72

Your Answer: I guess you're anxious about being left without any financial support.

> You've reflected one aspect of the client's feelings, but not the mixed nature of these feelings. You should help the client to clarify the mixed state of her emotions and explore all of them. Return to 4.69 and try again.

4.73

> Failure to identify and reflect a client's mixed emotions can result in undue attention on a single aspect of a problem to the exclusion of other equally important facets.

Client: I didn't do well in the exams. I'm going home next week. I'm looking forward to seeing my parents, but I don't know what they will say about my grades.

> Choose the response that best reflects the client's feelings.

Interviewer: It's really going to be great for you to be home with your parents again.　　　　　Go to 4.74

Interviewer: You're quite anxious about your parents' reaction to your grades.　　　　　Go to 4.75

Interviewer: You're excited about seeing your parents again, but you're anxious about their reaction to your grades.
　　　　　Go to 4.76

4.74

Your Answer: It's really going to be great for you to be home with your parents again.

> You've responded to only one aspect of the mixed emotions the client has displayed. You should help the client sort out these mixed emotions. Return to 4.73 and try again.

4.75

Your Answer: You're quite anxious about your parents' reaction to your grades.

The client has mixed feelings about the proposed trip home. You've responded to one of these feelings, but you haven't helped the client to clarify his confused feelings. Return to 4.73 and try again.

4.76

Your Answer: You're excited about seeing your parents again, but you're anxious about their reaction to your grades.

Correct. You've captured the mixed feelings the client has expressed. Proceed to 4.77.

4.77

Occasionally, a client may say one thing with words while saying something entirely different with actions.

Client (a widow talking about her only son, and crying): I'm really glad my son is going away to college.

Choose the response that best reflects the client's feelings.

Interviewer: You must be extremely proud of him. Where is he going?   Go to 4.78

Interviewer: You're happy that he's going to college, but you'll be lonely without him.   Go to 4.79

Interviewer: You're very unhappy about his decision to go to college.   Go to 4.80

4.78

Your Answer: You must be extremely proud of him. Where is he going?

You've interpreted, rather than reflected, the client's feelings. Moreover, you've changed the topic. Return to 4.77 and try again.

4.79

Your Answer: You're happy that he's going to college, but you'll be lonely without him.

Correct. Your statement reflects the feeling the client discussed as well as the emotion she displayed. Proceed to 4.81.

4.80

Your Answer: You're very unhappy about his decision to go to college.

Although this reflection of feeling identifies the emotion associated with the client's nonverbal behavior, it fails to identify the feeling associated with her verbal message. Return to 4.77 and try again.

4.81

Client   (fidgeting in his chair and wringing his hands): I'm glad I got in to see you today.

Choose the response that best reflects the client's feelings.

Interviewer: You're pleased to be here, but you're somewhat anxious at the same time.   Go to 4.82

Interviewer: I'm glad you were able to see me.   Go to 4.83

Interviewer: You seem to be fairly anxious today.   Go to 4.84

4.82

Your Answer: You're pleased to be here, but you're somewhat anxious at the same time.

Correct. Your response reflects the mixed emotions the client is feeling at the moment. He is showing his anxiety by his behavior while telling you that he is glad to see you. Proceed to 4.85.

4.83

Your Answer: I'm glad you were able to see me.

Although your response reflects the verbal content of the client's communication, it ignores the message of his bodily movements—fidgeting and wringing his hands. Adequate reflection of feeling brings to a person's attention *all* the feelings that he or she communicates. Return to 4.81 and try again.

4.84

Your Answer: You seem to be fairly anxious today.

You've accurately reflected the client's anxiety, but not his feelings about being glad to see you. Return to 4.81 and try again.

4.85

Client	(smiling pleasantly): He doesn't know what the word *share* means. He believes that what's his is his and what's mine is his, too.

Choose the response that best reflects the client's feelings.

Interviewer:	And you don't agree with that, I suppose.
	Go to 4.86
Interviewer:	I'm puzzled. You're smiling, but you sound so resentful. Go to 4.87
Interviewer:	Because you're smiling, I get the feeling his attitude doesn't bother you very much. Go to 4.88

4.86

Your Answer: And you don't agree with that, I suppose.

In making this response, you judge rather than reflect the client's feelings. Pay close attention to the client's verbal and nonverbal behavior, and select a response that reflects them both. Return to 4.85 and try again.

4.87

Your Answer: I'm puzzled. You're smiling, but you sound so resentful.

Correct. You've reflected the fact that the client is smiling while telling you of a situation he resents. By reflecting his verbal and nonverbal communications, you've asked him to clarify for both of you what he is feeling. Proceed to 4.89.

4.88

Your Answer: Because you're smiling, I get the feeling his attitude doesn't bother you very much.

You've misunderstood either the client's smile or his comments. Your reflection is inaccurate and will probably irritate the client. Return to 4.85 and try again.

4.89

Reflection of feeling can be used effectively to help a client who is finding it difficult to continue in an interview.

Client: (has been fidgeting for several minutes)
        Choose the most appropriate response.

Interviewer: (Turn to your desk and take notes until the client is
ready to continue.)   Go to 4.90

Interviewer: Surely it can't be that difficult to talk about it; I
can't help you until you do.   Go to 4.91

Interviewer: You seem very anxious about whatever it is you want
to discuss with me.   Go to 4.92

4.90

Your Answer: (Turn to your desk and take notes until the client is
ready to continue.)

    Your response closes down all communication between yourself and the client, who is already finding it difficult to discuss his problem. Return to 4.89 and try again.

4.91

Your Answer: Surely it can't be that difficult to talk about it; I
can't help you until you do.

    The client already realizes that you can't help him unless he discusses his problem. However, when he realizes that you understand his difficulty in discussing his problem, he will be able to open up to you. Return to 4.89 and try again.

4.92

Your Answer: You seem very anxious about whatever it is you want
to discuss with me.

    Correct. You've reflected the feeling the client is expressing by his behavior. This reflection will allow him to relax and discuss his concerns with you. Proceed to 4.93.

4.93

    It isn't necessary to use one phrase repeatedly when you reflect feelings; there are introductory phrases that provide some variation. Some of these phrases are: *It seems that you feel . . ., You believe . . ., It sounds like . . ., In other words, you feel . . ., I gather that . . ., You really are . . ..* In your own experience, you will come across many other introductory phrases.

Write a reflection of feeling for each of the following statements. Then compare your responses with the examples that follow this list.

1. I'm just fed up with my father. He's always telling me what to do.
2. The future looks really good; I'm looking forward to it.
3. I can't stand those long lines in the bank.
4. Each time I go to the dentist, I tremble.
5. It's going to be so great—I can't wait to get started.
6. There's no future, so why should I do anything?
7. By the time he does get home, I'm just so concerned.
8. I just lost my job because of those politicians and their economic mismanagement.

The following reflections of feeling could be used in response to the preceding statements. Note the various introductory phrases and the range of emotions.

1. You sound irritated (angry, hostile).
2. You're really hopeful (happy, optimistic) about your future.
3. Waiting makes you feel very impatient (fed up, annoyed).
4. You feel very tense (anxious, perturbed) on those occasions.
5. It sounds as though you're full of enthusiasm (excitement, eagerness).
6. You seem to be depressed (down, discouraged) right now.
7. In other words, you become anxious (tense, uptight) when he is delayed.
8. You're really bitter (resentful, frustrated) about what's happened to you.

If you had difficulty producing appropriate reflections of feeling for three or more of these situations, you should work through this chapter again.

POINTS TO REMEMBER ABOUT REFLECTING FEELING

1. **WHEN IDENTIFYING FEELINGS:**
   a. Attend to the affective component of what the client says.
   b. Attend to the client's behavior (posture, voice tone, rate of delivery, and other mannerisms).
   c. Use a wide range of words to label emotions appropriately.
   d. Identify *all* of the client's emotions.
2. **WHEN REFLECTING FEELINGS:**
   a. Use an appropriate introductory phrase followed by a clear

and concise summary of the feelings the client seems to be experiencing.
  b. Reflect mixed emotions.
  c. Don't repeat the client's exact words.
  d. Focus on current feelings, using the present tense.
  e. Use a wide range of introductory phrases, not just a few overworked ones.

3. **REFLECTION OF FEELING:**
  a. Helps clients to become aware of their feelings.
  b. Helps clients to accept and explore their feelings.
  c. Helps you demonstrate that you understand how the client is experiencing the world.
  d. Helps develop a strong relationship between yourself and the client.

4. **REFLECT FEELING:**
  a. In response to all types of emotion (positive, negative, or ambivalent).
  b. Regardless of the direction of the emotion (toward the client, the interviewer, or others).
  c. When the client has feelings about the interview that may impede its progress.
  d. When the client is having difficulty continuing in an interview.

MULTIPLE-
CHOICE
TEST

In order to evaluate your mastery of the material in this chapter, you should answer the following multiple-choice questions. In each case, select the most appropriate response based on the content of this chapter. The correct answers are presented in the Appendix.

1. Client: After the way they treated me in that store, I wouldn't go back there if it was the last store in town.
    Select the emotion that best represents the client's feelings.

    a. Irritated
    b. Angry
    c. Humiliated

2. Client: Can you believe this? I got a job today that I really wanted but I didn't think I could get.

    a. Interviewer: It's great that you got the job.
    b. Interviewer: You must be very happy about that.
    c. Interviewer: It sounds as though you're really excited about getting that job.

3. Client: When I first started coming to talk with you about my problems, I sometimes found it very difficult to open the door to your office.

    a. Interviewer: Initially, you felt apprehensive about coming to see me.
    b. Interviewer: Were you afraid to come and see me?
    c. Interviewer: It sounds as though you resigned yourself to the fact that you needed to come.

4. Client (a student with average grades): How can I ever live up to the accomplishments of my older brother and sister?

    a. Interviewer: You must feel frustrated.
    b. Interviewer: I hear you saying that you feel inadequate when compared to your brother and sister.
    c. Interviewer: Their accomplishments seem to overwhelm you.

5. Client: Mother is always complaining about being too sick to go anywhere or do anything. She's been to several doctors who have told her she is fine. I don't know what to do to convince her that she isn't sick.

    a. Interviewer: You sound annoyed because your mother always uses the excuse that she's sick.
    b. Interviewer: In other words, you become angry with her because she won't go anywhere.
    c. Interviewer: Have you talked with your father about helping her?

6. Client: I'm glad I told him how angry I was with him, but I don't know whether I've lost him or not. I don't want to lose him.

    a. Interviewer: You told him how you felt, but now you think he might leave you.
    b. Interviewer: You seem surprised that you were able to tell him, but you wonder whether he'll leave you.
    c. Interviewer: It sounds as though you feel good about telling him how you felt, but now you're afraid of losing him as a result.

Chapter 5
REFLECTING CONTENT

The material in this chapter is intended to help you acquire the ability to reflect content. When reflecting content, you either paraphrase a single statement or summarize a number of statements. After completing this chapter, you should be able to do the following:

1. Paraphrase a client's statement.
2. Explain the rationale for paraphrasing.
3. Decide whether paraphrasing is appropriate in a given situation.
4. Summarize a series of client statements.
5. Explain the rationale for summarizing.
6. Decide whether summarizing is appropriate in a given situation.

Interviewer trainees sometimes confuse the restatement of the content or cognitive aspects of a client's statement with the repetition of a client's message, or "parroting." When parroting occurs, interviews become circular rather than progressive and clients become uncomfortable and are unable to continue. Therefore, careful attention should be paid to the essence of a client's statement rather than the words a client uses.

The program in this chapter focuses on an interview that takes place in the personnel office of an insurance firm. The client—an insurance agent who is married and has one daughter—has been employed by the firm for approximately 20 years. Until recently, when his work began to deteriorate, he was regarded as a reliable and efficient employee. An interview has been arranged by the personnel manager to discuss the employee's tardiness and absenteeism. Proceed to 5.1.

5.1

In order to reflect the content of a client's statement, an interviewer must paraphrase the main idea contained in the statement without changing it.

Client: I'm not really sure why you've asked me to see you today, unless it's because I've been late a few times this month.

Choose the response that best reflects the content of the client's comments.

Interviewer: I'm sure you know why I've called you in to see me.
Go to 5.2

Interviewer: You think that your tardiness is causing problems.
Go to 5.3

Interviewer: We do have to talk about your tardiness.   Go to 5.4

5.2

Your Answer: I'm sure you know why I've called you in to see me.

This response fails to acknowledge the content of the client's statement. It detracts from his comment and indicates that you weren't focusing on what he was saying. Try to identify the essence of the client's statement. Return to 5.1 and try again.

5.3

Your Answer: You think that your tardiness is causing problems.

Correct. You have paraphrased the essence of the client's communication without changing its meaning. Proceed to 5.5.

5.4

Your Answer: We do have to talk about your tardiness.

         Your response acknowledges the fact that you've heard the client, but it significantly detracts from his communication and will probably increase his apprehension. Return to 5.1 and choose a response that focuses on the main thought expressed by the client.

5.5

         As an interviewer, you should reflect the essence of a client's communication, no matter where it occurs in his or her response.

Client: Well, it's one of the problems I'm concerned about, and I know you people worry about attendance and punctuality.

         Choose the response that best reflects the content of the client's comments.

Interviewer: There are a number of problems bothering you right now.   Go to 5.6

Interviewer: You seem to be aware of my position as personnel manager.   Go to 5.7

Interviewer: Then you know that the firm is interested in your attendance and punctuality.   Go to 5.8

5.6

Your Answer: There are a number of problems bothering you right now.

         Correct. This reflection of content focuses on the most important aspect of the client's comment. Proceed to 5.9.

5.7

Your Answer: You seem to be aware of my position as personnel manager.

         This is an inappropriate reflection of content. The essence of a client's response isn't always contained in his or her last comment. You should be concerned with the client's problems, not his knowledge of your position. Return to 5.5 and try again.

5.8

Your Answer: Then you know that the firm is interested in your attendance and punctuality.

You've parroted the last part of the client's comment and ignored the message contained in his response. Although your response isn't totally inappropriate, it won't help you or the client to explore his problem in any depth; instead, it concentrates on the interests of the firm. Return to 5.5 and try again.

5.9

By appropriately reflecting content, you assure clients that you understand what they're talking about.

Client: I guess all my problems are caused by what's going on at home.

Choose the response that best reflects the content of the client's comments.

Interviewer: You have a problem with your marriage.   Go to 5.10

Interviewer: You think that your problems stem from your difficulties at home.   Go to 5.11

Interviewer: You don't seem to be concerned about your status in the firm.   Go to 5.12

5.10

Your Answer: You have a problem with your marriage.

You've assumed too much. With this reflection of content, you've gone beyond the essence of what the client has said. He may have a number of problems at home. It's unwise to assume that you know what his problem is before he tells you about it. If he has no problem with his marriage, the client is likely to react negatively to your comment. Return to 5.9 and try again.

5.11

Your Answer: You think that your problems stem from your difficulties at home.

Correct. By accurately reflecting the content of his last statement, you've confirmed that you've heard the client's communication and that you want him to continue. Proceed to 5.13.

5.12

Your Answer: You don't seem to be concerned about your status in the firm.

      Your response gives no indication to the client that you've heard his communication. You've ignored the essence of his message. Return to 5.9 and try again.

5.13

      A reflection of content may take the form of a simple, compound, or complex sentence, or a sentence fragment. The reflection should be similar in grammatical structure to the client's statement.

Client: Yes. It's my daughter. She's fifteen, you know, and we're having trouble with her. She stays out all night.

      Choose the response that best reflects the content of the client's comments.

Interviewer: Has your daughter ever been in trouble with the law?
                   Go to 5.14

Interviewer: I guess you've had a lot of problems with your daughter.
                   Go to 5.15

Interviewer: The fact that your daughter doesn't come home at night is a major problem.   Go to 5.16

5.14

Your Answer: Has your daughter ever been in trouble with the law?

      This is a closed-ended question that focuses on the client's daughter rather than on the client and his problems. Your reflection should be grammatically similar to the client's comment; therefore, you should respond with a statement, not a question. Return to 5.13 and try again.

5.15

Your Answer: I guess you've had a lot of problems with your daughter.

      You've assumed too much and changed the focus from a discussion of the client's present difficulty with his daughter to his past experience with her. Return to 5.13 and try again.

5.16

Your Answer: The fact that your daughter doesn't come home at night is a major problem.

Correct. This reflection of content paraphrases the client's comments and, like his response, deals with the present tense. Proceed to 5.17.

5.17

The emphasis in reflecting content is on the cognitive aspect of a client's remarks.

Client: That, and the effect it's having on my wife's heart condition. She's already had one heart attack.

Choose the response that best reflects the content of the client's comments.

Interviewer: So you also have your wife's health to consider.
Go to 5.18

Interviewer: You're really worried about your wife.   Go to 5.19

Interviewer: Your daughter must be a real problem for your wife.
Go to 5.20

5.18

Your Answer: So you also have your wife's health to consider.

Correct. This reflection of content focuses on the cognitive aspect of the client's comment—his consideration of his wife's health. Proceed to 5.21.

5.19

Your Answer: You're really worried about your wife.

This response is a good reflection of feeling; however, you were asked for a reflection of content. Return to 5.17 and try again.

5.20

Your Answer: Your daughter must be a real problem for your wife.

Although this response relates to the content of the client's comments, it shifts the focus of the interview from his problems to problems his wife may be having. Return to 5.17 and try again.

5.21

Reflection of content can be used to summarize an interview and pull together the essence of a number of the client's statements.

Client: I know I'm having problems at work, but what am I going to do?

Choose the response that best summarizes the client's comments to this point.

Interviewer: I understand that you have problems at home, but can we focus on your attendance problems here?

Go to 5.22

Interviewer: Now let me see if I understand your problem. You realize that you're having difficulties at work, but, as you understand it, these are related to your problems at home.

Go to 5.23

Interviewer: It seems that you're finding it difficult to do your job satisfactorily and, at the same time, cope with the problems caused by your daughter and your wife's health.

Go to 5.24

5.22

Your Answer: I understand that you have problems at home, but can we focus on your attendance problems here?

This response is too brief and abrupt. The client has revealed three of his problems, and you should allow him to talk about these problems. A good summarization gives equal emphasis to the various themes covered in clients' previous statements and allows them to select the problem that they want to discuss further. Return to 5.21 and try again.

5.23

Your Answer: Now let me see if I understand your problem. You realize that you're having difficulties at work, but, as you understand it, these are related to your problems at home.

You've focused on the apparent problems of the client rather than on his actual problems. The client is your main focus, and his concerns must be reflected in your summary. Return to 5.21 and try again.

5.24

Your Answer: It seems that you're finding it difficult to do your job satisfactorily and, at the same time, cope with the problems caused by your daughter and your wife's health.

    Correct. This summary accurately reflects the essence of the client's statements up to this point in the interview. Proceed to 5.25.

5.25

    Accurate reflection of content encourages and reassures those clients who are threatened by discussion of feelings.

Client: Yes, but the major difficulty is with my daughter. I think she's been sleeping around, and I'm at my wit's end to know what to do about it.

    Choose the most appropriate response (assuming that this client has difficulty talking about his feelings).

Interviewer: It sounds as though you feel desperate about the situation.   Go to 5.26

Interviewer: That must be an awful situation.   Go to 5.27

Interviewer: Your major concern, then, is what to do to help your daughter.   Go to 5.28

5.26

Your Answer: It sounds as though you feel desperate about the situation.

    This is an accurate reflection of feeling; however, this client is not yet in touch with his feelings, and your reflection at this point could be threatening to him. If the client does feel threatened, he may decide that he's telling you too much too soon and that he should avoid this particular topic. Return to 5.25 and try again.

5.27

Your Answer: That must be an awful situation.

    This is an accurate reflection of feeling; however, you were asked to assume that the client has difficulty discussing feelings. Whenever the client finds it difficult to discuss feelings, you should reflect content and gradually introduce reflections of feeling only when he or she becomes comfortable talking about feelings. Return to 5.25 and try again.

5.28

Your Answer: Your major concern, then, is what to do to help your daughter.

Correct. This reflection of content is the most appropriate response for this particular client. Proceed to 5.29.

5.29

    By reflecting content, you communicate to the client that you are following and attempting to understand what is being said.

Client: Yes. You see, we've tried everything. We've promised to give her things if she'll agree to stay home. We've tried to ground her. What else can I do?

    Choose the response that best reflects the content of the client's comments.

Interviewer: You've tried a lot of things, but nothing has worked.
Go to 5.30

Interviewer: Well, maybe your minister could help you.
Go to 5.31

Interviewer: You think you should do more. There must be something else you can do.   Go to 5.32

5.30

Your Answer: You've tried a lot of things, but nothing has worked.

Correct. This reflection of content indicates that you're attempting to understand the message the client is conveying to you. If there is a misunderstanding, this will give him an opportunity to clarify what he has said. Proceed to 5.33.

5.31

Your Answer: Well, maybe your minister could help you.

This advice changes the topic and indicates to the client that you aren't focusing on what he is saying. Return to 5.29 and try again.

5.32

Your Answer: You think you should do more. There must be something else you can do.

This reflection of content ignores the essence of the client's message. He has just told you about his attempts to help his daughter and his failure to do so; your reflection of content should mirror this fact, not belittle it. Return to 5.29 and try again.

5.33

The main purpose of summarizing content is to help clients collect their thoughts. Clients often present their ideas in a haphazard way. In order to help clients organize their concerns, interviewers should present a concise, accurate, and timely summary.

Client: I lost my temper and almost hit her. But my wife got so upset, I started worrying about her heart condition. Anyway, I realized that I wouldn't solve anything by losing my temper.

Choose the response that best summarizes the client's comments up to this point.

Interviewer: So, your problems at work stem from the problems you're having with your daughter. Go to 5.34

Interviewer: So, the stress caused by your wife's heart condition and your daughter's promiscuity is affecting your ability to work, and you're searching for a solution. Go to 5.35

Interviewer: You're aware of the fact that your work isn't what it used to be. You seem to think that your problems with your daughter are contributing to your problems at work and putting a considerable strain on your wife. Your daughter is becoming promiscuous and, despite your efforts to control her, she continues to act out. Go to 5.36

5.34

Your Answer: So, your problems at work stem from the problems you're having with your daughter.

As an interviewer, you should focus on the client's main problem. This summary reflects only a small portion of the client's discussion and fails to help him organize his disclosures. Return to 5.33 and try again.

5.35

Your Answer: So, the stress caused by your wife's heart condition and your daughter's promiscuity is affecting your ability to work, and you're searching for a solution.

Correct. Your response is brief, accurate, and well organized. It will help the client deal with his problems in an orderly fashion. Proceed to 5.37.

5.36

Your Answer: You're aware of the fact that your work isn't what it used to be. You seem to think that your problems with your daughter are contributing to your problems at work and putting a considerable strain on your wife. Your daughter is becoming promiscuous and, despite your efforts to control her, she continues to act out.

Although this reflection of content contains the essence of what the client has discussed, it is fragmented. A summary should be brief, well organized, and to the point. Return to 5.33 and try again.

5.37

Reflection of content provides direction for an interview.

Client: I guess I'm going to have to find some help in dealing with my daughter's problem. I suppose I should be discussing my work-related problems.

Choose the response that best reflects the content of the client's comments.

Interviewer: I wonder if your daughter really needs help.
Go to 5.38

Interviewer: Yes. Your problems here at work should be the focus of our discussion. Go to 5.39

Interviewer: Your daughter's problem is important, but your problems at work are important, too. Go to 5.40

5.38

Your Answer: I wonder if your daughter really needs help.

This reflection of content is inaccurate. It shifts the focus of the interview from the client's concerns to your thoughts. Moreover, this response focuses on only part of the client's statement. When you reflect content, you should focus on main themes so that the direction of the interview is clear. Return to 5.37 and try again.

5.39

Your Answer: Yes. Your problems here at work should be the focus of our discussion.

You've ignored an important portion of the client's message—his problems at home. Return to 5.37 and try again.

5.40

Your Answer: Your daughter's problem is important, but your problems at work are important, too.

Correct. By concisely reflecting the content of the client's statement, you've made the direction of the interview clear to him. Proceed to 5.41.

5.41

By reflecting content, you can check and clarify your perceptions of what a client has said. Before you can help a client, you need to understand what he or she is trying to say to you.

Client: Well, since I found out about my daughter's problem, I've spent more time at home, and we've had more and more late-night arguments. As a result, I can't get up early in the morning, so I'm late. Then, sometimes I just don't feel like coming to work.

Choose the response that best reflects the content of the client's comments.

Interviewer: It sounds as though you've lost interest in your work.
                                                    Go to 5.42

Interviewer: Your problems with your daughter have been interfering with your work.   Go to 5.43

Interviewer:	It sounds as though your wife should take more responsibility for what's going on at home. Go to 5.44

5.42

Your Answer:	It sounds as though you've lost interest in your work.

This response doesn't paraphrase the client's comments. You've assumed, perhaps incorrectly, that he has lost interest in his work. Return to 5.41 and try again.

5.43

Your Answer:	Your problems with your daughter have been interfering with your work.

Correct. By reflecting the content of the client's comments, you've clarified your own perceptions of his remarks. If your perceptions are incorrect, the client will supply you with additional information. Proceed to 5.45.

5.44

Your Answer:	It sounds as though your wife should take more responsibility for what's going on at home.

This may or may not be true. In either case, this response will be of little benefit to the client, who is trying to tell you about his problem. Your responsibility at this point is to check and clarify your perceptions of what the client has told you. Return to 5.41 and try again.

5.45

Reflection of content should be interspersed with other types of interviewer responses. The overuse of reflecting has a parrot-like effect that can inhibit a client's communication.

Client:	Yes. And even when I try to keep my mind on my work, I find that my attention drifts back to the problems I'm having with my daughter. I've lost a few accounts lately. I lost some of them because I just couldn't get involved enough. And the others . . . well, there were times when my wife called, and I just had to break appointments and go home.

Choose the response that best reflects the content of the client's comments.

Interviewer (having previously responded with an open inquiry): Even when you're at work, your problems at home interfere with what you're doing. Go to 5.46

Interviewer (having previously responded with seven reflections of content): Even when you're at work, your problems at home interfere with what you're doing. Go to 5.47

Interviewer (having reflected content for five minutes): Even when you're at work, your problems at home interfere with what you're doing. Go to 5.48

5.46

Your Answer (having previously responded with an open inquiry): Even when you're at work, your problems at home interfere with what you're doing.

Correct. This response indicates your awareness of the fact that reflection of content shouldn't be overused. Proceed to 5.49.

5.47

Your Answer (having previously responded with seven reflections of content): Even when you're at work, your problems at home interfere with what you're doing.

Continuous reflection of content will give the client the impression that you are simply parroting what he is saying. Return to 5.45 and try again.

5.48

Your Answer (having reflected content for the previous five minutes): Even when you're at work, your problems at home interfere with what you're doing.

Reflection of content should be interspersed with other types of responses if communication between yourself and the client is to be facilitated. Return to 5.45 and try again.

5.49

Summarization of content is a systematic integration of the important themes in a client's statements, not a mechanical means of pulling a number of facts together. It helps a client to review what has been said and stimulates a thorough exploration of particular themes.

Client: Just the other day, I heard that one of my best clients is moving his insurance business to the Comprehensive Life Insurance Company.

Choose the response that best summarizes the client's comments up to this point.

Interviewer: It seems that your tardiness, your frequent absence, and your inability to attend to your work have lost the company considerable business. Go to 5.50

Interviewer: It seems that, at the moment, your problems at home take precedence over your job. Go to 5.51

Interviewer: You seem to be aware of the fact that the problems you're having at home are having serious effects on your business activities. Go to 5.52

5.50

Your Answer: It seems that your tardiness, your frequent absence, and your inability to attend to your work have lost the company considerable business.

Throughout the interview, the client has related his problems at home to his problems at work. This response will indicate to him that you've heard only his comments about his job. This inaccurate summarization of the client's comments represents your own perceptions rather than those of the client. Return to 5.49 and try again.

5.51

Your Answer: It seems that, at the moment, your problems at home take precedence over your job.

You've attempted to summarize the main facts in the client's discussion, but your integration of these facts has resulted in a misinterpretation of the underlying themes. The client has indicated concern for his business competence as well as an awareness of the relationship between his problems at home and his problems at work. Return to 5.49 and try again.

5.52

Your Answer: You seem to be aware of the fact that the problems you're having at home are having serious effects on your business activities.

     Correct. This brief summary reviews the essential ideas that are contained in the client's comments, promotes further exploration, and will lead toward solution of his problems. Proceed to 5.53.

5.53

     You can bring an interview to an effective conclusion by summarizing the major themes covered during the session.

Client: Speaking of business, I have an appointment in a few minutes.

     Choose the response that best concludes the interview.

Interviewer: I guess you'd better go. You seem really concerned about this business appointment.   Go to 5.54

Interviewer: I guess you'd better go. What do you think you should do about your problem?   Go to 5.55

Interviewer: I guess you'd better go. Let's see . . . we've discussed your family problems, their effect on your business activities, and your need to find solutions.

     Go to 5.56

5.54

Your Answer: I guess you'd better go. You seem really concerned about this business appointment.

     This reflection of feeling will probably initiate discussion of the client's appointment rather than close the interview. A brief summarization is often a good way to close down an interview. It allows a mutual review of the themes covered and sets the scene for the next interview. Return to 5.53 and try again.

5.55

Your Answer: I guess you'd better go. What do you think you should do about your problem?

     The client has indicated that he has a business appointment. As personnel manager, you should realize the importance of his appointments, and your response should serve to review and terminate the interview. Return to 5.53 and try again.

5.56

Your Answer: I guess you'd better go. Let's see . . . we've discussed
your family problems, their effect on your business
activities, and your need to find solutions.

Correct. This brief reflection of content summarizes the essence
of the interview and sets the scene for the next interview. Proceed to
5.57.

5.57

After you've investigated the client's need to discuss any problems that have come up since your last meeting, you should briefly
summarize that meeting as a means of giving direction to the present
interview.

Interviewer: If you've experienced any major difficulties since our
last meeting, maybe we should discuss those first.

Client: Well, not really. Things are much the same as they
were yesterday.

Choose the response that best initiates and gives direction to the
interview.

Interviewer: Yesterday, you discussed some of your problems at
home and their effects on your work. You also discussed your need to solve these problems.

Go to 5.58

Interviewer: The major concern we dealt with yesterday is the fact
that your personal problems are beginning to affect
your work.   Go to 5.59

Interviewer: Yesterday, we were discussing the problems you're
having at home. You indicated that you think your
daughter's problem is serious, and the question of
whether she needs professional care came up.

Go to 5.60

5.58

Your Answer: Yesterday, you discussed some of your problems at
home and their effects on your work. You also discussed your need to solve these problems.

Correct. This brief, accurate summary reviews your last session
and enables the client to resume his discussion. Proceed to 5.61.

5.59

Your Answer: The major concern we dealt with yesterday is the fact that your personal problems are beginning to affect your work.

This may be your major concern, but it isn't the client's. By focusing on your major concern you're distorting what the client has told you. As personnel manager, you can best help the client by accurately summarizing his major disclosures. Only when you understand the nature of his problem will you be able to help him resolve it. Return to 5.57 and try again.

5.60

Your Answer: Yesterday, we were discussing the problems you're having at home. You indicated that you think your daughter's problem is serious, and the question of whether she needs professional care came up.

You've added your own ideas to those discussed by the client. When you reflect content in the form of a summary, you should try to be accurate and avoid adding to or changing the client's message by focusing on your own ideas. You should summarize the client's comments accurately. Return to 5.57 and try again.

5.61

Summarization can be used to clarify a client's confusing, lengthy, or rambling comments.

Client: My sister took her daughter to their family physician, and he had a long chat with her.

Interviewer: Your sister found help.

Client: Yes. I still don't know whether I should see the school counselor about my daughter. It might be a good idea. I just don't know.

Interviewer: It's difficult to know what to do.

Client: John, across the road, said something about getting her into a detention home, but that's kind of drastic. I don't know whether there is any solution. Maybe I could send her to live with my brother in Los Angeles.

Choose the most appropriate response.

Interviewer: I'm sure there are other solutions.   Go to 5.62

Interviewer: Your sister sent her daughter to the family doctor. You wonder about taking your daughter to see a school counselor. Your neighbor has suggested a detention home. And you've thought of involving your brother. Go to 5.63

Interviewer: It seems that you're thinking about a number of solutions to your problem, and you're not sure which solution you should choose. Maybe we can discuss each one of them separately. Go to 5.64

5.62

Your Answer: I'm sure there are other solutions.

You've ignored the client's efforts to solve his problems. By suggesting that his thoughts on the matter are limited, you've failed to help him investigate the solutions he *has* thought of. Return to 5.61 and try again.

5.63

Your Answer: Your sister sent her daughter to the family doctor. You wonder about taking your daughter to see a school counselor. Your neighbor has suggested a detention home. And you've thought of involving your brother.

When you reflect content, you should be brief and well organized, and you should focus on the essential ideas contained in the client's comments. This rambling, parrot-like reflection of content misses the essence of what the client has communicated to you. Return to 5.61 and try again.

5.64

Your Answer: It seems that you're thinking about a number of solutions to your problem, and you're not sure which solution you should choose. Maybe we can discuss each one of them separately.

Correct. This summary helps the client identify the meaning behind his rambling thoughts and directs him toward the next phase of the interview—exploration of possible alternatives. In a similar manner, summarization may be used to help a client explore and set goals. Proceed to 5.65.

5.65

Indicate whether each of the following statements is true or false.

1. When reflecting content, it's important to accurately repeat everything a client has said.
2. Effective reflections of content confirm for the client that his or her message has been understood.
3. Frequent use of reflection of content may cause a parrot-like effect and inhibit a client's communication.
4. When clients are threatened by discussion of their feelings, the interviewer should use less intense reflections of feeling.
5. In framing a reflection of content, an interviewer should concentrate on a client's most recent remarks, because these are usually most important.
6. Summarization is appropriate when a client's comments have been confusing, lengthy, or rambling.
7. When summarizing, an interviewer must include all of the topics discussed by a client.
8. Summarization is inappropriate at the conclusion of an interview.
9. Reflection of content should be concise and should capture the essence of a client's comments.
10. Summarization may be used to give direction to an interview.

ANSWERS

1. *False.* If you answered *true,* go to 5.1 and review.
2. *True.* If you answered *false,* go to 5.9 and review.
3. *True.* If you answered *false,* go to 5.41 and review.
4. *False.* If you answered *true,* go to 5.21 and review.
5. *False.* If you answered *true,* go to 5.5 and review.
6. *True.* If you answered *false,* go to 5.57 and review.
7. *False.* If you answered *true,* go to 5.45 and review.
8. *False.* If you answered *true,* go to 5.49 and review.
9. *True.* If you answered *false,* go to 5.33 and review.
10. *True.* If you answered *false,* go to 5.53 and review.

If seven or more of your responses are wrong, you should return to 5.1 and review this chapter.

1. **WHEN PARAPHRASING:**
   a. Restate the main ideas contained in a client's communication.
   b. Don't add to or change the meaning of a client's statement.
   c. Avoid parroting a client's comments.

2. **PARAPHRASING:**
   a. Indicates that you're attending to and attempting to understand what a client is saying.
   b. Helps to develop a working relationship between you and the client.
   c. Serves to check your understanding of the client's statement.
   d. Helps the client crystallize his or her thoughts.
   e. Gives direction to an interview.

3. **YOU CAN PARAPHRASE:**
   a. When a client is threatened by discussion of feelings.
   b. To check and clarify your perceptions of what a client is saying.
   c. To indicate to a client that you understand what has been said, thereby facilitating further discussion.

1. **WHEN SUMMARIZING:**
   a. Systematically integrate the important ideas contained in a client's comments and restate them.

2. **SUMMARIZING:**
   a. Provides a concise, accurate, and timely summary of clients' statements and helps them to organize their thoughts.
   b. Helps a client review what has been said.
   c. Stimulates a thorough exploration of themes that are important to the client.
   d. Provides organization for an interview.

3. **YOU CAN SUMMARIZE:**
   a. When a client's comments are lengthy, rambling, or confused.
   b. When a client presents a number of unrelated ideas.
   c. To add direction and coherence to an interview.
   d. To move from one phase of an interview to the next.
   e. To conclude an interview.
   f. To provide an introduction to an interview by reviewing the previous interview.

MULTIPLE-
CHOICE
TEST

In order to evaluate your mastery of the material in this chapter, you should answer the following multiple-choice questions. In each case, choose the most appropriate response based on the content of this chapter. The correct answers are presented in the Appendix.

1. A mother (Client) has called a public-health nurse (Interviewer) concerning the problems she's having with her new baby. Choose the response that best initiates and gives direction to the interview.

   a. Interviewer: You mentioned on the phone the other day that you were having some problems. How are you feeling today?
   b. Interviewer: On the phone the other day, you mentioned several problem areas that you would like to discuss with someone.
   c. Interviewer: The other day on the phone, we briefly discussed some of the problems you're experiencing at home with your baby and the changes that have taken place in your relationship with your husband.

2. Client: Yes, I feel overwhelmed by my new responsibilities and by the complete dependence of my child. I have to do everything—wash clothes, prepare bottles, change diapers . . . .

   a. Interviewer: Your child takes up a lot of your time and energy.
   b. Interviewer: There are a lot of things to do when taking care of a new baby.
   c. Interviewer: You're finding it difficult to organize your time.

3. Client: I don't seem to have any time for myself or my husband.

   a. Interviewer: What would you like to do for yourself and your husband?
   b. Interviewer: You seem to have little time to do anything else but take care of your child.
   c. Interviewer: You have no time for yourself or your husband.

4. Client: And my husband just doesn't understand how much time is involved in taking care of a baby.

   a. Interviewer: Your husband doesn't appreciate the efforts involved in caring for a new baby.
   b. Interviewer: Does he want a lot of time and energy that you don't have right now?

c. Interviewer: The fact that your husband doesn't understand your situation must be frustrating.

5. Client: When I was working, he used to do his share of work around the house and fix dinners. Now, since I'm home all day, it seems he expects me to take care of the baby and do all of the work around the house.

    a. Interviewer: It sounds as though you used to share the chores around the house, but now you have the baby to take care of and all of the chores to do as well.

    b. Interviewer: Now that you're home, you have to take care of the baby and do all of the work around the house.

    c. Interviewer: Before the baby arrived, you used to share the house-work with your husband.

6. Client: I don't know why he's stopped doing his share around the house. He doesn't help with the baby, either. He's worried about a new project at work that seems to be taking up a lot of his time.

    a. Interviewer: Although your husband is under pressure at work, you would like him to do his share of work around the house.

    b. Interviewer: You say there is a new project at work that takes up a lot of your husband's time.

    c. Interviewer: Do you think that your husband's job is interfering with his life at home?

Chapter 6
PUTTING
IT TOGETHER

In each of the previous chapters, we focused on only one skill. The material in this chapter is intended to help you develop the ability to integrate these skills. After completing this chapter you should be able to do the following:

1. Focus on and follow the essence of what a client communicates during an interview.
2. Use and integrate open inquiry, minimal encouragement, and reflection of feeling and content throughout an interview.
3. Decide when it is appropriate for you to use a given skill in response to a client.

In the first five chapters of this book, you developed the skills of focusing and following, open inquiry, minimal encouragement, reflection of feeling, paraphrasing, and summarizing. The method of training followed in these chapters is known as *the single skills approach.* This kind of training has been used to teach individuals a number of leisure activities, such as golf, skiing, and bowling, each of which consists of a number of single skills. For example, a golfer has to learn stance, grip, wrist action, leg action, head position, and so on. When golfers concentrate on only one skill at a time, their game remains imperfect. However, after they have mastered a number of skills and are able to integrate them, there is a dramatic improvement in their game. Just as beginning golfers reach a point at which it is necessary to integrate single skills into a fluid, cohesive whole, beginning interviewers must also reach that point of integration.

This chapter is divided into two sections. The first section is designed to help you review and consolidate the interviewing skills learned in previous chapters. The second section of the chapter is designed to help you integrate these specific skills in an interview.

The program in this chapter focuses on an interview between a man and a social worker (male or female) in a community agency. The man has requested the interview, saying only that the matter is urgent. Proceed to 6.1.

6.1

Focusing and following—the basic interviewing skill—consists of natural, direct eye contact, a relaxed, attentive body posture, and verbal responses that indicate you understand the client's message.

Interviewer:	What would you like to talk about today?
Client:	Well, it's my son. I just don't know what to do with him.

Choose the most appropriate response.

Interviewer:	How old is your son?	Go to 6.2
Interviewer:	(after a brief silence): Your son?	Go to 6.3
Interviewer:	How does your son feel about you?	Go to 6.4

6.2

Your Answer: How old is your son?

This question may be appropriate later in the interview, but it's inappropriate at this point. You should focus on what the client is communicating and respond in a way that indicates you are following him. Return to 6.1 and try again.

6.3

Your Answer   (after a brief silence): Your son?

Correct. Your brief silence invited the client to continue. However, when you sensed that he wasn't going to continue, you repeated a portion of his statement. This response indicates that you are following his comments. Proceed to 6.5.

6.4

Your Answer: How does your son feel about you?

You've changed the topic. When you focus and follow, you help the client tell you about his problem in his own way. Return to 6.1 and try again.

6.5

In the early stages of working with a client it's important to listen; problem solving and information giving come much later.

Client: Yes, my son. Last year he became unmanageable.
And then, just recently, he's been shoplifting.
Choose the most appropriate response.

Interviewer:	He's been shoplifting	Go to 6.6
Interviewer:	Were you able to put a stop to that?	Go to 6.7
Interviewer:	Well, I'm sure we can deal with that.	Go to 6.8

6.6

Your Answer: He's been shoplifting . . . .

Correct. You've indicated that you're following the client and are interested in what he's saying. Proceed to 6.9.

6.7

Your Answer: Were you able to put a stop to that?

This irrelevant question, with its implied advice, may irritate or anger the client. Return to 6.5 and try again.

6.8

Your Answer: Well, I'm sure we can deal with that.

This may be true, but the son is not the client, his father is. You should focus on what the client is saying and help him to explore and clarify his problem. After you've done this, you can help him identify the best way to handle the problem. Return to 6.5 and try again.

6.9

Your attention or lack of attention, as indicated by your responses and behavior, significantly influences your relationship with a client.

Client: Yes. Last week the police were around with a warrant. And it damn well wasn't for one offense, but fourteen!

Choose the most appropriate response.

Interviewer:	Did they arrest him?	Go to 6.10
Interviewer:	Is he sorry about what he's done?	Go to 6.11
Interviewer:	You sound angry about that.	Go to 6.12

6.10

Your Answer: Did they arrest him?

Though you may need this information, this is not the time to request it. You've indicated that your thoughts are elsewhere and that you aren't focusing on what the client is telling you. Return to 6.9 and try again.

6.11

Your Answer: Is he sorry about what he's done?

You've changed the topic to one that may be of interest to you but may not be important to the client at this time. Return to 6.9 and try again.

6.12

Your Answer: You sound angry about that.

Correct. The client has expressed considerable anger. By reflecting this anger, you've indicated that you're attending to what he is saying as well as how he feels about what he is saying. Proceed to 6.13.

6.13

Open inquiry encourages a client to discuss problems with you.

Client: Yes. I am. Because that means he's been doing it for some time. That, along with his other behavior, would make anyone angry.

Choose the most appropriate response.

Interviewer:	Is your son on drugs?	Go to 6.14
Interviewer:	Can you expand on that for me?	Go to 6.15
Interviewer:	Do you think your son realizes that you're angry?	
		Go to 6.16

6.14

Your Answer: Is your son on drugs?

This closed inquiry invites a "yes" or "no" answer and changes the topic. By using a closed inquiry, you assume responsibility for continuing the interview. An open inquiry, on the other hand, would help the client explore his problem and give him an opportunity to continue the discussion. Return to 6.13 and try again.

6.15

Your Answer: Can you expand on that for me?

Correct. This open inquiry invites the client to tell you more about his problems with his son. Proceed to 6.17.

6.16

Your Answer: Do you think your son realizes that you're angry?

This closed inquiry requires only a "yes" or "no" answer. The client can now sit back and wait for you to talk again. An open inquiry on the other hand, would help the client to discuss his problem with his son. Return to 6.13 and try again.

6.17

Open inquiries often begin with *what, how,* or *could. What* often elicits factual information; *how* is people oriented; *could* encourages a client to continue. Although *why* can be used effectively, its use often places a client on the defensive.

Client: Well, for about a year now, we've had trouble with him. He doesn't come home for meals, and he gets in late at night.

Choose the most appropriate response.

Interviewer:	How have you handled his behavior?	Go to 6.18
Interviewer:	Does he ever stay out all night?	Go to 6.19
Interviewer:	Why do you let him get away with it?	Go to 6.20

6.18

Your Answer: How have you handled his behavior?

Correct. This open inquiry invites the client to continue telling you about his son's behavior and how it has affected him. Proceed to 6.21.

6.19

Your Answer: Does he ever stay out all night?

This closed inquiry will lead to several follow-up questions. An open inquiry, on the other hand, would elicit more information and encourage the client to assume responsibility for the interview's progress. Return to 6.17 and try again.

6.20

Your Answer: Why do you let him get away with it?

You've assumed that the client hasn't tried to change his son's behavior. This assumption may make the client feel defensive, especially if he *has* tried to make his son come home at night. Return to 6.17 and try again.

6.21

Reflection of feeling focuses on the emotional aspects of a client's comments.

Client: We ignored his lateness at first, because it only happened occasionally. But lately, he's been out every night after midnight, and sometimes one or two o'clock. I stay up and give him a piece of my mind. I really chew him out.

Choose the most appropriate response.

Interviewer: When do you think he should be in?   Go to 6.22

Interviewer: How does your wife feel about all of this?

Go to 6.23

Interviewer: You really feel angry when he comes in late.

Go to 6.24

6.22

Your Answer: When do you think he should be in?

        This closed inquiry changes the topic. The client was telling you how he feels about his son coming in late. Return to 6.21 and try again.

6.23

Your Answer: How does your wife feel about all of this?

        You've changed the topic by asking a question that has nothing to do with the client's feelings. Return to 6.21 and try again.

6.24

Your Answer: You really feel angry when he comes in late.

        Correct. The client has been telling you how he reacts when his son comes in late, and you've reflected the feeling implied by his reaction. Proceed to 6.25.

6.25

        You should correctly identify a client's feelings before you attempt to reflect them.

Client: Yes, I feel angry when it happens, but the next morning I just feel upset about it all. After all, it's his life he's messing up. I wish I could just make him understand that we love him.

        Choose the most appropriate response.

Interviewer: So your feelings are mixed. You feel anger, concern, and love.   Go to 6.26

Interviewer: You don't feel angry the next morning.   Go to 6.27

Interviewer: Do you really love him?   Go to 6.28

6.26

Your Answer: So your feelings are mixed. You feel anger, concern, and love.

        Correct. The client has displayed a number of feelings, which you've identified and reflected. By doing so, you've given him a chance to observe his feelings and unravel them. Proceed to 6.29.

6.27

Your Answer: You don't feel angry the next morning.

Your response focuses on only one aspect of the client's statement. It's important for him to identify and explore all of the feelings he is exhibiting. Return to 6.25 and try again.

6.28

Your Answer: Do you really love him?

This closed inquiry focuses on only one aspect of the client's statement. You haven't encouraged him to explore his mixed feelings. Return to 6.25 and try again.

6.29

Summarization allows a client to review what has been said in an interview.

Client: Yes. I guess I'm concerned for him and for us. I don't know how we can get him to change.

Choose the most appropriate response.

Interviewer: Maybe you should encourage him to stay home.

Go to 6.30

Interviewer: So, he's in trouble with the law, he doesn't come home at night, and you want to find a solution for these problems. Go to 6.31

Interviewer: Well, the courts will probably decide that for you.

Go to 6.32

6.30

Your Answer: Maybe you should encourage him to stay home.

Your response indicates that you don't think the client has tried to do this. If he has, your interpretation could make him feel resentful. If he hasn't found a way to encourage his son to stay home, your comment may make him feel defensive and cause him to withdraw from his interaction with you. Return to 6.29 and try again.

6.31

Your Answer: So, he's in trouble with the law, he doesn't come home at night, and you want to find a solution for these problems.

Correct. This is a good summary of what the client has told you, and it focuses his attention on what he has discussed with you up to this point. Proceed to 6.33.

6.32

Your Answer: Well, the courts will probably decide that for you.

You've demonstrated your lack of attention to the client's comments and your disinterest in how he feels. Your reply doesn't help him clarify his problem. Return to 6.29 and try again.

6.33

Paraphrasing the content of statements made during an interview is another way to focus a client's attention on what he or she has told you.

Client: That's about it. My wife and I have tried just about everything, but nothing seems to work.

Choose the most appropriate response.

Interviewer: Perhaps you should bring your wife in to see me.
Go to 6.34

Interviewer: Do you think there is a possibility you may have overlooked? Go to 6.35

Interviewer: Everything you've thought of has failed. Go to 6.36

6.34

Your Answer: Perhaps you should bring your wife in to see me.

Your response indicates that you weren't following the client attentively. Return to 6.33 and try again.

6.35

Your Answer: Do you think there is a possibility you may have overlooked?

This closed inquiry calls for a "yes" or "no" answer. Return to 6.33 and try again.

6.36

Your Answer: Everything you've thought of has failed.

Correct. This restatement of what the client has told you focuses on the problem he is discussing. Proceed to 6.37.

6.37

Minimal encouragements indicate that you are following and invite a client to continue a discussion.

Client: Yes. Did I tell you he was adopted?

Choose the most appropriate response.

Interviewer:	Adopted!	Go to 6.38
Interviewer:	Errr	Go to 6.39
Interviewer:	Hmm hmm . . . go on.	Go to 6.40

6.38

Your Answer: Adopted!

This exclamation interrupts the client's discussion. Return to 6.37 and try again.

6.39

Your Answer: Errr . . . .

This response suggests uncertainty. Minimal encouragements should facilitate discussion, not confuse it. Return to 6.37 and try again.

6.40

Your Answer: Hmm hmm . . . go on.

Correct. This minimal encouragement invites the client to continue the discussion with you.

You have now finished the review section of this chapter.

In the remaining frames of this chapter, you are given an opportunity to integrate the interviewer skills discussed thus far. You will find that a number of alternative routes through the program are available. As a result, you may advance a number of frames, depending on the alternative you choose. After you've completed the program, you will return to 6.41 and follow an alternative route. By working through this section twice, you will see that different combinations of skills and responses can facilitate progress during an interview. You will also see that alternative responses are available: you may want to use these for further practice. Proceed to 6.41.

6.41

By integrating interviewing skills, you develop your own natural mode of interviewing; that is, you use each skill when you feel it is appropriate.

Client: We adopted him when he was 6 months old, because we couldn't have children of our own.

Choose an appropriate response.

Interviewer:	Was he a good baby?	Go to 6.42
Interviewer:	Could you tell me more about that?	Go to 6.43
Interviewer:	You really wanted a family.	Go to 6.44

6.42

Your Answer: Was he a good baby?

Your response requires only a "yes" or "no" answer, and it doesn't help the client to continue the discussion. Moreover, you've indicated that you're interested in what the baby was like, not in what the client is telling you. Return to 6.41 and try again.

6.43

Your Answer: Could you tell me more about that?

Correct. This open inquiry gives the client the responsibility for continuing the discussion. Proceed to 6.45.

6.44

Your Answer: You really wanted a family.

Correct. This reflection of feeling encourages the client to tell you his feelings about having a family. Proceed to 6.46.

6.45

Client: Well, my wife and I had been married for six years, and we didn't have any children. We really wanted to have a family.

Choose an appropriate response.

Interviewer:	Having a family was important to you.	Go to 6.50
Interviewer:	Did you see a doctor about your problem?	
		Go to 6.51

| Interviewer: | You felt very concerned because you had no children. |
| | Go to 6.52 |

6.46

Client:	Well, yes. For six years we'd been trying to have children.
	Choose an appropriate response.
Interviewer:	Could you tell me more about that? Go to 6.47
Interviewer:	Does anyone else in your family have this problem?
	Go to 6.48
Interviewer:	But without success. Go to 6.49

6.47

| Your Answer: | Could you tell me more about that? |
| | Correct. This open inquiry encourages the client to continue. Proceed to 6.54. |

6.48

| Your Answer: | Does anyone else in your family have this problem? |
| | This response won't help the client deal with his current problem. Return to 6.46 and try again. |

6.49

| Your Answer: | But without success. |
| | Correct. This minimal encouragement indicates that you're attending to the client's comments and invites him to continue. Proceed to 6.53. |

6.50

| Your Answer: | Having a family was important to you. |
| | Correct. This restatement indicates that you are attending to the discussion, and it invites the client to continue. Proceed to 6.56. |

6.51

| Your Answer: | Did you see a doctor about your problem? |
| | This closed inquiry doesn't help the client to expand on what he is telling you. As soon as he answers "yes" or "no," you have to |

assume responsibility for the next response. Return to 6.45 and try again.

6.52

Your Answer: You felt very concerned because you had no children.

Correct. This reflection focuses on the client's feelings about having a family. Proceed to 6.55.

6.53

Client: Right. So, finally we decided to see our doctor about our problem. That was a hard decision to make.
Choose an appropriate response.
Interviewer: How did you feel after you'd seen him?   Go to 6.66
Interviewer: Deciding to see him was difficult.   Go to 6.67
Interviewer: The doctor reassured you and your wife.   Go to 6.68

6.54

Client: My wife and I both had checkups, and there was no apparent reason for our inability to have children. So, we decided to do something about it . . . and we did.
Choose an appropriate response.
Interviewer: You finally came to a decision.   Go to 6.63
Interviewer: You decided . . .   Go to 6.64
Interviewer: Have you considered becoming foster parents?
Go to 6.65

6.55

Client: Yes. We really wanted children. And also, people began to leave us out of parties and things, because they had families and we didn't.
Choose an appropriate response.
Interviewer: So, it was a social concern as well as a personal problem.   Go to 6.60
Interviewer: Go on.   Go to 6.61
Interviewer: Your social life is very important to you.   Go to 6.62

6.56

Client: I guess so. All of our friends had families, and everyone kept asking us when we were going to start ours. We were so uncomfortable.

Choose an appropriate response.

Interviewer: Maybe you should have told them that it wasn't their concern. Go to 6.57

Interviewer: It became really embarrassing for you. Go to 6.58

Interviewer: And then what happened? Go to 6.59

6.57

Your Answer: Maybe you should have told them that it wasn't their concern.

Your response indicates that you've allowed your own feelings on the subject to interfere with your attentive listening. Clients profit from working on their own solutions to their problems. Return to 6.56 and try again.

6.58

Your Answer: It became really embarrassing for you.

Correct. This reflection focuses attention on the client's feelings and invites him to continue. Proceed to 6.69.

6.59

Your Answer: And then what happened?

Correct. This brief, open inquiry indicates that you are attending to the client, and it encourages him to expand on what he is telling you. Proceed to 6.70.

6.60

Your Answer: So it was a social concern as well as a personal problem.

Correct. This restatement of content indicates that you are following the client and gives him a point of departure for his next comments. Proceed to 6.71.

6.61

Your Answer: Go on.

Correct. This minimal encouragement indicates that you are following the client and would like him to continue. Proceed to 6.72.

6.62

Your Answer: Your social life is very important to you.

This leading statement will probably irritate the client. You can help the client explore his problem by indicating that you know how he feels. Return to 6.55 and try again.

6.63

Your Answer: You finally came to a decision.

Correct. This restatement of content indicates that you are following the client's comments and encourages him to continue the discussion with you. Proceed to 6.73.

6.64

Your Answer: You decided . . .

Correct. This minimal encouragement indicates that you are following the client and invites him to continue. Proceed to 6.74.

6.65

Your Answer: Have you considered becoming foster parents?

You've changed the topic of the discussion. Return to 6.54 and try again.

6.66

Your Answer: How did you feel after you'd seen him?

Correct. This open inquiry focuses on the client's comments and asks him to continue the discussion. Proceed to 6.75.

6.67

Your Answer: Deciding to see him was difficult.

        Correct. Your response accurately reflects the content of the client's statement and indicates that you're following what he is saying. At the same time, the information elicited by this response will enable you to check your understanding of the client's message. Proceed to 6.76.

6.68

Your Answer: The doctor reassured you and your wife.

        Your reflection is an inaccurate one, because you have no information on which to base it. The doctor may have confirmed their worst nightmares and made them feel very depressed. Return to 6.53 and try again.

6.69

Client: Yes. We didn't even go out much, because we were afraid that the topic would come up. We had to do something.

        Choose an appropriate response.

Interviewer:	You were ashamed, so you just hid.	Go to 6.98
Interviewer:	Um hmm.	Go to 6.99
Interviewer:	What did you decide to do?	Go to 6.100

6.70

Client: Well, we went to see a doctor, and he said that we would probably never have children of our own. So, after talking with him, we looked into adopting a child.

        Choose an appropriate response.

Interviewer:	And then . . .	Go to 6.95
Interviewer:	That was one alternative that offered some hope.	Go to 6.96
Interviewer:	Did you go to your family doctor?	Go to 6.97

6.71

Client: Yes. We felt that we had to do something.
Choose an appropriate response.

Interviewer: I'm not sure you had to feel that way.   Go to 6.92

Interviewer: And so . . .   Go to 6.93

Interviewer: What did you decide to do?   Go to 6.94

6.72

Client: I guess they didn't want to embarrass us by talking about their children in front of us. And that wouldn't happen if they just didn't invite us.

Interviewer: So you were left out of things.   Go to 6.89

Interviewer: I sense that their behavior hurt you.   Go to 6.90

Interviewer: I guess there were other things you could have done.

Go to 6.91

6.73

Client: Yes. It was a difficult decision to make, but we decided to adopt a child.
Choose an appropriate response.

Interviewer: Uhm hmm. And then . . .   Go to 6.86

Interviewer: How do you feel about that decision now?

Go to 6.87

Interviewer: How did your friends react?   Go to 6.88

6.74

Client: Yes. We decided to adopt. We had to wait while they checked us out, but we made it. What a day that was!
Choose an appropriate response.

Interviewer: What kinds of things did they check?   Go to 6.83

Interviewer: So you were able to adopt.   Go to 6.84

Interviewer: How exciting that must have been!   Go to 6.85

6.75

Client: Well, he told us that we could have children, but it would be difficult. He suggested that we adopt a child.
Choose an appropriate response.

Interviewer:	So, it seemed that adoption was the answer.	
		Go to 6.80
Interviewer:	Did you reject that idea at first?	Go to 6.81
Interviewer:	So, then . . .	Go to 6.82

6.76

Client:	It sure was, but after he told us, we were glad that we'd gone.	
	Choose an appropriate response.	
Interviewer:	What did he tell you?	Go to 6.77
Interviewer:	You really felt relieved then.	Go to 6.78
Interviewer:	It must have been good news.	Go to 6.79

6.77

Your Answer: What did he tell you?

      Correct. This open inquiry is on topic.

      Let's review your last few responses. In working your way from 6.41, you've reflected feeling, used a minimal encouragement, reflected content, and made an open inquiry. By now, you're aware of the fact that a variety of responses are appropriate at most points in an interview. Now return to 6.41 and choose another appropriate response. You've already chosen 6.44, so don't choose it again. If this is your second time through, go to 6.101.

6.78

Your Answer: You really felt relieved then.

      Correct. This is an appropriate reflection of feeling.

      Let's review your last few responses. In working your way from 6.41, you've reflected feeling, used a minimal encouragement, reflected content, and reflected feeling again. By now, you're aware of the fact that a variety of responses are appropriate at most points in an interview. Now return to 6.41 and choose another appropriate response. You've already chosen 6.44, so don't choose it again. If this is your second time through, go to 6.101.

6.79

Your Answer: It must have been good news.

      The client's previous statement doesn't suggest that the news he received was good; therefore, your statement is an assumption that may be incorrect. Return to 6.76 and try again.

6.80

Your Answer: So, it seemed that adoption was the answer.

Correct. This is an accurate paraphrase.

Let's review your last few responses. In working your way from 6.41, you've reflected feeling, used a minimal encouragement, made an open inquiry, and reflected content. By now, you're aware of the fact that a variety of responses are appropriate at most points in an interview. Now return to 6.41 and choose another appropriate response. You've already chosen 6.44, so don't choose it again. If this is your second time through, go to 6.101.

6.81

Your Answer: Did you reject that idea at first?

This question may irritate the client and hinder your interaction with him. Return to 6.75 and try again.

6.82

Your Answer: So, then . . .

Correct. This minimal encouragement will help the client continue.

Let's review your last few responses. In working your way from 6.41, you've reflected feeling, used a minimal encouragement, made an open inquiry, and used another minimal encouragement. By now, you're aware of the fact that a variety of responses are appropriate at most points in an interview. Now return to 6.41 and choose another appropriate response. You've already chosen 6.44, so don't choose it again. If this is your second time through, go to 6.101.

6.83

Your Answer: What kinds of things did they check?

This response is irrelevant to the discussion. Return to 6.74 and try again.

6.84

Your Answer: So you were able to adopt.

Correct. This is an appropriate reflection of content.

Let's review your last few responses. In working your way from 6.41, you've reflected feeling, made an open inquiry, used a minimal encouragement, and reflected content. By now, you're aware of the fact that a variety of responses are appropriate at most points in an interview. Now return to 6.41 and choose another appropriate response. You've already chosen 6.44, so don't choose it again. If this is your second time through, go to 6.101.

6.85

Your Answer: How exciting that must have been!
Correct. This is an appropriate reflection of feeling.
Let's review your last few responses. In working your way from 6.41, you've reflected feeling, made an open inquiry, used a minimal encouragement, and reflected feeling again. By now, you're aware of the fact that a variety of responses are appropriate at most points in an interview. Now return to 6.41 and choose another appropriate response. You've already chosen 6.44, so don't choose it again. If this is your second time through, go to 6.101.

6.86

Your Answer: Uhm hmm. And then . . .
Correct. This minimal encouragement will help the client continue the discussion.
Let's review your last few responses. In working your way from 6.41, you've reflected feeling, made an open inquiry, reflected content, and used a minimal encouragement. By now, you're aware of the fact that a variety of responses are appropriate at most points in an interview. Now return to 6.41 and choose another appropriate response. You've already chosen 6.44, so don't choose it again. If this is your second time through, go to 6.101.

6.87

Your Answer: How do you feel about that decision now?
Correct. This open inquiry is on topic.
Let's review your last few responses. In working your way from 6.41, you've reflected feeling, used open inquiry, reflected content, and used open inquiry again. By now, you're aware of the fact that a variety of responses are appropriate at most points in an interview. Now return to 6.41 and choose another appropriate response. You've already chosen 6.44, so don't choose it again. If this is your second time through, go to 6.101.

6.88

Your Answer: How did your friends react?

You've changed the topic, indicating to your client that you are more interested in pursuing your own thoughts than in focusing on what he was discussing. Return to 6.73 and try again.

6.89

Your Answer: So you were left out of things.

Correct. This is an appropriate reflection of content.

Let's review your last few responses. In working your way from 6.41, you've used open inquiry, reflected feeling, used a minimal encouragement, and reflected content. By now, you're aware of the fact that a variety of responses are appropriate at most points in an interview. Now return to 6.41 and choose another appropriate response. You've already chosen 6.43, so don't choose it again. If this is your second time through, go to 6.101.

6.90

Your Answer: I sense that their behavior hurt you.

Correct. This is an accurate reflection of feeling.

Let's review your last few responses. In working your way from 6.41, you've made an open inquiry, reflected feeling, used a minimal encouragement, and reflected feeling again. By now, you're aware of the fact that a variety of responses are appropriate at most points in an interview. Now return to 6.41 and choose another appropriate response. You've already chosen 6.43, so don't choose it again. If this is your second time through, go to 6.101.

6.91

Your Answer: I guess there were other things you could have done.

The client has just indicated that he and his wife felt left out. Your response indicates that you don't understand how he feels. You've interpreted his statement from your own point of view. Return to 6.72 and try again.

6.92

Your Answer: I'm not sure you had to feel that way.

This statement denies the client the right to his own feelings and thus prevents him from resolving any difficulties his feelings may have caused. Return to 6.71 and try again.

6.93

Your Answer: And so . . .

Correct. This minimal encouragement will help the client continue.

Let's review your last few responses. In working your way from 6.41, you've used open inquiry, reflected feeling, reflected content, and used a minimal encouragement. By now, you're aware of the fact that a variety of responses are appropriate at most points in an interview. Now return to 6.41 and choose another appropriate response. You've already chosen 6.43, so don't choose it again. If this is your second time through, go to 6.101.

6.94

Your Answer: What did you decide to do?

Correct. This open inquiry focuses on the topic the client is discussing.

Let's review your last few responses. In working your way from 6.41, you've used open inquiry, reflected feeling, reflected content, and used open inquiry again. By now, you're aware of the fact that a variety of responses are appropriate at most points in an interview. Now return to 6.41 and choose another appropriate response. You've already chosen 6.43, so don't choose it again. If this is your second time through, go to 6.101.

6.95

Your Answer: And then . . .

Correct. This minimal encouragement will help the client continue.

Let's review your last few responses. In working your way from 6.41, you've used an open inquiry, reflected content, used another open inquiry, and used a minimal encouragement. By now, you're aware of the fact that a variety of responses are appropriate at most points in an interview. Now return to 6.41 and choose another appropriate response. You've already chosen 6.43, so don't choose it again. If this is your second time through, go to 6.101.

6.96

Your Answer: That was one alternative that offered some hope.

Correct. This is an accurate reflection of feeling.

Let's review your last few responses. In working your way from 6.41, you've used an open inquiry, reflected content, used another open inquiry, and reflected feeling. By now, you're aware of the fact that a variety of responses are appropriate at most points in an interview. Now return to 6.41 and choose another appropriate response. You've already chosen 6.43, so don't choose it again. If this is your second time through, go to 6.101.

6.97

Your Answer: Did you go to your family doctor?

This closed inquiry changes the topic. If this information is important to the client, he will convey it to you in his own time. Return to 6.70 and try again.

6.98

Your Answer: You were ashamed, so you just hid.

This reflection of feeling is excessive. You shouldn't overinterpret or make assumptions about the client's comments. Return to 6.69 and try again.

6.99

Your Answer: Um hmm.

Correct. This minimal encouragement invites the client to continue the discussion.

Let's review your last few responses. In working your way from 6.41, you've used an open inquiry, reflected content, reflected feeling, and used a minimal encouragement. By now, you're aware of the fact that a variety of responses are appropriate at most points in an interview. Now return to 6.41 and choose another appropriate response. You've already chosen 6.43, so don't choose it again. If this is your second time through, go to 6.101.

6.100

Your Answer: What did you decide to do?

Correct. This open inquiry indicates that you're following and invites the client to continue.

Let's review your last few responses. In working your way from 6.41, you've used an open inquiry, reflected content, reflected feeling, and used another open inquiry. By now, you're aware of the fact that a variety of responses are appropriate at most points in an interview. Now return to 6.41 and choose another appropriate response. You've already chosen 6.43, so don't choose it again. If this is your second time through, go to 6.101.

6.101

The material in this chapter has been concerned with the consolidation and integration of specific interviewing skills. In an actual interview, the distinction between skills isn't always apparent. At times, it's appropriate to employ several skills in one statement. For example, "Um hmm .... You sound angry" (minimal encouragement, reflection of feeling). Or "You sound concerned. Could you tell me more about that?" (reflection of feeling, open inquiry). Your task is to integrate these skills with others you already have so that you will be a more effective interviewer.

The following client statements are derived from the interview you've been following. Develop a response for each of these statements and write it on a separate worksheet.

1. Perhaps when I consider his behavior I regret adopting him, but, given the enjoyment we've had over the years, I'm glad we did it. (Paraphrase)
2. Yes. If we'd just had some indication that it was happening. But, all of a sudden, the policeman was at the door. And it's not just one incident, but fourteen. (Reflection of feeling)
3. I guess if I look at it, the problem has been developing over the past three or four years. He started showing up late for school . . . . (Minimal encouragement)
4. I don't know. He stopped doing what we asked him to do. (Open inquiry)

5. Over the past couple of summers, he and I have agreed that he'd mow the lawn and get paid for it. Well, he's done it for a couple of weeks each summer, and then he just stops. It's things like that. What I consider to be his responsibilities around the house aren't responsibilities as far as he's concerned. He just thinks he's a boarder. (Summarization, covering responses 1 through 5.)

The following are examples of possible responses to the preceding statements.

1. The pleasure you've experienced over the years far outweighs the problems you're having now.
    Generally, you have few regrets about having adopted him, although your present difficulties have caused you to question that decision.
2. Finding out that way overwhelmed you.
    The suddenness and enormity of the problem seemed to alarm you.
3. Hmm . . . hmm . . . .
    And . . .
4. Can you give me an example of that?
    What other things caused you concern?
5. So, to summarize what you've told me up to this point, your son has given you a lot of joy, and, although you'd been concerned about his behavior, you were unprepared for this visit from the police.
    Let me see if I understand you correctly. Although you'd been concerned about your son's behavior, you were unprepared for this visit from the police. You've had a good relationship with him until recently.

POINTS TO REMEMBER ABOUT INTEGRATING SKILLS

1. **WHEN FOCUSING AND FOLLOWING, MAKING OPEN INQUIRIES, GIVING MINIMAL ENCOURAGEMENT, AND REFLECTING FEELING AND CONTENT:**
    a. Master each skill to the best of your ability. Effective integration of interviewing skills depends on your ability to use each individual skill.
2. **WHEN USING SINGLE SKILLS IN AN INTERVIEW:**
    a. Respond to clients in a way that is comfortable for you.
    b. Combine single skills when necessary.
    c. Don't overuse a particular skill or a limited range of skills.

3. **THE SKILLS COVERED THUS FAR ARE APPROPRIATE:**
   a. In response to most client statements, as long as they demonstrate good focusing and following.

In order to evaluate your mastery of the skills presented thus far, you should answer the following multiple-choice questions. In each case, choose the most appropriate response. The correct answers are listed in the Appendix.

1. Client: We've been divorced for a year, and I'm having an awful time.

   a. Interviewer (giving the client full attention): An awful time.
   b. Interviewer (silent, giving the client full attention).
   c. Interviewer (giving the client full attention): You've been divorced for a year.

2. Client: I just can't get used to all the things that go with being divorced.

   a. Interviewer: It's difficult being divorced, isn't it?
   b. Interviewer: It sounds as though you can't get used to being divorced.
   c. Interviewer: Could you give me an example of what you mean?

3. Client: One example is living in an apartment rather than my own house.

   a. Interviewer: Do you have a comfortable apartment?
   b. Interviewer: Uh hum.
   c. Interviewer: What are some other examples?

4. Client: And I find it hard to be alone so much. It's so different from when I was married. I'm used to having another person in the house.

   a. Interviewer: How does it feel to be alone?
   b. Interviewer: It's nice to have someone else around the house.
   c. Interviewer: Did you and your husband spend a lot of time together?

5. Client: It doesn't feel good at all. Most of my friends are married. I feel so isolated, and sometimes even unwanted.

   a. Interviewer: Your friends aren't interested in you anymore, now that you're divorced?
   b. Interviewer: Since you've been divorced, you feel lonely and left out.
   c. Interviewer: You feel isolated and unwanted.

6. Client: Yes. I felt awkward at one party given by friends of ours; and I haven't been invited to any others. And there have been other situations, too.

   a. Interviewer: Could you tell me what made you feel awkward at the party you attended?
   b. Interviewer: It sounds as though you've been left out of most of the parties.
   c. Interviewer: Was your former husband invited to these parties?

7. Client: I had trouble talking with them. It seemed like I didn't have much in common with them anymore. I ended up sitting by myself for a while, and then I left.

   a. Interviewer: What did you try to talk about?
   b. Interviewer: Does that happen to you in other situations?
   c. Interviewer: It must have been a difficult situation for you.

8. Client: Yes. I've started to avoid my old friends now. I want to make new friends, but I'm having trouble meeting new people.

   a. Interviewer: It sounds as though you'd like to make a new start for yourself.
   b. Interviewer: You're finding it difficult to make new friends.
   c. Interviewer: So you aren't seeing many of your old friends, but you're finding it difficult to make new ones.

9. Client: There aren't many places where people my age can go to make new friends . . . not the kind of friends I'd like to make, anyway.

   a. Interviewer: It sounds like a difficult situation.
   b. Interviewer: What kinds of people do you want to meet?
   c. Interviewer: You sound angry about the whole situation.

10. Client: I've tried singles groups, going places by myself, and being active in my church, but I haven't met any interesting people.

    a. Interviewer: It sounds as though you haven't had much success.
    b. Interviewer: Are there other things you could do to meet interesting people?
    c. Interviewer: How do you go about meeting new people?

Chapter 7
COMMUNICATING
FEELING AND IMMEDIACY

In Chapters 1 through 6, we focused on a number of basic interviewing skills that enable you to develop a good working relationship and open communication with a client. In Chapters 7 through 10, we focus on advanced interviewing skills—communicating feeling and immediacy, confronting, self-disclosing, and structuring—that enable you to help a client focus on problems and act on them. Chapter 11 is designed to help you integrate the basic and advanced skills into an effective interviewing style.

The material in this chapter is intended to help you master the skills of communicating feeling and immediacy. After completing this chapter, you should be able to do the following:

1. Identify your feelings as you interact with a client.
2. Communicate your feelings to a client.
3. Decide whether communication of feelings is appropriate in a given situation.

135

4. Focus the communication between yourself and a client on immediate concerns.
5. Decide when it's appropriate to focus an interview on immediate concerns.

The ability to recognize your own feelings will increase your ability to identify the feelings of others. The first section of this chapter is intended to help you identify your own feelings. Then, you will be presented with material that will help you communicate your feelings and concerns about what is occurring in the immediate relationship between yourself and the client.

Most of the frames in this chapter are complete in themselves; that is, each frame focuses on a different client. Proceed to 7.1.

7.1

People often find it difficult to identify their feelings and communicate them appropriately. During an interview, you should be able to identify your feelings and communicate them to a client. Communicating feeling is similar to reflecting feeling, except that the emphasis is on the interviewer's feelings rather than on the client's.

Client: I was just getting into my job, and then they let me go. When I first applied for the job, I knew it was for me. When they called to tell me I had it, I was so excited. I really worked hard at it, and everyone said I was doing so well . . . . I really tried. Last Friday the manager called me in, gave me my severance pay, and said he was sorry, but cutbacks made it necessary for him to let me go.

Choose the most appropriate response.

Interviewer: I'm glad you were able to land the job. That's what's important.   Go to 7.2

Interviewer: Damn! Some companies make me so mad.   Go to 7.3

Interviewer: I'm really sorry to hear about your misfortune.
                                        Go to 7.4

7.2

Your Answer: I'm glad you were able to land the job. That's what's important.

You may be glad to hear of the client's success in obtaining a job; however, the expression of this emotion is inappropriate, because the client no longer has the job. This response suggests that you aren't listening to the client's entire message. Return to 7.1, attend to the client's message and your own feelings, and then respond with an appropriate expression of feeling.

7.3

Your Answer: Damn! Some companies make me so mad.

This response is excessive and far too general. When you express your feelings, the intensity of your statement should be appropriate to the particular situation. Moreover, the response you've selected will change the topic from the client to a general discussion of the unfairness of some companies and their personnel policies. Return to 7.1 and try again.

7.4

Your Answer: I'm really sorry to hear about your misfortune.

Correct. Given the nature of the client's disappointing experience, this is an appropriate expression of feeling. Proceed to 7.5.

7.5

An important aspect of communicating feelings is the ability to identify them. As you listen attentively to a client, you should be aware of your reactions to what is being said.

Client (having failed to bring important information concerning his problem): I'm sorry. I left my records at home again. They aren't that important, are they? I'm sure I'll remember next week.

Choose the most appropriate response.

Interviewer: I'm upset that you forgot your records. It's the only way we can evaluate your progress.   Go to 7.6

Interviewer: Not again. Well, I guess we can work around it.   Go to 7.7

Interviewer: How are we supposed to get anywhere? Clients who don't cooperate make me angry.   Go to 7.8

7.6

Your Answer: I'm upset that you forgot your records. It's the only way we can evaluate your progress.

Correct. You've communicated your feelings in a way that will be useful to the client. Proceed to 7.9.

7.7

Your Answer: Not again. Well, I guess we can work around it.

The initial part of your response suggests that you aren't sharing all of your feelings with the client. In order to effect some change in the client's behavior, it is necessary that you share these feelings. Otherwise, they will interfere with your efforts to establish an open relationship with the client. Return to 7.5 and try again.

7.8

Your Answer: How are we supposed to get anywhere? Clients who don't cooperate make me angry.

You've expressed not only your anger toward this client but also the anger you've accumulated from your interactions with other clients. You should note your reactions to each client and express your feelings in an appropriate and facilitative manner. Return to 7.5 and try again.

7.9

You should be aware of your bodily reactions as well as your thoughts and feelings.

Client (a student who has come to discuss poor grades): Last Saturday the apartment manager found me cooking hot dogs and told me they smelled terrible. I never heard of them smelling. How can she think that what I cook is causing the smells? When did hot dogs ever cause smells? I don't think I'm the culprit.

Choose the most appropriate response.

Interviewer (fidgeting and looking out the window while the client is talking): It seems you're having real difficulties with the apartment manager.   Go to 7.10

Interviewer (fidgeting and looking out the window while the client is talking): I get angry when people smell up a place with food.   Go to 7.11

Interviewer (fidgeting and looking out the window while the client is talking): I feel quite distracted by what you're saying, and I'm puzzled about how it relates to your problem.   Go to 7.12.

7.10

Your Answer (fidgeting and looking out the window while the client is talking): It seems you're having real difficulties with the apartment manager.

The client has come to talk about poor grades. Since discussion of this area is probably very difficult, the client may sometimes focus on irrelevant issues. You've responded to the client's inappropriate discussion. Return to 7.9 and try again.

7.11

Your Answer (fidgeting and looking out the window while the client is talking): I get angry when people smell up a place with food.

You've ignored your fidgeting and expressed an irrelevant bias that will probably lead to further discussion of hot dogs and cooking. You should recognize your bodily reactions and share your feelings with the client so that they can be utilized. Return to 7.9 and try again.

7.12

Your Answer (fidgeting and looking out the window while the client is talking): I feel quite distracted by what you're saying, and I'm puzzled about how it relates to your problem.

Correct. This response effectively communicates your feelings to the client. Proceed to 7.13 to continue.

7.13

In Chapter 2, we stressed the importance of maintaining natural eye contact and a relaxed posture while listening to a client. Eye contact and posture are also important when you communicate information to a client.

Client (discussing improved behavior of her son): I'm really glad I came to see you. John was just unmanageable when I first came, but now he's absolutely no problem. He's doing well at school. I don't know how I can thank you . . . . It's all due to you.

Choose the most appropriate response.

Interviewer (relaxed and looking warmly at the client): It makes me feel good to hear you say that.   Go to 7.14

Interviewer (fidgeting and looking away from the client): It makes me feel . . . really good to hear you say that.

Go to 7.15

Interviewer (looking directly at the client): You did all the work.

Go to 7.16

7.14

Your Answer (relaxed and looking warmly at the client): It makes me feel good to hear you say that.

Correct. Your posture, eye contact, and mode of delivery complement your verbal message and indicate to the client that you are happy to hear her remarks. Proceed to 7.17.

7.15

Your Answer (fidgeting and looking away from the client): It makes me feel . . . really good to hear you say that.

This reaction may confuse and disconcert the client. You should use your body and your eyes to complement your verbal message while speaking directly to the client. Return to 7.13 and try again.

7.16

Your Answer (looking directly at the client): You did all the work.

When interviewers are embarrassed by a client's positive or complimentary remarks, they sometimes contradict the client. When this happens, the client is denied the right to express positive feelings. As an interviewer, you should be aware of your reactions to positive feedback. Return to 7.13 and try again.

7.17

While maintaining natural eye contact and a relaxed posture, you should keep your communication of feelings on topic.

Client (discussing failure with a weight-reducing program): I really have been doing all the things we decided on, but I'm just not losing any weight. And I'm so afraid that, if I don't lose weight soon, I'll have another heart attack. I'm getting so depressed. I'm doing all the things I'm supposed to do, but it just isn't working . . . . (sighing) I don't know.

Choose the most appropriate response.

Interviewer: I'm worried about a number of things that are going on here. I guess we just have to go on trying.

Go to 7.18

Interviewer: What you're saying concerns me very much.

Go to 7.19

Interviewer: I'm pleased to see you today. I wasn't sure that you would come. Go to 7.20

7.18

Your Answer: I'm worried about a number of things that are going on here. I guess we just have to go on trying.

Your response should show that you are listening to the client and are interested in what he or she has to say. This response ignores the client's concerns and offers false reassurance. Return to 7.17 and try again.

7.19

Your Answer: What you're saying concerns me very much.

Correct. You've demonstrated your understanding of the importance of communicating feelings that are on topic. Proceed to 7.21.

7.20

Your Answer: I'm pleased to see you today. I wasn't sure that you would come.

This response is off topic. You should focus on what the client is saying. Return to 7.17 and try again.

7.21

When interviewers communicate their feelings, they clarify their reactions, demonstrate how to recognize and express feelings, and facilitate the development of trusting, open relationships with their clients.

Client (a widow who has been seeing her minister regularly to discuss her husband's recent death): I got it! I got it! I just had to come and tell you. I actually got the job. I start on Monday.

Choose the most appropriate response.

Interviewer: I'm so surprised. I wasn't sure that you'd be able to do it.   Go to 7.22

Interviewer: I'm so relieved. It was beginning to bother me that you seemed to be getting nowhere.   Go to 7.23

Interviewer: I'm so glad . . . so happy for you. I think that's the greatest news.   Go to 7.24

7.22

Your Answer: I'm so surprised. I wasn't sure that you'd be able to do it.

Your response is a communication of feeling, but not one that is likely to build a trusting, open relationship. The client is likely to view your surprise as a put-down. Return to 7.21 and try again.

7.23

Your Answer: I'm so relieved. It was beginning to bother me that you seemed to be getting nowhere.

What the client has just told you is likely to produce feelings of happiness, which are the most appropriate to express at the moment. The communication of your negative feelings won't serve to develop a trusting, open relationship. Return to 7.21 and try again.

7.24

Your Answer: I'm so glad . . . so happy for you. I think that's the greatest news.

Correct. The client's enthusiasm in wishing to share this news with you suggests a good relationship, and your communication of feeling will further this relationship. Proceed to 7.25.

7.25

When you, as an interviewer, begin to suspect that your biases are interfering with your relationship with the client, you should inform the client of this and make alternative arrangements if he or she wishes.

Client (discussing her feelings about her pregnancy): Our first child was retarded. The doctor thinks that it's genetic and that I should have an abortion. That's easy for him to say . . . . I'm just not comfortable with the idea. I can't get it out of my mind. I know it would be hard to raise two retarded children. Maybe it would be better for us all if I were to have an abortion . . . . I just don't know.

Choose the most appropriate response.

Interviewer: Abortion may be the only answer to your problem.
Go to 7.26

Interviewer: Hearing of your difficult decision makes me feel really concerned for you. Go to 7.27

Interviewer: I'm really concerned to hear you talk about abortion. I get upset when people encourage abortions.
Go to 7.28

7.26

Your Answer: Abortion may be the only answer to your problem.

This statement suggests that you have strong feelings in favor of abortion and have permitted them to influence your response. Return to 7.25 and try again.

7.27

Your Answer: Hearing of your difficult decision makes me really concerned for you.

Correct. This response communicates unbiased feelings concerning the client's problem. Proceed to 7.29.

7.28

Your Answer: I'm really concerned to hear you talk about abortion. I get upset when people encourage abortions.

This response communicates your personal bias. If you do feel antagonistic toward the idea of abortion, your views will interfere with your interaction with the client. You should encourage the client to seek counseling elsewhere. Return to 7.25 and select a more appropriate response.

7.29

Immediacy, or direct mutual communication—the ability to discuss directly and openly what is happening in a relationship—is closely related to the skill of communicating feeling.

Client   (a young woman who wishes to leave home and is having difficulty achieving this goal): I really don't know where to begin today (pauses and glances out the window). I chatted with my mother about finding a place of my own (glances out the window). We had a real long talk (looks down at the floor). It was a good talk (fidgets and looks down at the floor).

       Choose the most appropriate response.

Interviewer: Do you think you'll be moving soon, then?

Go to 7.30

Interviewer: I get the feeling that you're having difficulty telling me what occurred.   Go to 7.31

Interviewer: It sounds as though you had quite a good talk.

Go to 7.32

7.30

Your Answer: Do you think you'll be moving soon, then?

     The client's behavior suggests that she is having some difficulty talking to you. You should resolve this difficulty in order to make her feel more comfortable. Return to 7.29 and try again.

7.31

Your Answer: I get the feeling that you're having difficulty telling me what occurred.

     Correct. By focusing on the discomfort the client is experiencing, you've encouraged her to discuss this discomfort and explore its meaning. Proceed to 7.33.

7.32

Your Answer: It sounds as though you had quite a good talk.

     You've accurately reflected the content of the client's statement, but you haven't focused on her behavior and your reaction to it. By focusing on the meaning of her behavior, you can help the client to explore her problem more directly. Return to 7.29 and try again.

7.33

     In order to engage in direct mutual communication, you need to focus not only on what is being said but, more importantly, on what is not being said. For example, you might focus on the way in which a client expresses himself or herself, the feelings that develop between you and the client, or the nonverbal behavior that accompanies your discussion. Moreover, when you engage in direct mutual communication, you should respond in the present tense.

Client (referred to a psychologist because of difficulty with social relationships): Gee, am I ever mad. I went to the employment office on Tuesday—nothing. And I didn't get anywhere by looking in the paper. I've been coming here for three months, and I still don't have a job. What the hell are you doing? I came here so that you could help me get a job.

Choose the most appropriate response.

Interviewer: From what you've said, it seems that you made some effort to find a job but were disappointed again.
Go to 7.34

Interviewer: From what you're saying, I get the feeling that you don't think I'm doing my job. It seems that I'm not doing what you want me to do. Go to 7.35

Interviewer: As I remember, you weren't very comfortable with our decision of last week. Go to 7.36

7.34

Your Answer: From what you've said, it seems that you made some effort to find a job but were disappointed again.

You've attended to the content of the client's statement, but you've ignored an area of greater concern—the immediate feelings between you and the client. Until you help the client to communicate and resolve his hostility toward you, there can be little progress toward resolution of his problems. Return to 7.33 and try again.

7.35

Your Answer: From what you're saying, I get the feeling that you don't think I'm doing my job. It seems that I'm not doing what you want me to do.

Correct. This is a good response in which you communicate, in the present tense, the message underlying the client's statement. Proceed to 7.37.

7.36

Your Answer: As I remember, you weren't very comfortable with
our decision of last week.

One important aspect of immediacy is dealing with what is
going on at the present moment in a relationship. This response deals
with issues that were important in the past. Return to 7.33 and try
again.

7.37

The client is likely to engage in frank, open discussion when
you use immediacy. Therefore, you must be willing to converse in an
open, nondefensive manner.

Client (continuing from the last interaction): You're damned
right. As the weeks go by, I'm getting more and more
scared that I'll never get a job again. And all you do is
give me these silly assignments. You aren't helping me
a bit.

Choose the most appropriate response.

Interviewer: I don't think we should discuss what I do. Let's get
back to your problem.   Go to 7.38
Interviewer: You just don't do what I ask you to do.   Go to 7.39
Interviewer: You're becoming so anxious that you're afraid I
won't be able to help you after all.   Go to 7.40

7.38

Your Answer: I don't think we should discuss what I do. Let's get
back to your problem.

When you focus on the immediate situation, you must be prepared to help the client in a frank and open discussion. By being defensive, you haven't allowed the client to deal with the hostility that
is preventing him from cooperating with you. Return to 7.37 and try
again.

7.39

Your Answer: You just don't do what I ask you to do.

When you counterattack, the client will either back off or come
back with an even more aggressive response. In either case, the client
will assume that it's impossible to carry on a frank and open discus-

sion of his immediate feelings with you. Remember, when you initiate immediacy, you must be ready to follow through with open discussion. Return to 7.37 and try again.

7.40

Your Answer: You're becoming so anxious that you're afraid I won't be able to help you after all.

    Correct. By focusing in an open and nondefensive manner on what the client has said, you've encouraged further discussion. Proceed to 7.41.

7.41

    Discussing what is occurring in a relationship is often a new and difficult experience for the client. If you are too direct, the client will likely withdraw from the discussion, whereas, if you are careful and sensitive, the client will likely feel comfortable with you.

Client (a woman who has established a positive relationship with the therapist): I just can't get to sleep at night. . . . I keep having these awful thoughts. I know you're going to ask me what they are, but I can't tell you. I get along well with you, but, if I told you, you might not want to see me anymore. . . . Can't you just tell me what to do?

    Choose the most appropriate response.

Interviewer: You feel that we share a good relationship but that discussing these thoughts with me could alter it.
        Go to 7.42

Interviewer: You feel that we share a good relationship, but you're afraid to discuss these thoughts with me.   Go to 7.43

Interviewer: If you feel that we share a good relationship, why can't you tell me about these thoughts?   Go to 7.44

7.42

Your Answer: You feel that we share a good relationship but that discussing these thoughts with me could alter it.

    Correct. This response will help the client to feel more comfortable in discussing a sensitive subject. Proceed to 7.45.

7.43

Your Answer: You feel that we share a good relationship, but you're afraid to discuss these thoughts with me.

Because discussion of this subject with you is obviously difficult for the client, your response is far too direct. In order to help the client, you should be cautious in your response. Return to 7.41 and try again.

7.44

Your Answer: If you feel that we share a good relationship, why can't you tell me about these thoughts?

The client has told you that she's finding it difficult to discuss these thoughts with you. This attempt to shame her into revealing her thoughts will probably cause her to feel guilty and defensive. Your response should invite the client to discuss the reasons behind her reluctance to reveal her thoughts. Return to 7.41 and try again.

7.45

When the interviewer engages in direct mutual communication, the client develops a sensitivity to his or her own behavior and its effect on other people.

Client (having previously made similar comments): From what I said before, I'm sure you have a bad impression of my wife. I really didn't mean to portray her like that. She's actually a very good person. I hope you don't think badly of her.

Choose the most appropriate response.

Interviewer: Of course not. I'm sure she's a very good person.

Go to 7.46

Interviewer: You seem to be content with your wife.   Go to 7.47

Interviewer: You often find it necessary to apologize for your comments. It seems as though you have difficulty accepting responsibility for your statements.

Go to 7.48

7.46

Your Answer: Of course not. I'm sure she's a very good person.

By focusing on the content of the client's message, you reinforce his behavior. It is important that the client take responsibility for his own comments and feelings. By focusing on his present behavior and talking about it, you will help him to realize what he is doing. Return to 7.45 and try again.

7.47

Your Answer: You seem to be content with your wife.

Although you may placate the client with this response, you won't help him to develop the ability to communicate directly and honestly. Return to 7.45 and choose a response that focuses on your observations of the interaction between yourself and the client.

7.48

Your Answer: You often find it necessary to apologize for your comments. It seems as though you have difficulty accepting responsibility for your own statements.

Correct. This response gives the client feedback concerning the way in which he expresses himself and invites him to reconsider his responsibility for his manner of expression. Proceed to 7.49.

7.49

When the client engages in immediacy, his or her concerns should be discussed directly.

Client: I keep coming here and discussing the same things week after week. I'm sure you must be getting fed up with me.

Choose the most appropriate response.

Interviewer: Of course I'm not getting fed up with you. Could you tell me what's been happening to you this week?

Go to 7.50

Interviewer: You're not sure that you're getting anywhere, and you're wondering what I think about that.

Go to 7.51

Interviewer: That's really not important. I'm here to help you.

Go to 7.52

7.50

Your Answer: Of course I'm not getting fed up with you. Could you tell me what's been happening to you this week?

    When the client expresses a concern about the immediate situation, you need to enter into a discussion of this issue. Your response should demonstrate your willingness to discuss the client's immediate concerns about his progress. Return to 7.49 and try again.

7.51

Your Answer: You're not sure that you're getting anywhere, and you're wondering what I think about that.

    Correct. This response focuses directly on the client's immediate concern, thus encouraging discussion of this issue. Proceed to 7.53.

7.52

Your Answer: That's really not important. I'm here to help you.

    The client has raised a concern that requires your immediate attention. Your response not only ignores the client's concern but also belittles it. When a client focuses on the interaction between himself or herself and the interviewer, it is the responsibility of the interviewer to assist in the expression of this concern. Return to 7.49 and try again.

7.53

    Differences in age, sex, race, viewpoints, religion, and socioeconomic background often affect the degree of compatibility between the interviewer and the client and give rise to situations in which the interviewer needs to use immediacy responses.

Client   (an elderly man who finds himself in the presence of a young interviewer): I don't feel quite right discussing my problem with you. How long have you been doing this work?

    Choose the most appropriate response.

Interviewer: Because I'm young, you're wondering whether I have enough experience to be able to help you. Go to 7.54

Interviewer: I'm sure I can help you. Could you tell me what brings you here?   Go to 7.55

Interviewer: My age has nothing to do with my abilities. I have excellent credentials.   Go to 7.56

7.54

Your Answer: Because I'm young, you're wondering whether I have enough experience to be able to help you.

    Correct. You've identified the client's immediate concern and encouraged frank and open discussion of his worry over your age. Proceed to 7.57.

7.55

Your Answer: I'm sure I can help you. Could you tell me what brings you here?

    You are likely to gain the confidence of the client only after you have responded to his immediate concern and have helped to resolve it. Return to 7.53 and try again.

7.56

Your Answer: My age has nothing to do with my abilities. I have excellent credentials.

    Although you've identified the client's concern, your authoritative and defensive tone will probably alienate him further. Your response should invite the client to discuss his concern in a frank and open manner. Return to 7.53 and try again.

7.57

    Immediacy responses are a useful means of establishing trust between the interviewer and the client.

Client: I don't know whether I want to answer that question or not. After all, you're the personnel manager, and this information is highly personal. How do I know what you'll do with it?

    Choose the most appropriate response.

Interviewer: I can assure you that everything you say here will be held in confidence.   Go to 7.58

Interviewer: I didn't realize that my question would have such an effect on you. You should have nothing to hide from me.   Go to 7.59

Interviewer: You find it difficult to trust me with this information. I understand your concern, but I'll have difficulty making a fair decision without these facts.

Go to 7.60

7.58

Your Answer: I can assure you that everything you say here will be
held in confidence.

Whenever there is a question concerning the degree to which
either the interviewer or the client can be trusted, it is important that
the issue of trust be considered immediately. Return to 7.57 and try
again.

7.59

Your Answer: I didn't realize that my question would have such an
effect on you. You should have nothing to hide from
me.

You've responded to the immediate situation between yourself
and the client, but your response infers that the client does indeed
have something to hide. In order to gain the client's trust, you need
to focus on the issue of trust in a more tentative, nonthreatening manner. Return to 7.57 and try again.

7.60

Your Answer: You find it difficult to trust me with this information. I understand your concern, but I'll have difficulty making a fair decision without these facts.

Correct. This response encourages the client to discuss the issue
of trust. Proceed to 7.61.

7.61

While some clients become overdependent, others resist the interviewer's help. Immediacy responses are appropriate when the degree of dependence becomes a cause of concern for the client or the
interviewer.

Client: I did all the things you suggested last week, and they
worked well. But some other things have just come
up, and I need you to tell me what to do about them.

Choose the most appropriate response.

Interviewer: Why don't you tell me about them so that we can de-cide which one is most important.   Go to 7.62

Interviewer: I wonder if you could apply some of the things you learned last week to these problems and solve them yourself.   Go to 7.63

Interviewer: I'm concerned about the fact that you see me as the one who solves your problems. I see you as having a role in that, too. What do you think?   Go to 7.64

7.62

Your Answer: Why don't you tell me about them so that we can de-cide which one is most important.

This response suggests that you are comfortable when the client is dependent on you. In order to establish an equal working relation-ship with the client, you need to engage in an open, frank discussion of the dependency issue. Return to 7.61 and try again.

7.63

Your Answer: I wonder if you could apply some of the things you learned last week to these problems and solve them yourself.

This is a laudable goal, but your abrupt response will probably frighten the client. Moreover, you haven't attempted to discuss the client's increasing dependency on you. Return to 7.61 and try again.

7.64

Your Answer: I'm concerned about the fact that you see me as the one who solves your problems. I see you as having a role in that, too. What do you think?

Correct. This response focuses on the fact that the client de-pends on you to solve problems. Moreover, it invites frank and open discussion of this issue. Proceed to 7.65.

7.65

Immediacy responses are called for when the client engages in aimless, circular discussion or agrees to achieve a particular goal but does nothing to attain it.

Client   (having spent the first ten minutes of the session dis-
            cussing his uneventful week): It's been a pretty quiet
            week. I guess I just sat around most of the time.
            Choose the most appropriate response.

Interviewer: As I listen to you, I find myself wondering why we're
               not discussing more important things.   Go to 7.66

Interviewer: What else would you like to talk about today?
                                                        Go to 7.67

Interviewer: I don't think that this is getting us anywhere. Why
               don't you come back in another week.   Go to 7.68

7.66

Your Answer: As I listen to you, I find myself wondering why we're
               not discussing more important things.

               Correct. By raising your concern about the apparent lack of di-
               rection in the client's statements, you've opened the way for an
               open, relevant discussion. Proceed to 7.69.

7.67

Your Answer: What else would you like to talk about today?

               This response invites more aimless chatter. Your response
               should focus on your concern and invite an open discussion of it. Re-
               turn to 7.65 and try again.

7.68

Your Answer: I don't think that this is getting us anywhere. Why
               don't you come back in another week.

               Although this response focuses on your immediate concern, it's
               too abrupt to be of any benefit. Return to 7.65 and try again.

7.69

               Clients frequently experience some discomfort during the ini-
               tial and final stages of a relationship with an interviewer. When this
               happens, the interviewer should focus on these feelings and help the
               client to resolve them.

Client: I won't be coming any more .... Won't that be
               strange? I'm used to coming here .... It's been so
               good. But I guess you'll be glad to get rid of me.

Choose the most appropriate response.

Interviewer: You've been seeing me for a long time, but you're well in control now.   Go to 7.70

Interviewer: We've been meeting for a long time, and we have a good relationship. I guess you're telling me that you'll miss me. I'll miss you too.   Go to 7.71

Interviewer: I won't be glad to get rid of you, but you don't need me any more. You're strong enough now to manage things by yourself.   Go to 7.72

7.70

Your Answer: You've been seeing me for a long time, but you're well in control now.

This response is somewhat cold and abrupt. Your response should encourage the discussion of feelings about the conclusion of your relationship with the client. Return to 7.69 and try again.

7.71

Your Answer: We've been meeting for a long time, and we have a good relationship. I guess you're telling me that you'll miss me. I'll miss you too.

Correct. This response encourages the client to engage in direct mutual communication. Proceed to 7.73.

7.72

Your Answer: I won't be glad to get rid of you, but you don't need me any more. You're strong enough now to manage things by yourself.

When the relationship between the interviewer and the client has been a good one, separation is often difficult for the client. Your response prohibits any discussion of the client's feelings, as well as any possibility of resolving them. Return to 7.69 and try again.

7.73

Indicate whether each of the following statements is true or false.

1. The interviewer's communication of feeling facilitates the client's communication of feeling.

2. It's appropriate for the interviewer to communicate all his or her feelings to the client.
3. In order to use immediacy responses appropriately, the interviewer needs to attend to the client's verbal message.
4. In order to communicate feeling, the interviewer must be aware of not only the client's message but also his or her own reaction to that message.
5. Immediacy focuses on what is happening in the here-and-now of a relationship.
6. Direct rather than tentative communications of immediacy lead to frank and open discussion.
7. The interviewer should wait for the client to initiate discussion of their relationship.
8. Discussion of the issue of trust between the interviewer and the client can be damaging to their relationship.
9. Interpersonal relationships are enhanced by the skill of immediacy.
10. When the interviewer initiates immediacy, he or she should be prepared to enter into a direct, honest discussion.

ANSWERS
1. *True.* If you answered *false,* go to 7.21 and review.
2. *False.* If you answered *true,* go to 7.25 and review.
3. *False.* If you answered *true,* go to 7.33 and review.
4. *True.* If you answered *false,* go to 7.5 and review.
5. *True.* If you answered *false,* go to 7.29 and review.
6. *False.* If you answered *true,* go to 7.41 and review.
7. *False.* If you answered *true,* go to 7.49 and review.
8. *False.* If you answered *true,* go to 7.57 and review.
9. *True.* If you answered *false,* go to 7.45 and review.
10. *True.* If you answered *false,* go to 7.37 and review.

If seven or more of your responses were incorrect, you should return to 7.1 and work through this chapter again.

POINTS
TO
REMEMBER
ABOUT
COMMUNICAT-
ING
FEELING
AND
IMMEDIACY

1. **WHEN IDENTIFYING YOUR FEELINGS**:
   a. Identify the feelings evoked by your thoughts about what the client is communicating.
   b. Identify the feelings associated with your bodily reactions to the client's message.
2. **WHEN COMMUNICATING YOUR FEELINGS**:
   a. Maintain appropriate eye contact and a relaxed posture.
   b. Communicate feelings that are relevant to the topic being discussed.
   c. Use an appropriate form of expression.
3. **COMMUNICATE FEELINGS**:
   a. When you wish to clarify your reactions for the client, act as a model for the client, or develop a trusting, open relationship with the client.
   b. When your feelings are provoked by an unbiased response to the client's message.
4. **WHEN COMMUNICATING IMMEDIATE CONCERNS**:
   a. Focus on both what is being said and also on what is *not* being said.
   b. Respond in the present tense.
   c. Express yourself carefully and sensitively.
   d. Be ready to follow up openly and nondefensively.
5. **COMMUNICATE IMMEDIATE CONCERNS TO**:
   a. Promote direct mutual communication.
   b. Resolve tensions and discomforts.
   c. Focus on and resolve incompatibilities.
   d. Clarify the issues concerning trust.
   e. Focus on and resolve the client's dependence.
   f. Resolve circular discussion and client inactivity.
   g. Resolve the client's feelings during the initial and final stages of the interviewing process.

MULTIPLE-
CHOICE
TEST

In order to evaluate your mastery of the material presented in this chapter, you should answer the following multiple-choice questions. In each case, select the most appropriate response based on the content of this chapter. The correct answers are presented in the Appendix.

1. Client: Guess what! You know all those blood tests they've been doing on Johnny? They came back negative. Boy, are we relieved!

   a. Interviewer: That's very good. I'm pleased for you.
   b. Interviewer: I'm really happy to hear that. I'm relieved, too.
   c. Interviewer: That's really great to hear. You must be happy that it turned out that way for Johnny.

2. Client: When I think back on how my parents used to treat me, I get so angry that I'd do anything to get back at them. One time I even hid some tickets they had for a play so they couldn't go.

   a. Interviewer: You seem to be feeling a lot of that anger right now.
   b. Interviewer: So, you used to get very angry with them, and you've even done some things to get even.
   c. Interviewer: You seem angry with them, even now.

3. Client: I've told you about a lot of things that bother me, but there are some other things that I haven't told you . . . things that I'm afraid to tell anyone. I'm afraid you'll think I'm crazy.

   a. Interviewer: You've shared a lot of things about yourself, but you're not sure that I could handle this.
   b. Interviewer: At some point, you're going to have to tell me and see what happens.
   c. Interviewer: There are some things you'd like to share with me, but you're afraid I might not be able to accept or understand you.

4. Client (female): I'd been living with Judy for three years. We'd had a wonderful life together, and I thought everything was fine between us. Then, one weekend she moved out and said our relationship was over. I really love her, and I don't know what to do to get her back.

   a. Interviewer: I have to admit that I don't know very much about dealing with lesbian relationships. I think it would be more helpful if you were to talk with another counselor.
   b. Interviewer: I feel uncomfortable talking with you about your relationship. I suggest that you talk with another counselor on our staff about it.
   c. Interviewer: I think I would have trouble being objective with you because of some of my own views. I suggest you talk with another one of our counselors about your concern.

5. Client (looking down and fidgeting): Last weekend was the worst weekend I've ever had . . . . I've never felt so low (begins to cry). For the first time in my life, I thought about suicide . . . and that scared me.

    a. Interviewer: I'm wondering if you're feeling as low now as you did on the weekend?
    b. Interviewer: Could you tell me the feelings you had about suicide?
    c. Interviewer: You're really low now. Do you still feel that suicide is the way out?

6. Client (his first interview with a female counselor): There are several things that have been bothering me for quite a while . . . . And they have been bothering me more lately. My worrying has even been affecting my work. But I don't know if I can talk about my problems with a woman.

    a. Interviewer: It appears that you're surprised to have a female counselor and that you're finding it difficult to talk to me.
    b. Interviewer: It seems that you're feeling uncomfortable talking with me about your concerns because I'm a woman.
    c. Interviewer: I get the feeling that you expected a male counselor.

Chapter 8
CONFRONTING

The material in this chapter is intended to help you master the skill of confronting. After completing this chapter, you should be able to do the following:

1. Identify discrepancies in a client's communication.
2. Confront a client with discrepancies you've identified.
3. Explain the purpose of confrontation.
4. Decide whether confronting is appropriate in a given situation.

Confrontation is often seen as hostile or punitive. However, a skilled interviewer confronts clients in order to make them aware of discrepancies in their communication. Once they are acquainted with discrepancies, clients are frequently able to work toward their resolution.

The first half of this chapter is designed to acquaint you with the mechanics of confrontation. The second half illustrates situations in which confrontation is appropriate. The initial sequence of frames in this program focuses on an interview between a counselor and a middle-aged woman whose marriage has failed. The client is seeking assistance because of her inability to manage her finances. Each of the following frames is complete in itself. Proceed to 8.1.

8.1

When confronting, interviewers bring specific discrepancies to the attention of clients—discrepancies in their actions, in their words, and between their actions and words. Effective confrontation often leads to a better understanding of problems and constructive change on the part of the client.

Client: (having indicated that she has just bought an expensive dress): I'm really worried about how I'm going to pay this month's rent.

Choose the most appropriate response.

Interviewer: Not having enough money can be really stressful.
Go to 8.2

Interviewer: Maybe the bank would give you a loan.　　Go to 8.3

Interviewer: I'm a bit confused. Earlier, you talked about buying an expensive dress, but now you say that you're worried about paying your rent. It seems hard for you to manage your money.　　Go to 8.4

8.2

Your Answer: Not having enough money can be really stressful.

Although your response accurately reflects the client's distress, you've failed to confront her questionable behavior. Your implied acceptance of the client's behavior may lead her to believe that her actions are appropriate. Return to 8.1 and try again.

8.3

Your Answer: Maybe the bank would give you a loan.

Although a loan might provide a solution to the client's immediate financial difficulty, it won't help her to deal with her underlying money-management problems. Moreover, you've failed to confront her with the money-management issue and have avoided discussion of this relevant topic. Return to 8.1 and try again.

8.4

Your Answer: I'm a bit confused. Earlier, you talked about buying an expensive dress, but now you say that you're worried about paying your rent. It seems hard for you to manage your money.

    Correct. This response focuses on a specific discrepancy in the client's communication. Proceed to 8.5.

8.5

    The interviewer who uses confrontation effectively becomes a model for honest communication. You shouldn't avoid the use of confrontation because you're concerned that the client will be hurt or because you're afraid of endangering your relationship with the client. On the other hand, confrontation shouldn't be used as a means of punishment or revenge.

Client: It's really my former husband's fault. He refused to give me what I asked for when we divorced.

    Choose the most appropriate response.

Interviewer: You say that your former husband has caused your financial problems, yet you spend money on expensive clothing. It's very hard for you to look at your role in this situation.   Go to 8.6

Interviewer: People who spend money the way you do and then blame someone else are just fooling themselves.   Go to 8.7

Interviewer: A fair settlement in a divorce is very important. Could you help me to understand why your settlement was insufficient?   Go to 8.8

8.6

Your Answer: You say that your former husband has caused your financial problems, yet you spend money on expensive clothing. It's very hard for you to look at your role in this situation.

    Correct. By bringing the client's attention to the discrepancy between her behavior and her verbal message, you are helping her to focus on the situation she is avoiding—her own role in her financial dilemma. Proceed to 8.9.

8.7

Your Answer: People who spend money the way you do and then
blame someone else are just fooling themselves.

This is an expression of feeling and opinion, not a confrontation. Moreover, this response won't help the client to examine her behavior. Return to 8.5 and try again.

8.8

Your Answer: A fair settlement in a divorce is very important. Could you help me to understand why your settlement was insufficient?

You are in the midst of confronting the client about her inability to manage money. This response changes the focus and allows her to avoid her real problem. Return to 8.5 and try again.

8.9

When confronted, the client is required to consider other than her present way of acting, thus employing untried resources. In using confrontation, you feed back discrepancies in behavior and communication and help the client to explore these discrepancies.

Client: I need to get enough money to pay the rent. My unemployment check comes in next week, and I plan to buy a better tape deck with that.

Choose the most appropriate response.

Interviewer: You told me that you already have a tape deck. Why do you want to buy another one?   Go to 8.10

Interviewer: Shouldn't you spend your money on other things?   Go to 8.11

Interviewer: You're short of money, but you really find it difficult to stop spending.   Go to 8.12

8.10

Your Answer: You told me that you already have a tape deck. Why do you want to buy another one?

This confrontation focuses on a minor discrepancy. Your response should direct the client's attention to her overall problem. Return to 8.9 and try again.

8.11

Your Answer: Shouldn't you spend your money on other things?

This response may seem judgmental to the client and will probably cause her to feel defensive rather than open. Return to 8.9 and try again.

8.12

Your Answer: You're short of money, but you really find it difficult to stop spending.

Correct. By confronting the client with her difficulty, you ask her to consider her present behavior and the possibility of changing. Proceed to 8.13.

8.13

Confrontation should be used only when a good relationship exists between the interviewer and the client. Good rapport is important; when confronting, the interviewer focuses on material that was previously avoided by the client. As a result, the client may become distressed or confused when confrontation is used.

Client   (tearfully): I know my debts are my responsibility, but it's so hard to admit it. Since my marriage broke up, I've just gone out and bought things without thinking. It has given me something to do.

Once she has faced her responsibility, the client, along with the interviewer, sets up a program to resolve her budgeting problems. The client is also concerned about obtaining a job in order to supplement her limited income.

Client   (discussing a job for which she isn't qualified): That's another reason I want that job. I thought it would help me to meet people. I really want that job.

Choose the most appropriate response.

Interviewer: That is a good job, isn't it? Perhaps another opening like that will come up soon. I'm sure that it would be good for you.   Go to 8.14

Interviewer: There seems to be some discrepancy between the type of job you look for and your actual qualifications. It seems hard for you to explore jobs that match your qualifications.   Go to 8.15

Interviewer: With your qualifications and experience, you shouldn't
expect to get that sort of job.   Go to 8.16

8.14

Your Answer: That is a good job, isn't it? Perhaps another opening
like that will come up soon. I'm sure that it would be
good for you.

Your failure to confront the client with her inappropriate
choice of jobs will reinforce her behavior. She may be distressed by a
confrontation; however, unless you confront her, she will probably
continue to seek unsuitable jobs. Return to 8.13 and try again.

8.15

Your Answer: There seems to be some discrepancy between the
type of job you look for and your actual qualifications. It seems hard for you to explore jobs that
match your qualifications.

Correct. By focusing on the discrepancy between her qualifications and those required by the job, you help the client to focus on
an issue that she has either avoided or failed to recognize. Proceed to
8.17.

8.16

Your Answer: With your qualifications and experience, you shouldn't
expect to get that sort of job.

This confrontation is far too abrupt and direct. Clients often
feel threatened by confrontation. Your response should be helpful,
not abusive or punitive. Return to 8.13 and try again.

8.17

Clients are often more receptive to tentative than direct or
abrupt confrontations. Tentative confrontations often begin with
phrases such as "Could it be" and "You tend to suggest."

Client: Well, the job was just what I wanted. I'm not going to
apply for something I don't want.

Choose the most appropriate response.

Interviewer: You tend to suggest that the only thing you are considering is whether or not you want the job. It's difficult for you to think about other factors. Go to 8.18

| Interviewer: | Could it be that yours is a short-sighted way to select a job? Go to 8.19 |
| Interviewer: | Could it be that you just want your own way? Go to 8.20 |

8.18

Your Answer: You tend to suggest that the only thing you are considering is whether or not you want the job. It's difficult for you to think about other factors.

Correct. This tentative confrontation will help the client to explore her behavior with respect to job hunting. Proceed to 8.21.

8.19

Your Answer: Could it be that yours is a short-sighted way to select a job?

Although you began your response tentatively, you concluded by directly confronting the client with your own feelings and opinions about her behavior. Your response should invite the client to examine her behavior rather than react in her own defense. Return to 8.17 and try again.

8.20

Your Answer: Could it be that you just want your own way?

Your tentative opening should be followed by an equally tentative confrontation. This response is blunt and direct and will be of no help to the client. Return to 8.17 and try again.

8.21

You should be aware of the client's feelings both during and after a confrontation. Good confrontations, then, often include reflections of feeling concerning the client's difficulty in facing the discrepancy being discussed.

Client: That's all that's important. For years I've done what everybody else wanted me to do. Now it's time for me to do what I want to do.

Choose the most appropriate response.

Interviewer: But what would happen if everyone acted that way?

Go to 8.22

Interviewer: It sounds as though your life has been absolute hell.
Could you tell me about it?   Go to 8.23

Interviewer: Having been given little choice in the past, you're
now determined to do what you want to do. It's hard
for you to realize that there is more to getting a job
than just wanting it.   Go to 8.24

8.22

Your Answer: But what would happen if everyone acted that way?

This confrontation is far too direct. Moreover, it invites the client to discuss society in general rather than her problems in particular. Return to 8.21 and try again.

8.23

Your Answer: It sounds as though your life has been absolute hell.
Could you tell me about it?

By attending to the client's past, you are helping her to avoid a difficult but important issue. Return to 8.21 and try again.

8.24

Your Answer: Having been given little choice in the past, you're
now determined to do what you want to do. It's hard
for you to realize that there is more to getting a job
than just wanting it.

Correct. You have confronted the client while attending to her feelings concerning the problem area. By confronting with such support, you invite the client to face her problem and deal with it. Proceed to 8.25.

8.25

You should base your confrontation on the client's statements or behavior, not on inferred information. Confrontations should not include accusations, evaluations, or solutions to problems.

Client: Yes. I guess I'm afraid of being pushed around again.
I don't know why they worry about my qualifica-
tions. Isn't it important that I want to do the job?
Choose the most appropriate response.

Interviewer: You've probably thought that, because you're not really qualified, you don't have to take responsibility for getting the job.   Go to 8.26

Interviewer: You're finding it difficult to face the fact that your qualifications interfere with your choice of jobs. Considering your own qualifications is threatening.
                                                    Go to 8.27

Interviewer: You seem to be forgetting that people have to work hard to get their qualifications.   Go to 8.28

8.26

Your Answer: You've probably thought that, because you're not really qualified, you don't have to take responsibility for getting the job.

   You have no information on which to base this statement. Your confrontation should be based on what the client has said or done. Return to 8.25 and try again.

8.27

Your Answer: You're finding it difficult to face the fact that your qualifications interfere with your choice of jobs. Considering your own qualifications is threatening.

   Correct. By focusing on the discrepancy between the type of job the client wants and the type of job for which she is qualified, you've helped her to look at her situation realistically. Proceed to 8.29.

8.28

Your Answer: You seem to be forgetting that people have to work hard to get their qualifications.

   This response will not help the client to explore her qualifications or her behavior. Your confrontation should focus on a discrepancy in the client's message. Return to 8.25 and try again.

8.29

   The client may try to discredit you, argue with you, or pretend to agree with you when you use confrontation. When this happens, you should continue to confront the client.

Client: You have a good job . . . . And I'm as much entitled to one as you are. You just don't want me to have a good job.

                    Choose the most appropriate response.

Interviewer: You seem to be angry with me because I've discussed your qualifications. It's easier to avoid that issue than it is to examine it.   Go to 8.30

Interviewer: I worked hard for my qualifications. You'll have to work hard for yours.   Go to 8.31

Interviewer: Of course I want you to have a good job. I'll help you look for one.   Go to 8.32

8.30

Your Answer: You seem to be angry with me because I've discussed your qualifications. It's easier to avoid that issue than it is to examine it.

        Correct. You've continued to confront the client while inviting her to examine and discuss her behavior in terms of her feelings. This method of confronting is supportive. Proceed to 8.33.

8.31

Your Answer: I worked hard for my qualifications. You'll have to work hard for yours.

        Your response gives the client an opportunity to change topics. You haven't helped her to examine her own behavior. Return to 8.29 and try again.

8.32

Your Answer: Of course I want you to have a good job. I'll help you look for one.

        This response is not a confrontation. Although you may have assuaged the client's anger, you haven't helped her to confront and examine her behavior. Return to 8.29 and try again.

8.33

        The use of confrontation is often required in crisis situations, in which the client's behavior is threatening to his or her welfare or the welfare of others.

Client: What's the point? It's no use . . . . It's hopeless. I'll
never get what I want. Why should I even go on?
Choose the most appropriate response.

Interviewer: It all seems really difficult for you right now. Finding
a job seems to be an impossible task.   Go to 8.34

Interviewer: You talk positively about finding a good job, but you
say that it's all hopeless. Sometimes it's hard to keep
trying.   Go to 8.35

Interviewer: I'm really concerned about you. It sounds as though
you might do something drastic.   Go to 8.36

8.34

Your Answer: It all seems really difficult for you right now. Finding
a job seems to be an impossible task.

This is a good reflection of feeling, but, in order to quickly explore the gravity of her feelings, you should confront the client about the meaning of her previous comments. Return to 8.33 and try again.

8.35

Your Answer: You talk positively about finding a good job, but you
say that it's all hopeless. Sometimes it's hard to keep
trying.

Correct. This supportive confrontation is the most effective way to quickly explore the gravity of the client's feelings. Proceed to 8.37.

8.36

Your Answer: I'm really concerned about you. It sounds as though
you might do something drastic.

Your confrontation is too direct and threatening. It could cause the client to feel even more depressed. Confrontation should focus on discrepancies and lead to positive change. Return to 8.33 and try again.

8.37

Confrontation can be directed at discrepancies that are related to the client's strengths and resources as well as his or her weaknesses and limitations.

Client: It's just that . . . I know I have the ability to retrain and get the sort of job I want . . . but I guess I find it easier to stay home and collect money from my former husband.

Choose the most appropriate response.

Interviewer: You know that you have the ability to earn money to buy the things you want, but something seems to make it hard for you to do that.   Go to 8.38

Interviewer: Don't you think that you should try to change your attitude? With your ability, you could be out earning money for yourself.   Go to 8.39

Interviewer: Don't you think that you're trying to get even with your former husband?   Go to 8.40

8.38

Your Answer: You know that you have the ability to earn money to buy the things you want, but something seems to make it hard for you to do that.

Correct. This confrontation focuses on an ability that the client isn't using at this time. By confronting the client in this way, you encourage her to explore her strengths and take some positive action. Proceed to 8.41.

8.39

Your Answer: Don't you think that you should try to change your attitude? With your ability, you could be out earning money for yourself.

This confrontation is too blunt; it may provoke defensive or aggressive behavior on the part of the client. Return to 8.37 and try again.

8.40

Your Answer: Don't you think that you're trying to get even with your former husband?

This confrontation implies something that may or may not be true. Confrontations must be based on information, not on assumptions. Return to 8.37 and try again.

8.41

It is important for an interviewer to know when the use of confrontation is appropriate. The following frames offer examples of situations in which confrontation should be employed. Each frame is independent and represents a separate interview.

Client (whose records indicate that his smoking has increased slightly during the past two weeks): I know smoking is bad for my health. I'm cutting down.

Choose the most appropriate response.

Interviewer: If you want to stop smoking, you'll have to try harder.
Go to 8.42

Interviewer: It's good to hear you say that you're cutting down. You sound committed to that. Go to 8.43

Interviewer: You say that you've cut down, but your records show that your smoking has increased. Go to 8.44

8.42

Your Answer: If you want to stop smoking, you'll have to try harder.

The client has probably heard this advice many times. You should confront him about the discrepancy between his stated goals and his behavior and thereby help him to resolve this discrepancy and take responsibility for reducing his smoking. Return to 8.41 and try again.

8.43

Your Answer: It's good to hear you say that you're cutting down. You sound committed to that.

Although it's good to respond positively to the client's efforts, you've ignored the discrepancy between his words and his actions. In order to help him, you need to confront the client with this discrepancy. Return to 8.41 and try again.

8.44

Your Answer: You say that you've cut down, but your records show that your smoking has increased.

Correct. By confronting the client about the discrepancy between his comments and his actions, you will help him to resolve the discrepancy and take responsibility for his behavior. Proceed to 8.45.

8.45

Interviewers often note a discrepancy between clients' self-perception and their actual appearance.

Client (whose looks are above average): I just can't stand myself. I'm so ugly.

Choose the most appropriate response.

Interviewer: You know, you're quite wrong. You really are very attractive. I'm sure you've been told that before.

Go to 8.46

Interviewer: You say that you're ugly, but I'm impressed by how attractive you are. I wonder if you could sort out this contradiction. Go to 8.47

Interviewer: I think you've been watching too much television. We don't all have to be sex symbols, you know.

Go to 8.48

8.46

Your Answer: You know, you're quite wrong. You really are very attractive. I'm sure you've been told that before.

You are probably correct in assuming that the client has been told that she is attractive; therefore, it is unlikely that you will help her by telling her this again. You need to direct her attention to the discrepancy between what she sees and what you see. Return to 8.45 and try again.

8.47

Your Answer: You say that you're ugly, but I'm impressed by how attractive you are. I wonder if you could sort out this contradiction.

Correct. This confrontation focuses the client's attention on the discrepancy between what she sees and what you see and asks her to examine it. Proceed to 8.49.

8.48

Your Answer: I think you've been watching too much television. We don't all have to be sex symbols, you know.

You've discounted the client's feelings and made it difficult for her to examine her perception of herself. You should confront her with the discrepancy between her perception and yours. Return to 8.45 and try again.

8.49

Confrontations can be used to draw a client's attention to incongruous or contradictory comments and behaviors.

Client   (who asserts that there are no problems in his marriage): My wife's going away again this weekend. As I've told you before, I'm really lucky to have such a good marriage.

Choose the most appropriate response.

Interviewer: You feel that you have a good marriage.   Go to 8.50

Interviewer: In my experience, good marriages don't involve separations every weekend.   Go to 8.51

Interviewer: You maintain that you have a good marriage, but you don't seem to be comfortable with your wife's absence on weekends.   Go to 8.52

8.50

Your Answer: You feel that you have a good marriage.

This is a good reflection of feeling, but you should confront the client about the incongruity between his wife's behavior and his apparent belief that all is well with his marriage. Return to 8.49 and try again.

8.51

Your Answer: In my experience, good marriages don't involve separations every weekend.

This confrontation is likely to produce defensive behavior on the part of the client. Your confrontation should be supportive and helpful. Return to 8.49 and try again.

8.52

Your Answer: You maintain that you have a good marriage, but you don't seem to be comfortable with your wife's absence on weekends.

    Correct. Your response confronts the client with the discrepancy between his statements about his marriage and his feelings about his wife's behavior. Proceed to 8.53.

8.53

    Confrontation can be used to draw clients' attention to discrepancies between what they say and how they express themselves.

Client (head down, low, flat, expressionless voice): I'm really very happy. I don't know why I'm sitting here. Everything is going so well.

    Choose the most appropriate response.

Interviewer: You say that you're happy, but your expression and tone of voice suggest otherwise.   Go to 8.54

Interviewer: It's really good to hear you say that everything is going so well. People don't often feel that way.
    Go to 8.55

Interviewer: I just can't believe that. How can you sit there looking depressed and tell me that you're happy?
    Go to 8.56

8.54

Your Answer: You say that you're happy, but your expression and tone of voice suggest otherwise.

    Correct. By focusing on the discrepancy between the client's statements and her way of expressing them, you've confronted her with an inconsistency and encouraged her to explore it. Proceed to 8.57.

8.55

Your Answer: It's really good to hear you say that everything is going so well. People don't often feel that way.

    You've ignored a large portion of the client's total message. She needs feedback about her behavior if she is to confront any difficulties that she is avoiding. Return to 8.53 and try again.

8.56

Your Answer: I just can't believe that. How can you sit there looking depressed and tell me that you're happy?

 This confrontation is too abrupt and will probably cause the client to become defensive. Your confrontation should encourage the client to explore her behavior, not defend it. Return to 8.53 and try again.

8.57

 Rather than attempt to change their behavior, clients often find excuses, blame others, forget a problem, or simply apologize for their behavior. Confrontation can be used to draw these defensive strategies to the clients' attention.

Client (overweight): I don't see why I can't eat whatever I want to eat. Everybody else does. I like to eat.

 Choose the most appropriate response.

Interviewer: You must realize that it's important for you to lose weight. The sooner you get on with it, the better.

Go to 8.58

Interviewer: Could it be that eating is more important to you than losing weight?   Go to 8.59

Interviewer: It seems that you really don't want to do anything about your weight problem.   Go to 8.60

8.58

Your Answer: You must realize that it's important for you to lose weight. The sooner you get on with it, the better.

 Since the client is defending his behavior, it is unlikely that he will heed your advice. You should draw the client's attention to his behavior and encourage him to deal with it. Return to 8.57 and try again.

8.59

Your Answer: Could it be that eating is more important to you than losing weight?

 Correct. This confrontation focuses the client's attention on his behavior and invites him to explore it. Proceed to 8.61.

8.60

Your Answer: It seems that you really don't want to do anything about your weight problem.

This expression of your own opinion will probably cause the client to become defensive. Return to 8.57 and try again.

8.61

It's often necessary to confront clients with contradictions in their personal and social values.

Client: I believe that women have the right to work and contribute to society. I work with some very competent women. But I'm happy that my wife stays home to help me entertain clients. I could never let her work . . . . How would it look?

Choose the most appropriate response.

Interviewer: You think it's very important that your wife supports you in your business activities.   Go to 8.62

Interviewer: Isn't your attitude toward your wife a bit chauvinistic?
                                                    Go to 8.63

Interviewer: You say that you think women should work, but you find it hard to extend this attitude to include your wife.   Go to 8.64

8.62

Your Answer: You think it's very important that your wife supports you in your business activities.

You should confront the client with the contradictory statements he has made so that he can examine his attitudes. Return to 8.61 and try again.

8.63

Your Answer: Isn't your attitude toward your wife a bit chauvinistic?

This response will cause the client to become defensive or hostile. You should confront the client with the discrepancy between his personal and social values and help him to resolve this discrepancy. Return to 8.61 and try again.

8.64

Your Answer: You say that you think women should work, but you find it hard to extend this attitude to include your wife.

Correct. This response confronts the client with the discrepancy between his personal and social values. Proceed to 8.65.

8.65

You need to confront clients about their unrealistic goals in order to help them formulate workable goals.

Client (who is on a fixed income and is in debt): I've been looking at houses. I'm sure that, if we had a house, the children would settle down.

Choose the most appropriate response.

Interviewer: It's important to you to own a house, but I wonder how realistic that is for someone in your financial situation. Go to 8.66

Interviewer: It's important that you give your children the security of a home. You've identified a goal for yourself. Go to 8.67

Interviewer: I'm not sure that's a good idea. Your children are more likely to improve if you settle down and stop creating debts. Go to 8.68

8.66

Your Answer: It's important to you to own a house, but I wonder how realistic that is for someone in your financial situation.

Correct. This confrontation encourages the client to examine his aspirations and set realistic goals for himself. Proceed to 8.69.

8.67

Your Answer: It's important that you give your children the security of a home. You've identified a goal for yourself.

If you don't confront the client, he will assume that you support his unrealistic goals. Return to 8.65 and try again.

8.68

Your Answer: I'm not sure that's a good idea. Your children are
                more likely to improve if you settle down and stop
                creating debts.
                    Confrontation, rather than advice, will enable the client to ex-
                amine his goals and change them. Return to 8.65 and try again.

8.69

                    Because of its strong effects on clients, confrontation should al-
                ways be used in context, and it should never be used excessively.
Client: I hope it's all right with you if we talk today about a
                problem that's caused me a lot of anxiety this week.
                    Choose the most appropriate response.
Interviewer: Last week we agreed to continue discussing an impor-
                tant area, but now you want to discuss something else.
                I get the feeling that you're avoiding the problem we
                were talking about last week.   Go to 8.70
Interviewer: That's fine. It sounds like a matter of real concern to
                you. Start wherever you want to start.   Go to 8.71
Interviewer: I think that we should continue to work on the area
                we were discussing last week.   Go to 8.72

8.70

Your Answer: Last week we agreed to continue discussing an impor-
                tant area, but now you want to discuss something else.
                I get the feeling that you're avoiding the problem we
                were talking about last week.
                    This confrontation would be appropriate if you were able to
                evaluate the importance of the problem the client wishes to discuss.
                The client's behavior seems appropriate at this time; a confrontation
                isn't needed. Return to 8.69 and try again.

8.71

Your Answer: That's fine. It sounds like a matter of real concern to
                you. Start wherever you want to start.
                    Correct. No confrontation is required at this time. You've en-
                couraged the client to discuss the source of his new difficulties. Pro-
                ceed to 8.73.

8.72

Your Answer: I think that we should continue to work on the area
we were discussing last week.

It is inappropriate for you to confront the client at this point.
You should listen to what he has to say and, if necessary, confront
him when you have evidence that warrants the use of confrontation.
Return to 8.69 and try again.

8.73

Indicate whether each of the following statements is true or false.

1. Confrontation draws the client's attention to specific instances of discrepant behavior.
2. Whether or not the interviewer confronts a client is determined by his or her feelings about the client.
3. Rapport between the interviewer and the client is irrelevant to the appropriateness of confrontation.
4. Tentative rather than direct confrontations are more likely to be considered by the client.
5. The client's feelings should be respected both during and after a confrontation.
6. Confrontations often include evaluative comments or solutions to problems.
7. Confrontations should only be used in dealing with the client's weaknesses or limitations.
8. Interviewers should not confront clients about discrepancies between their own perceptions and those of the client.

ANSWERS
1. *True.* If you answered *false,* go to 8.1 and review.
2. *False.* If you answered *true,* go to 8.5 and review.
3. *False.* If you answered *true,* go to 8.13 and review.
4. *True.* If you answered *false,* go to 8.17 and review.
5. *True.* If you answered *false,* go to 8.21 and review.
6. *False.* If you answered *true,* go to 8.25 and review.
7. *False.* If you answered *true,* go to 8.37 and review.
8. *False.* If you answered *true,* go to 8.45 and review.

If six or more of your responses were incorrect, you should return to 8.1 and review this chapter.

POINTS TO REMEMBER ABOUT CONFRONTING

1. **WHEN IDENTIFYING DISCREPANCIES:**
   a. Focus on observed discrepancies.
   b. Focus on discrepancies that are related to clients' strengths as well as their limitations.
2. **WHEN YOU CONFRONT:**
   a. State the discrepant elements in the client's message and encourage the client to explore these discrepancies.
   b. Be tentative.
   c. Be prepared to explore feelings.
   d. Don't use this skill as a means of punishment or revenge.
   e. Your comments shouldn't include accusations, judgments, or solutions to problems.
3. **USE CONFRONTATION:**
   a. To show the client how to recognize contradictions and resolve them.
   b. To help the client identify and resolve discrepancies.
   c. After you've established a good relationship with a client.
   d. Whenever a client's behavior is a threat to his or her welfare or the welfare of others.
   e. When you recognize discrepancies between the client's words and actions, between the client's perceptions and your own, between the client's message and the way in which that message is communicated, or between the client's personal and social values.
   f. When the client exhibits incongruous or contradictory behavior patterns.
   g. When the client employs defensive strategies.
   h. When the client sets unrealistic goals.

MULTIPLE-CHOICE TEST

In order to evaluate your mastery of the material in this chapter, you should answer the following multiple-choice questions. In each case, select the most appropriate response based on the material in this chapter. The correct answers are listed in the Appendix.

1. Client (who has indicated that he makes friends easily and gets along well with people): I've had to move again. It's the third time this year. I always seem to wind up with a strange roommate.

a. Interviewer: You said earlier that you make friends easily, but you seem to have difficulty living with anyone for a very long time.

b. Interviewer: It seems strange to me that you make friends so easily but have so much trouble living with anyone.

c. Interviewer: You said earlier that you make friends easily. Now you're moving for the third time this year because of difficulties with your roommate.

2. Client (who is always late for interviews): I look forward to these sessions with you, because I get so much out of them.

a. Interviewer: You indicate that you enjoy our sessions, but you're always late. This doesn't make sense to me.

b. Interviewer: I have trouble understanding what you mean when you say that you look forward to our sessions; you're always late.

c. Interviewer: If you benefit from our sessions so much, I wonder why you're always late.

3. Client (a 14-year-old boy who has been fighting with his classmates): I get along with the guys. I'm pretty easygoing. But if anybody tries to push me around or tell me what to do, they'd better be careful. Nobody messes around with me.

a. Interviewer: I can't figure out how you get along with the guys so well when they have to be so careful around you. In fact, I understand that you've been getting into fights lately.

b. Interviewer: You say that you get along with the guys, but at the same time you say that the guys had better be careful around you.

c. Interviewer: If people have to be so careful around you because you might start fighting, I can't understand why you think that you're easygoing.

4. Client (a young woman who has postponed her wedding date twice): I really love him . . . . I think he's the greatest guy in the world. We have so many plans for our future together. It has just happened that I've had to postpone the wedding.

a. Interviewer: You've postponed the wedding twice, but you say you love the fellow. I could be wrong, but I don't think you're absolutely sure that you want to marry this man.

b. Interviewer: It's hard to understand how you could postpone the wedding if you care for the fellow as much as you say you do.

c. Interviewer: It sounds as though you might be afraid of marriage. I wonder how much you really do love the fellow.

5. Client (an unassertive person): I can handle myself and not get walked on in most situations.

   a. Interviewer: You see yourself as an assertive person, but I haven't seen that assertiveness. Could you help me to understand this discrepancy?
   b. Interviewer: If you are an assertive person, could you help me to understand how you got into the situations you've told me about?
   c. Interviewer: I may be wrong, but I don't see you as an assertive person.

6. Client (a high school dropout who is discussing job advancement with a personnel manager): Even though the company only takes the cream of the crop from the university for its management-training program, I don't see why I can't apply. I've had a good record with this company for ten years. People say that I'm a leader.

   a. Interviewer: You should be proud of your record with the company. But I wonder if that record is sufficient to overcome your lack of qualifications for the management-training program.
   b. Interviewer: You do have a good record with the company. But I wonder if it's realistic for you to apply for this particular program.
   c. Interviewer: You do have a good record with the company. But I wonder if your goal is realistic, considering the educational requirements for the training program.

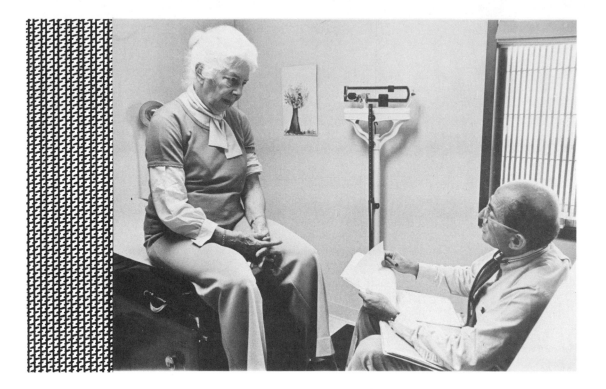

Chapter 9
SELF-DISCLOSING

The material in this chapter is intended to help you master the skill of self-disclosing. After completing this chapter, you should be able to do the following:

1. Self-disclose to a client.
2. Explain the purpose of self-disclosing.
3. Decide whether self-disclosure is appropriate in a given situation.

There is a great deal of evidence to substantiate the facilitative effects of an interviewer's self-disclosure on the interviewing process. In this chapter, you will learn how to formulate self-disclosures, how self-disclosures affect clients, and when it is appropriate to use self-disclosure. In this material, one self-disclosure follows another in order to help you develop this skill. In an actual interview, the interviewer should not use one self-disclosure after another.

The frames in this chapter follow an interview between a high school counselor and a student. The counselor has helped the student in the past, and they have developed a good relationship. This interview was requested by the student. Proceed to 9.1.

9.1

Self-disclosure involves sharing personal information about yourself, your experiences, your attitudes, and your feelings. A good interviewer should be willing to disclose such information when it appears that it will help the client.

Client: I'm really upset. I just found out that my brother and sister are using drugs.

Choose the most appropriate response.

Interviewer: How can you be sure that they're on drugs?
Go to 9.2

Interviewer: I'm glad you found out about it. I can understand your concern. Go to 9.3

Interviewer: You must be worried. When my brother was on drugs, I was really worried about him. I can understand your concern. Go to 9.4

9.2

Your Answer: How can you be sure that they're on drugs?

This question could elicit important information; however, in this chapter, you are learning to self-disclose. A self-disclosure involves telling the client something personal about yourself that relates to his or her problem. Return to 9.1 and try again.

9.3

Your Answer: I'm glad you found out about it. I can understand your concern.

This self-disclosure reveals very little about yourself. Return to 9.1 and try again.

9.4

Your Answer: You must be worried. When my brother was on drugs, I was really worried about him. I can understand your concern.

Correct. You've revealed personal information that lets the client know that you understand his feelings. The client will now feel more comfortable discussing his problem with you. Proceed to 9.5.

9.5

Self-disclosure involves the use of pronouns such as *I* or *me.*

Client: Yes, I'm worried about them. And I don't know what to do about it. As you know, my father died two years ago. My mother would get upset if I told her about my brother and sister. I have to do something.

Choose the most appropriate response.

Interviewer: It must be difficult for you. Why don't you talk to a relative about it? I would.   Go to 9.6

Interviewer: It must be difficult for you. It's important for me to talk problems over with my family. I feel alone until I do.   Go to 9.7

Interviewer: It must be difficult for you. I really think that you should tell your mother. She'll have to know, eventually.   Go to 9.8

9.6

Your Answer: It must be difficult for you. Why don't you talk to a relative about it? I would.

This reflection of feeling, and the leading question that follows it, will be of little use to the client. You should use self-disclosure to help the client with his problem. Return to 9.5 and try again.

9.7

Your Answer: It must be difficult for you. It's important for me to talk problems over with my family. I feel alone until I do.

Correct. This is an appropriate self-disclosure that shows the client that you understand the situation. Proceed to 9.9.

9.8

Your Answer: It must be difficult for you. I really think that you should tell your mother. She'll have to know, eventually.

This reflection of feeling, followed by what could be inappropriate advice, won't help the client to solve the problem he has presented. Return to 9.5 and try again.

9.9

Good self-disclosures enable the client to go on with the interview without distraction. As an interviewer, you need to make self-disclosures that are relevant to the client's concerns and the topic under discussion.

Client: I'm planning to go away to college in the fall. If I have to worry about this problem, I don't see how I can go.

Choose the most appropriate response.

Interviewer: That certainly complicates things. I have the same kind of problem at the moment. I may have to move soon, and I will have to consider my family.

Go to 9.10

Interviewer: You must feel considerable pressure. When I'm faced with a problem like yours, I try to identify its central aspect. It's hard to face the whole thing at once.

Go to 9.11

Interviewer: I find that, as soon as one problem crops up, it leads to a string of others. I wish someone would come up with an explanation of why that happens.

Go to 9.12

9.10

Your Answer: That certainly complicates things. I have the same kind of problem at the moment. I may have to move soon, and I will have to consider my family.

This is an irrelevant self-disclosure that will distract the client. As the interviewer, your role is to facilitate discussion, not divert it. Return to 9.9 and try again.

9.11

Your Answer: You must feel considerable pressure. When I'm faced with a problem like yours, I try to identify its central aspect. It's hard to face the whole thing at once.

Correct. This self-disclosure is on topic and will help the client to sort out his problem. Proceed to 9.13.

9.12

Your Answer: I find that, as soon as one problem crops up, it leads to a string of others. I wish someone would come up with an explanation of why that happens.

This kind of irrelevant self-disclosure has no place in an interview. Return to 9.9 and try again.

9.13

When using self-disclosure, you can share information that relates to your experiences, your current situation, or possible events in your future. Self-disclosures that relate to your current situation are most powerful, because they help the client to focus on a particular problem and deal with it concretely.

Client: I *am* a little overwhelmed. I suppose I just have to do something about my brother and sister. If I don't do something about them, I'll have a hard time going off to college. I don't know how they would manage . . . . I guess I should tell my mother and let her deal with it, but I just don't know how she would cope.

Choose the most appropriate response.

Interviewer: At times, I feel responsible for one or both of my parents. When that happens, I often underestimate how well they can cope. When I discuss problems with them, I'm surprised at how well they can deal with them.   Go to 9.14

Interviewer: When my father dies, I know that I'll have to assume responsibility in the same way that you have. And that will create problems in my life. I guess I'll try to find solutions to problems on my own.   Go to 9.15

Interviewer: When I was your age, I often found it hard to discuss things with my mother. I tried to solve problems on my own, but later I wished that I had asked her for help.   Go to 9.16

9.14

Your Answer: At times, I feel responsible for one or both of my parents. When that happens, I often underestimate how well they can cope. When I discuss problems with them, I'm surprised at how well they can deal with them.

Correct. This self-disclosure focuses on your present situation and helps the client to identify an important aspect of his problem. Proceed to 9.17.

9.15

Your Answer: When my father dies, I know that I'll have to assume responsibility in the same way that you have. And that will create problems in my life. I guess I'll try to find solutions to problems on my own.

This response indicates that you don't understand or empathize with the client's situation. Your response should encourage the client, not inhibit him. Return to 9.13 and try again.

9.16

Your Answer: When I was your age, I often found it hard to discuss things with my mother. I tried to solve problems on my own, but later I wished that I had asked her for help.

Your self-disclosure is appropriate, but it isn't as powerful as one that focuses on the present. Return to 9.13 and try again.

9.17

The way in which you present self-disclosure affects its impact on the client.

Client: I don't really think that my mother can cope with my brother's and sister's problem. I don't really know, though. I haven't let her handle very many responsibilities since my father died.

Choose the most appropriate response.

Interviewer (leaning back in the chair, speaking in a monotone): My uncle is dead, and my aunt has a major problem right now—her son's truancy. I think coping with that problem is helping her to get over my uncle's death.

Go to 9.18

Interviewer (leaning toward the client with a warm expression): My uncle is dead, and my aunt has a major problem right now—her son's truancy. I think coping with that problem is helping her to get over my uncle's death.

Go to 9.19

Interviewer (leaning toward the client, laughing awkwardly): My uncle is dead, and my aunt has a major problem right now—her son's truancy. I think coping with that problem is helping her to get over my uncle's death.

Go to 9.20

9.18

Your Answer (leaning back in the chair, speaking in a monotone): My uncle is dead, and my aunt has a major problem right now—her son's truancy. I think coping with that problem is helping her to get over my uncle's death.

The content of a disclosure and the way in which it is presented are both important. You've negated the positive effect of your self-disclosure by presenting it in a manner that indicates you aren't interested in what you're saying. This could suggest that your response is rehearsed rather than spontaneous. Return to 9.17 and try again.

9.19

Your Answer (leaning toward the client, with a warm expression): My uncle is dead, and my aunt has a major problem right now—her son's truancy. I think coping with that problem is helping her to get over my uncle's death.

Correct. Because your demeanor and self-disclosure are congruous, the client will feel that you are sharing information about meaningful events. Proceed to 9.21.

9.20

Your Answer (leaning toward the client, laughing awkwardly): My uncle is dead, and my aunt has a major problem right now—her son's truancy. I think coping with that problem is helping her to get over my uncle's death.

Although your laughter may be due to the fact that you are uncomfortable with what you are about to say, the client could interpret your behavior as an indication of insincerity. When you feel uncomfortable about making a self-disclosure, it is best not to make it. Return to 9.17 and try again.

9.21

When an interviewer discloses personal information, the client often responds by disclosing specific, personal information.

Client: I hadn't looked at things that way. Maybe I'm protecting my mother too much. It sure would help me if I thought she could look after my brother and sister. I'm tired of trying to help them.

Choose the most appropriate response.

Interviewer: I find it difficult to help my brothers and sister, too. I try, but I just don't have the influence that my mother has. They respect her, but I guess they see me as just one of them. Go to 9.22

Interviewer: Everyone fights with brothers and sisters. We've had some massive battles over the years, and some of them are still going on. Go to 9.23

Interviewer: My brothers and sister fight about everything. They never stop. There is always an argument when they get together. Go to 9.24

9.22

Your Answer: I find it difficult to help my brothers and sister, too. I try, but I just don't have the influence that my mother has. They respect her, but I guess they see me as just one of them.

Correct. This self-disclosure is relevant to the client's problem. It will encourage more specific discussion of his role in his situation. Proceed to 9.25.

9.23

Your Answer: Everyone fights with brothers and sisters. We've had some massive battles over the years, and some of them are still going on.

This self-disclosure may suggest that you are comfortable discussing generalities rather than the specific aspects of one person's problems. Return to 9.21 and try again.

9.24

Your Answer: My brothers and sister fight about everything. They never stop. There is always an argument when they get together.

Your response changes the focus to your family disputes. Return to 9.21 and try again.

9.25

Self-disclosure allows the client to know the interviewer as a person, thereby facilitating a greater level of trust and open discussion between the two.

Client: Well, maybe I should tell my mother about all of this, but I've always found it hard to talk to her. I don't really know how to go about it.

Choose the most appropriate response.

Interviewer: I can't talk to my mother, either. She's always busy.
Go to 9.26

Interviewer: You know, my mother's funny. When I think she's listening, she doesn't hear a thing. Go to 9.27

Interviewer: I find it hard to talk to my mother, too. It's all right once I'm started, but it's always difficult for me at the beginning. Go to 9.28

9.26

Your Answer: I can't talk to my mother, either. She's always busy.

There is little in this self-disclosure that is relevant to the client's problem. Your response will distract him from considering the feelings he has about communicating with his mother. Return to 9.25 and try again.

9.27

Your Answer: You know, my mother's funny. When I think she's listening, she doesn't hear a thing.

This self-disclosure doesn't necessarily relate to the client's problem. The client has told you that he has difficulty discussing things with his mother, but you don't know anything about his mother's listening abilities. In order to build mutual trust, you need to share personal information that relates to the topic under discussion. Return to 9.25 and try again.

9.28

Your Answer: I find it hard to talk to my mother, too. It's all right once I'm started, but it's always difficult for me at the beginning.

Correct. This self-disclosure focuses on your reaction to a situation that is similar to the client's. By revealing this information, you help to develop mutual trust and stimulate relevant discussion. Proceed to 9.29.

9.29

Clients often find it difficult to share personal information. They may be afraid that sharing such information is inappropriate, they may be uncomfortable with self-disclosure, or they may not know how to self-disclose. Under these circumstances, the interviewer should model the skill of self-disclosing for the client.

Client: I really should discuss my concerns with my mother. I've known that for ages. I guess it's just like the other times I've had to discuss things with her. I keep putting it off, thinking about it . . . worrying about it . . . and then when I talk to her, I wonder why I waited so long. I'll tell her when I go home. It won't be easy. But I need to consider my plans for college.

Choose the most appropriate response.

Interviewer: I often find that worrying about something is more stressful than actually doing it. And worrying keeps me from doing other things.   Go to 9.30

Interviewer: Thinking about things beforehand is really a problem for me. I don't know what I can do about it.
                                        Go to 9.31

Interviewer: I've been thinking about college as well, but I can't decide whether to go back or not. It's a difficult decision.   Go to 9.32

9.30

Your Answer: I often find that worrying about something is more stressful than actually doing it. And worrying keeps me from doing other things.

    Correct. Your self-disclosure invites the client to stay on topic and consider the relevant aspects of his problem. Hence, your self-disclosure is an appropriate model for the client. Proceed to 9.33.

9.31

Your Answer: Thinking about things beforehand is really a problem for me. I don't know what I can do about it.

    This self-disclosure changes the topic to one of your problems and could easily lead to a discussion of your situation rather than the client's. Self-disclosures should be on topic and advance the interview. Return to 9.29 and try again.

9.32

Your Answer: I've been thinking about college as well, but I can't decide whether to go back or not. It's a difficult decision.

    Your self-disclosure changes the focus of the interview from the client to yourself. You've changed the topic and burdened the client with your problem. Return to 9.29 and try again.

9.33

    Self-disclosure should help the client to focus clearly and accurately on a particular problem and on the resources that can be used to solve that problem.

Client: You know, when I came in, I thought my problem with my brother and sister might prevent me from going to college. But now, as I'm talking about it, I don't think it's just that. I think I'm afraid to leave home.

    Choose the most appropriate response.

Interviewer: When I went to college, I think I found it difficult to leave home, too. Go to 9.34

Interviewer: I sometimes focus on the wrong reason for a problem, too. I often find that, after I solve one problem, I can move on to attend to others.   Go to 9.35

Interviewer: When I think about moving to a new position in a new city, I get uptight, too.   Go to 9.36

9.34

Your Answer: When I went to college, I think I found it difficult to leave home, too.

This self-disclosure is too general to help the client focus accurately on a particular problem or resource. Return to 9.33 and try again.

9.35

Your Answer: I sometimes focus on the wrong reason for a problem, too. I often find that, after I solve one problem, I can move on to attend to others.

Correct. This self-disclosure relates to the situation that the client is describing. Moreover, you've offered a method of approaching his situation. Proceed to 9.37.

9.36

Your Answer: When I think about moving to a new position in a new city, I get uptight, too.

This self-disclosure is off topic and provides no useful information to the client. Return to 9.33 and try again.

9.37

Self-disclosures shouldn't be used to overshadow, deny, or put down what the client has said.

Client: I really am afraid to leave home and go to college. I have a lot of difficulty making new friends. I'll be so lonely there. I suppose it really would help if I knew how to go about making new friends.

Choose the most appropriate response.

Interviewer: I find that I'm better off at home rather than out trying to find new friends.   Go to 9.38

Interviewer: Trying to make new friends and failing always makes me feel worse. I've found that it's better to stick with old friends.   Go to 9.39

Interviewer: Sorting out things ahead of time really helps me.
                                                Go to 9.40

9.38

Your Answer: I find that I'm better off at home rather than out trying to find new friends.

   Your self-disclosure discourages the client from exploring ways by which he can find a positive solution to his dilemma. Return to 9.37 and try again.

9.39

Your Answer: Trying to make new friends and failing always makes me feel worse. I've found that it's better to stick with old friends.

   In his previous statement, the client suggested a positive move that could reduce much of his anxiety about going away to college. This self-disclosure discounts that solution. Return to 9.37 and try again.

9.40

Your Answer: Sorting out things ahead of time really helps me.

   Correct. Your self-disclosure will encourage the client to explore appropriate means of working through his anxiety. Proceed to 9.41.

9.41

   The extensive use of interviewer self-disclosure is inappropriate during the early stages of an interview, at which time it is more important to *listen* to the client. When you do use this skill, you should use it in moderation. It's difficult to trust an interviewer who uses self-disclosure excessively. Proceed to 9.42.

9.42

Indicate whether each of the following statements is true or false.

1. Self-disclosure can be used to demonstrate that it is appropriate to reveal personal information during an interview.
2. Self-disclosure should be used frequently during the early stages of an interview.
3. Self-disclosure invites the client to share specific personal information with the interviewer.
4. Self-disclosure should be used to distract the client from specific problems.
5. Self-disclosure should be used as frequently as possible.
6. Self-disclosure generally facilitates trust between the interviewer and the client.
7. Self-disclosure is often used to help the client focus on a specific problem.
8. Self-disclosures that focus on past experiences are the most effective.

ANSWERS

1. *True.* If you answered *false,* go to 9.29 and review.
2. *False.* If you answered *true,* go to 9.41 and review.
3. *True.* If you answered *false,* go to 9.21 and review.
4. *False.* If you answered *true,* go to 9.9 and review.
5. *False.* If you answered *true,* go to 9.41 and review.
6. *True.* If you answered *false,* go to 9.25 and review.
7. *True.* If you answered *false,* go to 9.33 and review.
8. *False.* If you answered *true,* go to 9.13 and review.

If five or more of your responses were incorrect, you should return to 9.1 and review the material in this chapter.

POINTS
TO
REMEMBER
ABOUT
SELF-
DISCLOSING

1. **WHEN YOU SELF-DISCLOSE:**
   a. Your response must include relevant personal material.
   b. You should try to focus on your present circumstances.
   c. You should be spontaneous and make your response with appropriate affect.
2. **SELF-DISCLOSURE:**
   a. Encourages the client to share information that is personally meaningful.

b. Increases trust between the interviewer and the client.
c. Enhances the client's ability to share feelings and personal information.

3. **USE SELF-DISCLOSURE:**
   a. To help the client focus clearly and accurately on problems and available resources.
   b. When your response won't overshadow, deny, or negate the client's communication.
   c. After you have established a good relationship with the client.
   d. In moderation.

MULTIPLE-
CHOICE
TEST

In order to evaluate your mastery of the material in this chapter, you should answer the following multiple-choice questions. In each case, select the most appropriate response based on the material in this chapter. The correct answers are listed in the Appendix.

1. Client: I frequently have trouble making decisions about the most simple things. I think I must be a stupid person when I can't make up my mind about little things.

   a. Interviewer: You know, sometimes that happens to me. And I get so frustrated with myself.
   b. Interviewer: In what type of situations does this indecision occur?
   c. Interviewer: That kind of thing happens to my husband, and I can see how frustrated he gets.

2. Client: I get so angry with my husband when he doesn't show up on time. Sometimes I wait at least an hour. He always has some excuse. I wonder if other people get angry about that sort of thing.

   a. Interviewer: I don't know about everybody else, but sometimes I feel upset with my husband when I have to wait for him.
   b. Interviewer: I get angry with my husband about that. When he makes me wait longer than I think I should, I just go on without him.
   c. Interviewer: My husband does the same thing to me. How does your husband react when you tell him how angry you are?

3. Client: My best friend just told me that he has leukemia. I don't know how to act around him. I don't know whether I should talk about it or let him bring up the subject. I just want to be able to show him how much I care for him.

a. Interviewer: I have an idea of how hard that must be. It's hard under any circumstances to let another person know how much you care.

b. Interviewer: That's really a tough situation to be in. When a close cousin of mine was dying of cancer, I had real difficulty in letting her know how much I cared.

c. Interviewer: It's difficult to let someone know how much you care. What have you considered doing to show that you care?

4. People think it's funny, but I just can't stand to ride in airplanes.

a. Interviewer: I don't have problems in airplanes, but when I ride in a boat I feel really nervous.

b. Interviewer: I'm afraid to ride in airplanes, too. I use the train or car to get where I need to go.

c. Interviewer: I have some idea of how you feel. I feel very anxious when I fly in a small plane. It's almost like a panic feeling.

5. Client: I was really pleased when my son decided to go to a trade school rather than college, because he realized college wasn't right for him.

a. Interviewer: It has been my experience that, if you let children make their own decisions, they usually do a good job.

b. Interviewer: My son is wrestling with a similar issue. I hope he can make the best choice for himself, as your son did.

c. Interviewer: I worry about my children making that decision, even though they are a long way from facing it.

6. My wife died several months ago . . . . I feel so lost without her, and so do the kids. I can't get our lives sorted out and running again . . . . I don't think anyone has felt as inadequate as I do.

a. Interviewer: If I were in your situation, I would probably feel lonely and inadequate, too,

b. Interviewer: I hear you saying that you're not sure you can cope without your wife.

c. Interviewer: You *do* have a difficult situation to deal with.

Chapter 10
STRUCTURING

The material in this chapter is intended to help you master the skill of structuring. After completing this chapter, you should be able to do the following:

1. State the relationship objectives for each phase of an interview.
2. State the action objectives for each phase of an interview.
3. Decide when to make a structuring response.
4. Make structuring responses when they are required.

Structuring involves the ability to organize and pace a relationship with a client from its beginning to its conclusion. In each phase, the interviewer has a relationship objective and an action objective. In order to use the skill of structuring effectively, you need to become familiar with these objectives. (See Table 10-1.)

TABLE 10-1   **An Overview of the Interviewing Phases and
Their Related Relationship and Action Objectives**

Interviewing Phase	*Relationship Objective*	*Action Objective*
1. Development	Develop and facilitate open communication between the interviewer and the client.	Discover the client's problem(s) and assess the need for further action.
2. Inventory	Develop a more focused and facilitative relationship between the interviewer and the client.	Develop a mutually agreed upon definition of the client's specific problem(s).
3. Priority	Maintain a facilitative relationship between the interviewer and the client.	Achieve a mutually agreed upon order in which the client's problems are to be considered.
4. Goal Formulation	Maintain a facilitative relationship between the interviewer and the client. Use confrontation to help the client translate problems into goals.	Mutually redefine problems as attainable goals. Each goal may need to be restated as a set of subgoals.
5. Action Plan Formulation	Maintain a facilitative relationship between the interviewer and the client that emphasizes the client's responsibility.	Mutually generate action plans that are relevant to each goal and, based on the merits of each alternative, select the optimal plan.
6. Action	Maintain a facilitative relationship between the interviewer and the client by supporting or confronting as required.	Help the client to implement the optimal action plan and modify it as required to facilitate maintenance of new behaviors in the absence of the interviewer/client relationship.
7. Termination	Conclude the interviewer/client relationship, leaving it open to reinitiation if required.	Terminate the interviewer/client relationship after the stated goals have been attained.

In the preceding chapters, you've been exposed to a variety of basic interviewing skills. As an interviewer, you will be most effective when you are able to combine and organize these skills in a purposeful manner—when you are able to structure your relationships with clients.

An effective interviewer uses the skill of structuring throughout the interviewer/client relationship. Because of the varied nature of the decisions and problems that people will present to you, you need to remain *flexible* in your use of this skill. Occasionally, some phases of structuring may be unnecessary. On other occasions, each phase will be essential and will extend over a considerable period of time. In some cases, you may find that two phases blend together into a natural whole.

This chapter follows a series of interviews between a male student and a counselor at a student drop-in center. Proceed to 10.1.

10.1

The first phase of structuring is development. In this phase, the interviewer employs listening and reflecting skills to demonstrate that he or she is listening and to help the client discuss problems openly. The first action objective in this phase is to gain an overview of the client's problems so that the interviewer and the client can assess the situation together.

In this first session, the interviewer and the client have spent several minutes discussing the client's concerns about choosing a career.

Client: One of the most pressing concerns I have is deciding whether I should go into dentistry or medicine.

Choose the most appropriate response.

Interviewer: What does your father do?   Go to 10.2

Interviewer: A major concern for you is choosing the right profession. What are some of your other concerns?

Go to 10.3

Interviewer: That's a hard decision. I don't know which one I would choose.   Go to 10.4

10.2

Your Answer: What does your father do?

There was no indication in the client's statement that his father's profession is relevant to his decision. During this part of the development phase, you need to establish rapport with the client and try to understand the nature of his problems by employing listening skills and remaining on topic. Return to 10.1 and try again.

10.3

Your Answer: A major concern for you is choosing the right profession. What are some of your other concerns?

      Correct. During this part of the development phase, you need to establish rapport with the client and develop an initial understanding of his problems. By reflecting content and using open inquiry, you've shown that you're listening to the client and have encouraged him to discuss his problems with you. Proceed to 10.5.

10.4

Your Answer: That's a hard decision. I don't know which one I would choose.

      This self-disclosure won't help to facilitate an open relationship with the client, and it won't help him with the decision he has to make. Appropriate structuring at this point requires a response that indicates you have heard what the client has said and are willing to listen to his other concerns. Return to 10.1 and try again.

10.5

      The second action objective of the development phase is to decide whether or not the client needs further counseling. This decision must be mutually agreed upon by the interviewer and the client. In this particular case, the client now has an overview of his problems, and the interviewer and the client have agreed that these problems necessitate further counseling.

Client: Let me see . . . . I told you about trying to decide what to study. And then there's the issue of whether to live at home or not. And I suppose the dating thing's a problem, too. I don't think there are any others. I suppose if there are, they'll come up later.

      Choose the response that will bring the development phase of this interview to a conclusion.

Interviewer: You've just identified three areas of concern. To what extent are you willing to work on developing some solutions to these problems?   Go to 10.6

Interviewer: You've just identified three areas of concern. We need to look at and define each one individually.

               Go to 10.7

Interviewer: You've just identified three areas of concern, but I think that they are things you can work on yourself. Let's close the interview at this point. It was a good idea for you to check out whether or not you needed help.   Go to 10.8

10.6

Your Answer: You've just identified three areas of concern. To what extent are you willing to work on developing some solutions to these problems?

    Correct. This brief paraphrase, followed by an open inquiry, is the appropriate structuring response at this point. The open inquiry initiates a discussion that will help you and the client to reach a decision concerning further action. When this decision is reached, the development phase is completed. Proceed to 10.9.

10.7

Your Answer: You've just identified three areas of concern. We need to look at and define each one individually.

    This response is premature. Before moving to further discussion of his problems, you and the client need to reach a mutual decision concerning the need for further counseling. Return to 10.5 and try again.

10.8

Your Answer: You've just identified three areas of concern, but I think that they are things you can work on yourself. Let's close the interview at this point. It was a good idea for you to check out whether or not you needed help.

    You've made a unilateral decision to terminate the interview; however, you and the client need to reach a *mutual* decision concerning further counseling. Return to 10.5 and try again.

10.9

    In the second phase of structuring—the inventory phase—the interaction between the client and the interviewer becomes more focused. In this phase, you will find it necessary to use action-oriented skills in addition to listening and reflecting skills. The action objective in this phase is to explore the client's problem areas until you both reach an accurate and concrete definition of each problem.

Client: Well, I've tried to do something about my problems by myself for some time now. I really do need to talk them through with someone. I would like to talk with you about them if you would be willing to do that.

Choose the most appropriate response.

Interviewer: That seems like a good idea to me. As you indicated earlier, you have a number of problems. Perhaps we could talk about these in detail and come up with a precise definition of each one. How does that sound to you? Go to 10.10

Interviewer: That seems like a good idea to me. Now, let's see . . . . You've talked about deciding between medicine and dentistry. That's a big decision. And you've indicated that you'd like to get away from your family. And then you mentioned dating. And perhaps you have other problems. I think that we should solve the career problem first. Maybe you should go over and see the dean of medicine this afternoon. Go to 10.11

Interviewer: That seems like a good idea to me. About those other problems you think you have . . . I know it's hard to talk about them, but before we can move on, you're going to have to tell me about them. Go to 10.12

10.10

Your Answer: That seems like a good idea to me. As you indicated earlier, you have a number of problems. Perhaps we could talk about these in detail and come up with a precise definition of each one. How does that sound to you?

Correct. This response orients the client toward the next phase of the interview. Proceed to 10.13.

10.11

Your Answer: That seems like a good idea to me. Now, let's see . . . . You've talked about deciding between medicine and dentistry. That's a big decision. And you've indicated

that you'd like to get away from your family. And
then you mentioned dating. And perhaps you have
other problems. I think that we should solve the career
problem first. Maybe you should go over and see the
dean of medicine this afternoon.

In this phase, you should help the client to explore and define
specific problems. This response omits exploration of any specific
problem and offers a possibly inappropriate solution. Return to
10.12 and try again.

10.12

Your Answer: That seems like a good idea to me. About those other
problems you think you have . . . I know it's hard to
talk about them, but before we can move on, you're
going to have to tell me about them.

The client has already discussed his other problems and has decided that discussion of them isn't warranted at this time. Therefore,
you should move on to the next phase of the structuring process—the
inventory phase. Return to 10.12 and try again.

10.13

In the inventory phase, the interviewer and the client explore
problems until they agree on concrete solutions for each one. Usually,
a concrete solution takes the form of a specific action, such as making
a decision, learning a skill, or increasing or decreasing the frequency
of a behavior.

During the inventory phase, the interviewer needs to be able to
recognize the point at which the client formulates a precise and concrete definition of a problem. In the course of this interview, the
client has formulated a definition of his dating problem.

Choose the comment that best defines the problem.

Client: I guess I've got a poor self-concept that gets in my
way when I'm out with a woman.   Go to 10.14

Client: I guess it's my parents' fault. They've never let me go
out on dates.   Go to 10.15

Client: I guess I've just never learned how to arrange a date
or what to do if I get one.   Go to 10.16

10.14

Your Answer: I guess I've got a poor self-concept that gets in my
way when I'm out with a woman.

In order to help the client, you need to know specifically how
his self-concept affects his behavior. In this situation, further exploration of the problem is needed. Return to 10.13 and try again.

10.15

Your Answer: I guess it's my parents' fault. They've never let me go
out on dates.

This may be one aspect of the client's problem, but it isn't a
precise definition of the problem in concrete terms. You need to encourage exploration beyond this point in order to reach a precise definition of the client's problem. Return to 10.13 and try again.

10.16

Your Answer: I guess I've just never learned how to arrange a date
or what to do if I get one.

Correct. This is a precise definition of the client's problem.
After you have helped him to define his problems, you should move
on to the priority phase of the interview. Proceed to 10.17.

10.17

The third phase in structuring is the priority phase. During this
phase, the interviewer continues to maintain a facilitative relationship with the client. The action objective in this phase is to determine the order in which the client's problems should be considered.
The interdependence of problems may suggest a logical sequence. If a
logical sequence isn't apparent and the client has no preference, it is
advisable to move from the least severe problem to the most severe.

In the inventory phase of this interview, you and the client have
agreed to discuss the following specific problems: his failure to obtain
sufficient information on which to base his decision concerning his
course of study, his inability to communicate to his parents his desire
to leave home and attend college elsewhere, and his inability to arrange a date.

Choose the response that will initiate the priority phase of this
interview.

Interviewer: Now that we have a definition of your concerns, we need to consider the order in which to deal with them. Your parents seem to have an important role in all of this. Before we go any further, you should tell them about your desire to leave home.   Go to 10.18

Interviewer: First, I want you to go home and draw up a list of all the women you know. Then, beside each name, write the reason for your inability to ask her for a date.
                                                                   Go to 10.19

Interviewer: Now that we have a definition of your concerns, we need to consider the order in which to deal with them. It seems that you're very concerned about choosing a career. It might be appropriate to deal with that first. What do you think?   Go to 10.20

10.18

Your Answer: Now that we have a definition of your concerns, we need to consider the order in which to deal with them. Your parents seem to have an important role in all of this. Before we go any further, you should tell them about your desire to leave home.

You've imposed your priorities on the client and moved into problem solving much too quickly. The ranking of the client's problems must be mutually agreed upon by the client and the interviewer. Moreover, you have shifted the relationship from an open, facilitative one to a closed, authoritarian one. Return to 10.17 and try again.

10.19

Your Answer: First, I want you to go home and draw up a list of all the women you know. Then, beside each name, write the reason for your inability to ask her for a date.

During this phase of the interview, you need to help the client rank his concerns according to their priority. The ranking of the concerns must be mutually agreed upon by the client and the interviewer. You've assumed that the dating problem supersedes all others. Moreover, you've failed to tell the client what he might expect during this phase of the interview. Return to 10.17 and try again.

10.20

Your Answer: Now that we have a definition of your concerns, we need to consider the order in which to deal with them. It seems that you're very concerned about choosing a career. It might be appropriate to deal with that first. What do you think?

Correct. This response explains the priority phase of interviewing and initiates the ordering process in a way that invites the client's input. Proceed to 10.21.

10.21

Up to this point, you've helped the client to explore his concerns and the need for further counseling (development phase), to define his concerns in concrete terms (inventory phase), and to determine the order in which these concerns should be considered (priority phase). The remaining phases in structuring involve setting goals, planning action, implementing programs, and terminating the interviewer/client relationship. In order to illustrate these phases clearly, we have focused the remaining segments of this program on only one of the client's concerns. Proceed to 10.22.

10.22

After you and the client have determined the order in which his or her specific concerns should be dealt with, you move to the goal-formulation phase of structuring. The client's concern or problem, as stated in the inventory phase, defines his or her present situation. The aim of goal formulation is to redefine this problem in terms of an alternative situation that is both realistic and acceptable to the client. At the conclusion of the priority phase of this interview, the client makes the following statement.

Client: Choosing a career is a major concern of mine, but I've got a whole year to work that out. The thing that's really getting me down is never having a date. All my friends get dates, but I just can't seem to get one.

Interviewer: From what you've said, it sounds as though we should work on that first. What about that?

Client: I'd be happy if we did that.

Choose the response that will best structure the goal-formulation phase.

Interviewer: Maybe you'd better tell me about this dating problem again. I'm not sure that I understand it completely. Have you been on any dates recently?   Go to 10.23

Interviewer: We've discussed your dating problem. Now we need to use that information to develop a goal that you're willing to work toward. Could you describe a goal that you'd like to reach?   Go to 10.24

Interviewer: Before I see you again, I want you to do three things. Spend five minutes chatting with a woman after each of your classes. Have lunch with a mixed group every day. And invite a woman for coffee at least once during the next week.   Go to 10.25

10.23

Your Answer: Maybe you'd better tell me about this dating problem again. I'm not sure that I understand it completely. Have you been on any dates recently?

You've already collected the information that is relevant to this particular problem. When you ask a client to repeat information, you waste time and do little to facilitate your relationship or help the client to set appropriate goals. Return to 10.22 and try again.

10.24

Your Answer: We've discussed your dating problem. Now we need to use that information to develop a goal that you're willing to work toward. Could you describe a goal that you'd like to reach?

Correct. You've invited the client to redefine his problem as an attainable goal. Proceed to 10.26.

10.25

Your Answer: Before I see you again, I want you to do three things. Spend five minutes chatting with a woman after each of your classes. Have lunch with a mixed group every day. And invite a woman for coffee at least once during the next week.

This response violates the mutuality of the interviewing process. The client is more likely to work toward a goal that he has helped to formulate and to which he aspires. Moreover, in making this response, you've skipped both the goal-formulation and the action-plan-formulation phases of interviewing. All possibilities should be examined before an action plan is initiated. Return to 10.22 and try again.

10.26

A client may have difficulty translating a problem into an attainable goal. If this happens because the problem has been poorly defined, you will need to return to the inventory phase and develop a clearer definition. However, you may find that the client can define the problem but seems unwilling or unable to translate it into an attainable goal. When this occurs, you can use the skill of confronting to focus on this unwillingness or inability.

Client: I don't know about any goal. I don't think you understand. Maybe I'd better tell you more about it, but I'm not sure it's that much of a problem.

Choose the most appropriate response.

Interviewer: It's much easier to talk about your problems than it is to solve them. Deciding on a goal is a big step.
Go to 10.27

Interviewer: I think your goal should be to go out with women until you have a list of four or five who go out with you regularly. Go to 10.28

Interviewer: You don't seem to be too sure of what you want. Maybe we should talk about it some more. Where do you want to start? Go to 10.29

10.27

Your Answer: It's much easier to talk about your problems than it is to solve them. Deciding on a goal is a big step.

Correct. By confronting the client with the discrepancy between his stated desire to act and his apparent unwillingness to act, you encourage him to set appropriate, realistic goals. Proceed to 10.30.

10.28

Your Answer: I think your goal should be to go out with women until you have a list of four or five who go out with you regularly.

Your response should help the client explore his unwillingness to formulate a goal. You've ignored his unwillingness and suggested a goal that may or may not be realistic or appropriate. Although the client may cooperate with you temporarily, it is doubtful that he will persist if he is having difficulty moving into the action phase of interviewing. Return to 10.26 and try again.

10.29

Your Answer: You don't seem to be too sure of what you want. Maybe we should talk about it some more. Where do you want to start?

You've already explored the problem with the client and developed a definition of it. It is unlikely that you will alter the client's resistance to establishment of a goal by covering this information again. You need to confront him with his behavior in order to help him explore and clarify its meaning and work toward the establishment of a goal. Return to 10.26 and try again.

10.30

Goals should be formulated in concrete terms. In order to accomplish this, you may need to redefine a general goal as a series of specific subgoals, or steps, that lead to the attainment of the general goal.

Client: I hadn't looked at it that way. I guess I'm a little scared to think of going out with women. But I know I've got to do something about it.

Interviewer: Let's talk about the way you'd like things to be. How would you act toward women if you didn't have this problem?

Client: I'd like to be able to ask women out so that I could have some fun. My friends know women, and they all do things together.

Choose the response that will conclude the goal-formulation phase of this interview.

Interviewer: I think that's a reasonable goal. Perhaps we can move on now to identify some ways of doing that.

Go to 10.31

Interviewer: It seems that you envy your friends and what they do. Could you tell me about some of those things?

Go to 10.32

| Interviewer: | That's a reasonable goal. What might be the first step in learning to ask women out?   Go to 10.33 |

10.31

Your Answer: I think that's a reasonable goal. Perhaps we can move on now to identify some ways of doing that.

You're moving too quickly. This structuring response is inappropriate, because the client's goal is too vague to act as a reasonable focus for action planning or action initiation. Your response should help the client to define his goal in more concrete terms. Return to 10.30 and try again.

10.32

Your Answer: It seems that you envy your friends and what they do. Could you tell me about some of those things?

This response may be appropriate during some other phase of the interview, but not when you're helping the client to define goals. You've changed the topic and made an open inquiry that is irrelevant to the solution of the client's problem. Return to 10.30 and try again.

10.33

Your Answer: That's a reasonable goal. What might be the first step in learning to ask women out?

Correct. This response encourages the client to define his general goal in a series of concrete, attainable subgoals. Proceed to 10.34.

10.34

After a specific goal or set of subgoals have been identified, the interviewer and the client need to agree on an action plan that will enable the client to attain the goal or subgoals. It is important for the client to be responsible for the formulation of the action plan. The first step is to consider a number of plans that are relevant to the client's goal. Although the client should be mainly responsible for developing action plans, you may need to contribute possible alternatives.

The interviewer and the client have now agreed on a number of subgoals. First of all, the client is to have coffee with a woman. For purposes of illustration, this subgoal alone will be dealt with.

Choose the response that will initiate the action-plan-formulation phase of this interview.

Interviewer: I think it's important that you have coffee with a woman you don't know. That seems to be a good way to start. Go to 10.35

Interviewer: I suggest that you ask a woman to have coffee on the spur of the moment and go with her right away. That way, you'll keep anxiety to a minimum.

Go to 10.36

Interviewer: We need to think about how you might accomplish this goal. What ideas do you have? Go to 10.37

10.35

Your Answer: I think it's important that you have coffee with a woman you don't know. That seems to be a good way to start.

You should give the client an opportunity to formulate his own plan of action. By making this response, you limit his responsibility. At this point in the action-planning phase, your response should encourage the client to participate in the generation of possible alternatives. Return to 10.34 and try again.

10.36

Your Answer: I suggest that you ask a woman to have coffee on the spur of the moment and go with her right away. That way, you'll keep anxiety to a minimum.

You've taken full responsibility for generating the action plan. Action plans are most likely to be successful when clients generate and explore their own alternative routes to reaching their goals. Return to 10.34 and try again.

10.37

Your Answer: We need to think about how you might accomplish this goal. What ideas do you have?

Correct. You've encouraged the client to focus on possible action plans for the goal under discussion and to take responsibility for generating these plans. Proceed to 10.38.

10.38

> After relevant action plans have been established, the advantages and disadvantages of each one are explored, and an optimal plan is selected.
>
> The interviewer and the client have explored four relevant plans of action. Choose the response that will further structure the action plan-formulation phase of this interview.

Interviewer: We've decided on four possible methods by which you can attain your goal. You could choose someone ahead of time and arrange it over the phone the night before. You could ask a woman you know through your friends. You could casually ask someone in one of your classes as the class ends. Or you could ask someone who never seems to go out. We've discussed the consequences of each of these plans and how the plans themselves fit in with your values. From your perspective, which alternative seems most appropriate?
Go to 10.39

Interviewer: You said that you would find it difficult to ask a woman to have coffee with you if you'd met her through your friends. You seem to think that doing this would hurt your relationship with your friends. That seems out of place in this day and age. Maybe we should think about clarifying your values before we go any further. Go to 10.40

Interviewer: We've decided on four possible methods by which you can attain your goal. We've discussed the consequences of each of these plans and how the plans themselves fit in with your values. From my experience, and from what you've said, I think that you should ask someone ahead of time and set up the date over the phone the night before. Go to 10.41

10.39

Your Answer: We've decided on four possible methods by which you can attain your goal. You could choose someone ahead of time and arrange it over the phone the night before. You could ask a woman you know through your friends. You could casually ask someone in one of your classes as the class ends. Or you could ask someone who never seems to go out. We've discussed the consequences of each of these plans and how the plans themselves fit in with your values. From your perspective, which alternative seems most appropriate?

Correct. In this structuring response, you've briefly summarized the most promising plans of action and invited the client to choose the plan with which he feels comfortable. Proceed to 10.42.

10.40

Your Answer: You said that you would find it difficult to ask a woman to have coffee with you if you'd met her through your friends. You seem to think that doing this would hurt your relationship with your friends. That seems out of place in this day and age. Maybe we should think about clarifying your values before we go any further.

Action plans must be formulated with the client's values in mind. However, if the client's values are the cause of some problem, this problem should be defined and considered at another time. At this point, you should consider alternatives that are open to the client. Return to 10.38 and try again.

10.41

Your Answer: We've decided on four possible methods by which you can attain your goal. We've discussed the consequences of each of these plans and how the plans themselves fit in with your values. From my experience, and from what you've said, I think that you should ask someone ahead of time and set up the date over the phone the night before.

This response renders the discussion of alternatives and their consequences useless. The purpose of discussing alternatives is to expose clients to a number of possible methods by which goals can be attained and to permit them to select the method with which they are most comfortable. In attempting to impose a solution, you ignore the standards and values of the client. Return to 10.38 and try again.

10.42

During the action phase of interviewing, the interviewer helps the client to implement the action plan that has been selected. After the plan has been implemented, the interviewer and the client should evaluate its success according to the criteria established for the attainment of the goal. Based on this evaluation, they may agree to modify the action plan or to select a more appropriate one. If the plan is successful, the client and the interviewer need to consider ways by which the client's new behaviors can be maintained without the support of the interviewing relationship.

During the previous session, the client decided to ask a woman to have coffee with him at the conclusion of one of his classes. Now he is back to report on the results of this plan of action.

Client: Well . . . I did it. I asked the most attractive woman in my class to have coffee with me. I managed to do it. But she said she didn't have time. Then I asked her to go out with me the next day, and she made some other excuse.

Choose the most appropriate response.

Interviewer: Sounds like it was a disaster. I think we'd better go back and select another plan.   Go to 10.43

Interviewer: Sounds like asking her went well, but the rest didn't go so well. What could you do next time to achieve your goal?   Go to 10.44

Interviewer: Sounds like asking her went well. But did you really expect to succeed with the most attractive woman in your class?   Go to 10.45

10.43

Your Answer: Sounds like it was a disaster. I think we'd better go back and select another plan.

You need to discuss the client's failure to achieve his goal in order to help him decide what to do next. A slight adjustment in the plan could help him to attain his goal. The client should decide whether a new plan is needed. Return to 10.42 and try again.

10.44

Your Answer: Sounds like asking her went well, but the rest didn't go so well. What could you do next time to achieve your goal?

Correct. This response acknowledges the client's partial success and encourages him to consider what he can do to achieve his goal. Proceed to 10.46.

10.45

Your Answer: Sounds like asking her went well. But did you really expect to succeed with the most attractive woman in your class?

The initial part of your response is supportive, but then you belittle the client's attempt and thus remove the effect of your supportive statement. The client's choice of a potential companion may have contributed to his lack of success. As the interviewer, you should help him to recognize this fact. Return to 10.42 and try again.

10.46

Clients may fail to cooperate with you during the action phase of interviewing for a number of reasons: they may experience a conflict concerning the selected goal, they may lack the skills they need to attain the goal, they may not want to change their behavior, or they may experience problems in the client/interviewer relationship. When clients fail to cooperate, you need to help them confront and remove the impediments to goal attainment.

Several weeks have passed, and the client is regularly having coffee with women and talking with them on the phone. However, he has been unable to ask a woman for a date, despite several attempts to initiate an action plan for this goal.

Choose the most appropriate comment.

Interviewer: You seem to be having a great deal of difficulty reaching this goal. Perhaps we should work on something else for a while. Go to 10.47

Interviewer: You want to ask a woman for a date, but you've been unable to reach this goal. Could you help me to understand your difficulty? Go to 10.48

Interviewer:	Perhaps your difficulty in attaining your goal is caused by a fear of women. What do you think has contributed to that fear? Go to 10.49

10.47

Your Answer:	You seem to be having a great deal of difficulty reaching this goal. Perhaps we should work on something else for a while.

When a client experiences difficulty in carrying out a plan of action, you need to help him or her confront and resolve the difficulty. As an interviewer, it is your responsibility to help the client identify and explore difficulties rather than avoid them. Return to 10.46 and try again.

10.48

Your Answer:	You want to ask a woman for a date, but you've been unable to reach this goal. Could you help me to understand your difficulty?

Correct. This response confronts the client with his failure to reach the identified goal and invites him to explore the reasons for his failure. Proceed to 10.50.

10.49

Your Answer:	Perhaps your difficulty in attaining your goal is caused by a fear of women. What do you think has contributed to that fear?

You're jumping to conclusions. As we indicated in the introduction to this set of frames, a client may resist goal attainment for a number of reasons. You need to confront the client with his apparent resistance rather than guess at the reason behind it. By using confrontation at this point, you'll invite the client to discuss the reasons for his resistance. Return to 10.46 and try again.

10.50

In the termination phase of structuring, the interviewer and the client evaluate the degree to which the client has reached his or her overall goal. If the client has been unsuccessful, it may be necessary to formulate an alternative action plan or an alternative goal. If the client has successfully accomplished the goal, it may be necessary to move on to other goals. During the termination phase, you may want to review your relationship so that you and the client can gain insight into his relationships with others. While concluding the interview, you need to leave the relationship open so that the client will feel free to contact you again, if necessary.

Three months have passed since the preceding interview. The client dates regularly, has decided to study dentistry, and has told his parents that he is going away to college. They've accepted this idea very well.

Choose the response that will initiate the termination phase.

Interviewer: You've accomplished a great deal in the past three months. You've developed the ability to go out with women. You've decided to study dentistry. And you've reached a point of agreement with your parents concerning your plans for the future. I don't think we need to meet any more. I hope that you're successful in dentistry. Go to 10.51

Interviewer: You've accomplished a great deal in the past three months. You've developed the ability to go out with women. You've decided to study dentistry. And you've reached a point of agreement with your parents concerning your plans for the future. You must have problems we haven't discussed yet. Could we discuss them now? Go to 10.52

Interviewer: You've accomplished a great deal in the past three months. You've developed the ability to go out with women. You've decided to study dentistry. And you've reached a point of agreement with your parents concerning your plans for the future. Now that we've reached this point, I wonder if there are any other concerns you would like to discuss. Go to 10.53

10.51

Your Answer: You've accomplished a great deal in the past three months. You've developed the ability to go out with women. You've decided to study dentistry. And you've reached a point of agreement with your parents concerning your plans for the future. I don't think we need to meet any more. I hope that you're successful in dentistry.

Before you terminate the interview, you need to determine whether or not there are any other concerns the client wants to deal with. Moreover, when you conclude the interview, you should make it clear that the client can contact you again, if necessary. Return to 10.50 and try again.

10.52

Your Answer: You've accomplished a great deal in the past three months. You've developed the ability to go out with women. You've decided to study dentistry. And you've reached a point of agreement with your parents concerning your plans for the future. You must have problems we haven't discussed yet. Could we discuss them now?

The client has spent three months exploring and resolving his problems. At this and other stages of interviewing, your relationship with the client is best facilitated by open, nonjudgmental discussion. Your assumption that the client has other problems will inhibit his open discussion. Return to 10.50 and try again.

10.53

Your Answer: You've accomplished a great deal in the past three months. You've developed the ability to go out with women. You've decided to study dentistry. And you've reached a point of agreement with your parents concerning your plans for the future. Now that we've reached this point, I wonder if there are any other concerns you would like to discuss.

Correct. This response indicates that it is appropriate to discuss any other problems the client may have. This is an important step in the termination phase. Proceed to 10.54.

10.54

Remember that you must remain *flexible* when using the skill of structuring. The frames in this chapter were designed to illustrate the important phases of structuring. Whether or not you use each phase with a client will be determined by the nature of his or her problem. At times, it may be necessary to repeat the early phases of structuring. Proceed to 10.55.

10.55

Indicate whether each of the following statements is true or false.

1. During the inventory phase, an accurate description of the client's problems is developed.
2. It is important for the interviewer to offer solutions to the client's problems as soon as possible.
3. Interviewers should always encourage clients to deal with their easiest problem first.
4. Once the client's problems have been defined, an action plan for each one should be developed.
5. Difficulties in goal formulation often result from poor definition of goals or the client's resistance to change.
6. During the action-planning phase, the client should retain maximum responsibility.
7. The most appropriate action plan is the one that is most appealing to the client.
8. The interviewer can be the best judge of when the interview should terminate.
9. Every client should progress through each interviewing phase.

ANSWERS

1. *True.* If you answered *false,* go to 10.9 and review.
2. *False.* If you answered *true,* go to 10.1 and review.
3. *False.* If you answered *true,* go to 10.17 and review.
4. *False.* If you answered *true,* go to 10.21 and review.
5. *True.* If you answered *false,* go to 10.25 and review.
6. *True.* If you answered *false,* go to 10.33 and review.
7. *False.* If you answered *true,* go to 10.37 and review.
8. *False.* If you answered *true,* go to 10.49 and review.
9. *False.* If you answered *true,* go to 10.53 and review.

If six or more of your responses were incorrect, you should return to 10.1 and review the material in this chapter.

POINTS
TO
REMEMBER
ABOUT
STRUCTURING

1. **USE STRUCTURING TO**:
   a. Initiate or conclude an interviewing phase.
   b. Facilitate attainment of the objective for a given phase.
   c. Provide the client with information concerning the direction of the interview.

2. **WHEN STRUCTURING:**
   a. Initiate a new phase by stating its purpose and determining the client's willingness to participate.
   b. Use previously acquired skills to facilitate attainment of the objective for a given phase.
   c. Conclude a phase by reviewing what has been accomplished and ascertaining whether the client agrees that the objectives have been met.

MULTIPLE-CHOICE TEST

In order to evaluate your mastery of the material in this chapter, you should answer the following multiple-choice questions. In each case, select the most appropriate response based on the material in this chapter. The correct answers are listed in the Appendix.

1. Client (who has been asked to summarize the major concerns in his life): Well, we've talked about more areas of concern than I expected. I started to talk about my feelings of loneliness and depression. Then I talked about how dissatisfied I am with my job and what a poor father I am to my three children. I really wasn't aware that all of those things were bothering me until we started talking about them.

   a. Interviewer: We've identified several areas of concern. It seems that you're most concerned about how you get along with your children. Shall we look at that area first?
   b. Interviewer: We've focused on three areas of concern that seem to be important to you. How interested are you in making changes in these areas of your life?
   c. Interviewer: We've identified at least three areas of concern to you. Are there any more areas you are concerned about? Let's talk about them now.

2. Interviewer: We've defined your first two concerns clearly, and now it sounds as though you have a clear definition of the third. Could you state that definition again?

   a. Client: It seems that, when I'm with the children, I expect them to do things the way I do them. And if they don't, we argue.
   b. Client: It seems that, when I'm with the children, they don't do things correctly, so I have to tell them how to do everything.
   c. Client: It seems that, when I'm with the children, I feel uncomfortable and I'm not sure how to act.

3. The three concerns mentioned in the first question have been defined in precise and concrete terms. Choose the response that will initiate the priority phase.

   a. Interviewer: Now that we've clearly defined your concerns, we need to decide the order in which to approach them. From what you said about your job, I think it would be best to start there. Do you agree?
   b. Interviewer: Now that we've clearly defined your concerns, we need to decide the order in which to approach them. From what you said about feeling depressed and alone, I suggest we start with that, because it will be the most difficult to deal with. Do you agree?
   c. Interviewer: Now that we've clearly defined your concerns, we need to decide the order in which to approach them. From what you said about your job, it might be most useful to start with that concern. How do you see it?

4. During the priority phase, the interviewer and the client agreed to begin with a discussion of the client's relationship with his three children. Choose the response that will structure the goal-formulation phase.

   a. Interviewer: We have a definition of your concern with how you relate to your children. Now we need a positive goal to work toward in that area. How about a goal with regard to the way you argue with your children?
   b. Interviewer: Earlier, we developed a definition of your concern. Now we need to turn that definition into a positive goal that you would be willing to work toward. Could you try to do that for me?
   c. Interviewer: Earlier, we developed a definition of your concern for the way in which you relate to your children. Now we need to set a positive goal. Could you tell me more about the way in which the members of your family relate to one another?

5. The client and the interviewer have developed a set of subgoals that may help the client relate to his children. One subgoal is to allow one of the children to do a small task in his or her own way. Choose the response that will initiate the action-formulation phase.

   a. Interviewer: Why don't you try to do something other than you usually do the next time a typical situation arises?
   b. Interviewer: One possible situation you could try here would be to build something with one of your children—a model airplane, for example.
   c. Interviewer: How could you set up situations to reach this subgoal?

6. The client decided to ask one of his children to help him clear the table after dinner one night. The client reports that he let his child help with the task, but he found it difficult to tolerate the way in which she completed it. Choose the most appropriate response.

   a. Interviewer: It sounds as though you let your child complete the task, even though it was difficult for you to do so. What could you do next time to be more tolerant of reasonable alternatives to your own way of doing things?

   b. Interviewer: It sounds as though it was very difficult for you to tolerate your child's behavior. I wonder if we should aim toward an easier goal.

   c. Interviewer: It sounds as though things went reasonably well. Where should we go from here?

Chapter 11
PUTTING
IT ALL TOGETHER

The preceding chapters in this book dealt with a number of skills that are essential to good interviewing: focusing and following, using open inquiry, reflecting feeling and content, communicating feeling and immediacy, confronting, self-disclosing, and structuring. The material in this chapter is intended to help you integrate these skills.

After completing this chapter, you should be able to do the following:

1. Use the skills presented in this book in a systematic and integrated manner.
2. Decide when it is appropriate to use a given skill.

The program in this chapter focuses on an interview between an unemployed man and a counselor in a crisis center. The client has been unemployed since he and his family moved six months ago, and he now has a severe financial problem. This is the first time he has discussed his problem with anyone.

Since there are several routes through this program, more than one response may be correct in each frame. Proceed to 11.1.

11.1

Interviewer:	How can I help you today?
Client:	I'm not sure you can help me, but I've got to discuss this with someone . . . . I just can't find a job. I've been looking for six months now. I look through the want ads every day, but there's just nothing. We have three children, my wife isn't able to work right now, and our savings are just about gone.
	Choose an appropriate response.
Interviewer:	Have you gone to the unemployment office regularly? Go to 11.2
Interviewer:	You sound quite desperate. Could you help me to understand your situation better? Go to 11.3
Interviewer:	Your financial situation is grim, and you're wondering what to do next. Go to 11.4

11.2

Your Answer: Have you gone to the unemployment office regularly?

This closed inquiry diverts the client from an exploration of his problem and demonstrates poor focusing and following. At this point in the interview, you should encourage the client to explore his problem with you. Return to 11.1 and try again.

11.3

Your Answer: You sound quite desperate. Could you help me to understand your situation better?

Correct. This reflection of feeling followed by an open inquiry, enables the client to feel comfortable while discussing his problem with you. Proceed to 11.6.

11.4

Your Answer: Your financial situation is grim, and you're wondering what to do next.

Correct. This restatement indicates that you are following the client and invites him to continue discussing his problem with you. Proceed to 11.5.

11.5

Client:	It's really crucial that I get a job. I'm sure there must be some way for me to get back into the real estate business. There has to be something I can do.

Choose an appropriate response.

Interviewer:	It sounds as though you're under a great deal of pressure and that getting a job is of major importance to you. That kind of pressure often creates other difficulties. Go to 11.7
Interviewer:	Your situation sounds really stressful. Go to 11.8
Interviewer:	You could babysit while your wife goes out to work. Have you thought about that? Go to 11.9

11.6

Client:	I'm getting quite desperate. I lost my job about six months ago, so I thought I'd come here and get back into real estate. I renewed my license and went around to all the companies, but there just aren't any openings. I have to find work soon. I don't have any money left.

Choose an appropriate response.

Interviewer:	Have you thought about setting up your own business? That might be a reasonable way to solve your problem. Go to 11.10
Interviewer:	So, you've tried to make use of your skills. Go to 11.11
Interviewer:	You tried to improve your situation by moving, but things have grown worse. Go to 11.12

11.7

Your Answer:	It sounds as though you're under a great deal of pressure and that getting a job is of major importance to you. That kind of pressure often creates other difficulties.

Correct. This reflection of feeling and content indicates that you are following the client and are interested in what he is telling you. Also, you've invited him to explore other difficulties. Proceed to 11.15.

11.8

Your Answer: Your situation sounds really stressful.

Correct. This reflection of feeling indicates that you are listening to the client and encourages him to explore his situation further. Proceed to 11.16.

11.9

Your Answer: You could babysit while your wife goes out to work. Have you thought about that?

This response shows that you haven't been listening to the client: he has told you that his wife isn't able to work. Return to 11.5 and try again.

11.10

Your Answer: Have you thought about setting up your own business? That might be a reasonable way to solve your problems.

This may be a reasonable solution, but, at this early stage of the interview, you need more information about the client. Return to 11.6 and try again.

11.11

Your Answer: So, you've tried to make use of your skills.

Correct. Your brief restatement indicates that you are attending to the client and invites him to continue. Proceed to 11.13.

11.12

Your Answer: You tried to improve your situation by moving, but things have grown worse.

Correct. This reflection of content shows the client that you have heard what he has said and encourages him to discuss his difficulties further. Proceed to 11.14.

11.13

Client: I really don't want to go back to working in a factory. I want a clean job where there isn't noisy machinery going all the time, and one in which I can meet and mix with people. But, I'm so desperate, I'd take anything at the moment. I guess I've got two big problems right now: I can't find a job, and I don't have any money.

Choose an appropriate response.

Interviewer: So, you have two urgent problems. Could you help me to understand which one is more pressing?

Go to 11.17

Interviewer: Everyone seems to be in the same situation these days. Is there anyone you could borrow money from?

Go to 11.18

Interviewer: I get the feeling that you really haven't been trying hard enough to find a job. What things did you say you'd done so far? Go to 11.19

11.14

Client: Yes. We're a lot worse off. We're renting a small house that's cold and damp, and my wife and I can't go out, because we can't afford a sitter. But these are small problems compared to being broke and out of work. I guess my biggest problem right now is my inability to pay our bills.

Choose an appropriate response.

Interviewer: From what you say, you have two major problems. Perhaps the one we should look at first is your inability to pay your bills. Go to 11.20

Interviewer: You have two urgent problems: your inability to find a job, and your inability to pay your bills. Paying your bills seems to be your greater concern. To what extent should we deal with that concern first? Go to 11.21

Interviewer: It's often better to consider the easiest problem first. Maybe we should look for ways to get you and your wife out socially. Go to 11.22

11.15

Client: I have a lot of difficulties because I'm out of work. If I had a job, a lot of my problems would be settled. I'd really like to get back into real estate, but no one wants to hire me.

Choose an appropriate response.

Interviewer: The real estate market is slow right now. Do you have to go into that business? Go to 11.23

Interviewer: You seem really determined to go into real estate. Perhaps I'm wrong, but I'm getting the feeling that it's difficult for you to consider any other alternatives. Go to 11.24

Interviewer: It sounds as though you lost your license for some reason. Maybe that's why you're having trouble getting back into real estate. Go to 11.25

11.16

Client: That's why I contacted you. I can't go on like this. I've got debts building up, and they have to be paid. It's beginning to create problems at home. I'm sure that, if I got a job, my problems would be settled. The job's the key.

Choose an appropriate response.

Interviewer: From what you say, it seems that you're overreacting. There's no need to get so upset. Go to 11.26

Interviewer: Since you have so many debts, maybe you should see a debt counselor. Go to 11.27

Interviewer: Getting a job is vital if you're going to hold things together. What else do you think you could do to find a job? Go to 11.28

11.17

Your Answer: So, you have two urgent problems. Could you help me to understand which one is more pressing?

Correct. This restatement of content, followed by an open inquiry, constitutes a structuring response that will help the client to deal with his problems in order of their priority. Proceed to 11.33.

11.18

Your Answer: Everyone seems to be in the same situation these days. Is there anyone you could borrow money from?

The client has sought your assistance in a crisis and is in need of your understanding and support. He has probably exhausted all possible short-term solutions, including loans. Your response could negate the effort he made in contacting you. Return to 11.13 and try again.

11.19

Your Answer: I get the feeling that you really haven't been trying
hard enough to find a job. What things did you say
you'd done so far?

    You've berated the client for not doing enough to find a job,
and then you've suggested that you can't remember what he has done
in this regard. Also, you've neglected to discuss the order in which
his problems should be considered. Return to 11.13 and try again.

11.20

Your Answer: From what you say, you have two major problems.
Perhaps the one we should look at first is your inability to pay your bills.

    Correct. Your restatement indicates that you're following the
client. Furthermore, you've checked with the client on the appropriateness of attending to his financial problem first. Proceed to 11.32.

11.21

Your Answer: You have two urgent problems: finding a job, and
paying your bills. Paying your bills seems to be your
greater concern. To what extent should we deal with
that concern first?

    Correct. Your paraphrase demonstrates to the client that you've
heard his comments, and your open inquiry structures the situation
for him to consider the order in which his problems should be examined. Proceed to 11.31.

11.22

Your Answer: It's often better to consider the easiest problem first.
Maybe we should look for ways to get you and your
wife out socially.

    The client has said that his problems would be solved if he could
find a job. His lack of a social life has been alluded to, but only in
terms of a side effect of this major problem. In times of crisis, major
problems are the focus of attention. At other times, the interviewer
and the client decide on the order in which problems are to be considered. Return to 11.14 and try again.

11.23

Your Answer: The real estate market is slow right now. Do you have
to go into that business?

      This closed inquiry makes you responsible for the direction of
the interview. Your response should keep the discussion open and give
the client this responsibility. Return to 11.15 and try again.

11.24

Your Answer: You seem really determined to go into real estate.
Perhaps I'm wrong, but I'm getting the feeling that
it's difficult for you to consider any other alternatives.

      Correct. You have confronted the client with the discrepancy
between his need to find a job and his reluctance to consider a wider
choice of alternatives. Proceed to 11.30.

11.25

Your Answer: It sounds as though you lost your license for some
reason. Maybe that's why you're having trouble getting back into real estate.

      This overinterpretation and inaccurate reflection of content will
have negative effects on your relationship with the client. You need
to listen carefully to what the client is telling you. Return to 11.15
and try again.

11.26

Your Answer: From what you say, it seems that you're overreacting.
There's no need to get so upset.

      Your response denies the client the right to express and explore
his feelings and may cause him to think that you're unable to understand his problem. Return to 11.16 and try again.

11.27

Your Answer: Since you have so many debts, maybe you should see
a debt counselor.

      The client has stressed his concern about finding a job. His debts
may be important to him, but, at the moment, finding a job is even
more important. Return to 11.16 and try again.

11.28

Your Answer:	Getting a job is vital if you're going to hold things together. What else do you think you could do to find a job?

     Correct. You've accurately reflected the client's feelings of urgency about finding a job and interpreted this as a reasonable goal. Your open inquiry is a structuring response that will initiate the action plan-formulation stage of the interview. Proceed to 11.29.

11.29

Client:	Well, as I mentioned, there's real estate, but there really aren't any openings there. I hated working in a factory, and I can't see doing it again. My wife has suggested that I look for something new, even if it means retraining. I've thought a lot about that, and it seems to be the best route to take.

     Choose an appropriate response.

Interviewer:	As you look at the options that are available to you, retraining seems to be the most workable.	Go to 11.34
Interviewer:	Do you think it's wise to retrain just because your wife suggested it?	Go to 11.35
Interviewer:	I find it hard to believe that there aren't any openings in real estate.	Go to 11.36

11.30

Client:	I really would like to get into real estate, but I'm not having much success. I've had to look at other alternatives. I could go back into factory work, but I hated that. I'd be willing to take a job in which I'd move around and meet people, but I don't think I'm qualified for anything other than real estate. The whole situation is sort of frightening.

     Choose an appropriate response.

Interviewer:	Have you tried applying for outdoor jobs? You might be able to find work as a gardener. There are a number of nurseries and lawn-maintenance firms in this area.	Go to 11.37

Interviewer: There's a certain amount of fear involved in thinking about what to do. The jobs you can do seem to be impossible to find, and any other job represents an unknown. Go to 11.38

Interviewer: If you keep your fear under control, you'll be more likely to find a job. Go to 11.39

11.31

Client: Well, I guess we have to look at that first. I hate to think of what will happen if I don't pay our bills this week. I've thought of a number of alternatives, but the only one that seems reasonable is to go on unemployment. But I'm not sure you're here to help me with that.

Choose an appropriate response.

Interviewer: I'm a little concerned that you've ruled out a loan so hastily. It's your only solution right now.

Go to 11.40

Interviewer: You seem to have some reservations about going on unemployment. Could you tell me your thoughts about that? Go to 11.41

Interviewer: You're asking me whether I can help you to investigate the possibility of applying for unemployment benefits. Go to 11.42

11.32

Client: Yes. I really have to do something about that. By the end of next week, I need to find enough money to pay the rent and utilities, buy groceries, and buy shoes for the children. And then there's next month.

Choose an appropriate response.

Interviewer: You haven't told me anything about your family. Perhaps you could tell me a little bit about them now.

Go to 11.43

Interviewer: I don't think there's any way to solve your problems in one week. Go to 11.44

Interviewer: You seem to have a reasonable goal, but one that must be creating a lot of pressure for you. What do you think you could do to achieve that goal?

Go to 11.45

11.33

Client: They're both important, but I came to talk to you be-cause I don't even have enough money to pay the rent next week.

Choose an appropriate response.

Interviewer: Your most urgent problem is a lack of money. Could you tell me whether you're buying your house?

Go to 11.46

Interviewer: We should consider your money problems first. What do you need to do in order to resolve your financial crisis? Go to 11.47

Interviewer: We should attend to your money problems first. Per-haps you should find accommodations with your rela-tives. Go to 11.48

11.34

Your Answer: As you look at the options that are available to you, retraining seems to be the most workable.

Correct. This restatement enables you and the client to verify or modify the plan that is taking shape. Proceed to 11.54.

11.35

Your Answer: Do you think it's wise to retrain just because your wife suggested it?

The client told you that, after his wife suggested retraining, he gave the matter careful thought. By ignoring this part of the client's message, you've failed to use the most basic interviewing skill—focus-ing and following. Furthermore, your closed-ended question makes you responsible for the reestablishment of the discussion. Return to 11.29 and try again.

11.36

Your Answer: I find it hard to believe that there aren't any openings in real estate.

If you feel that it is important to discuss this topic, you should use an open inquiry or a reflection of content to initiate such a dis-cussion. However, the client has placed considerable stress on the possibility of retraining; you should pursue this topic. Return to 11.29 and try again.

11.37

Your Answer: Have you tried applying for outdoor jobs? You might
be able to find work as a gardener. There are a number
of nurseries and lawn-maintenance firms in this area.

    This closed inquiry, followed by advice, is inappropriate at this point in the interview. You need to help the client explore a variety of action plans and select the most appropriate one. Your response should stimulate his exploration of the alternatives available to him. Return to 11.30 and try again.

11.38

Your Answer: There's a certain amount of fear involved in thinking
about what to do. The jobs you can do seem to be
impossible to find, and any other job represents an
unknown.

    Correct. This reflection of feeling and content encourages the client to discuss his apprehensions, bring them under control, and continue his exploration of the alternatives available to him. Proceed to 11.53.

11.39

Your Answer: If you keep your fear under control, you'll be more
likely to find a job.

    Advice, however well-meaning, is generally ineffective. The client has told you that he is afraid. He will need your understanding and support in order to develop the ability to cope with his fears and find suitable work. Return to 11.30 and try again.

11.40

Your Answer: I'm a little concerned that you've ruled out a loan so
hastily. It's your only solution right now.

    Your task is to facilitate the client's exploration of his problem and selection of an action plan that is acceptable to him. Any attempt on your part to prescribe a solution is inappropriate. Return to 11.31 and try again.

11.41

Your Answer: You seem to have some reservations about going on unemployment. Could you tell me your thoughts about that?

Correct. You've reflected the client's concern about applying for unemployment benefits and invited him to explore this concern with you. Proceed to 11.51.

11.42

Your Answer: You're asking me whether I can help you to investigate the possibility of applying for unemployment benefits.

Correct. This communication of immediacy identifies the concern that the client has about his relationship with you. This response will help him to become aware of his concern and work toward its resolution. Proceed to 11.52.

11.43

Your Answer: You haven't told me anything about your family. Perhaps you could tell me a little bit about them now.

The client is trying to solve a major financial difficulty; your response distracts him from this task. Your failure to follow the client suggests that you aren't interested in the problem he is discussing. The client's progress toward solving his problem is likely to be adversely affected by your response. Return to 11.32 and try again.

11.44

Your Answer: I don't think there's any way to solve your problems in one week.

Your communication of feeling is inappropriate here and will do little to help the client solve his problem. You should try to generate alternative action plans with the client by discussing possible solutions with him. Return to 11.32 and try again.

11.45

Your Answer: You seem to have a reasonable goal, but one that must be creating a lot of pressure for you. What do you think you could do to achieve that goal?

Correct. You've confirmed the legitimacy of the client's goal in a supportive manner and structured the situation so that he can consider possible alternatives to his problem. Proceed to 11.50.

11.46

Your Answer: Your most urgent problem is a lack of money. Could you tell me whether you're buying a house?

Although you've agreed with your client concerning the order in which his problems should be dealt with, your closed inquiry changes the topic. At this point, you need to use a more open response that will encourage the client to engage in the goal-formulation process. Return to 11.33 and try again.

11.47

Your Answer: We should consider your money problems first. What do you need to do in order to resolve your financial crisis?

Correct. This structuring response demonstrates that you agree with the client. Your open inquiry encourages him to translate his problem into a goal. Proceed to 11.49.

11.48

Your Answer: We should attend to your money problems first. Perhaps you should find accommodations with your relatives.

Although you've agreed with the client concerning the high priority of his financial problems, you've attempted to solve his problem on your own and in a premature fashion. You've neglected goal formulation—a prerequisite to problem solving. Return to 11.33 and try again.

11.49

Client: I need enough money to pay the rent and utilities, buy groceries, and buy shoes for the children next week. And it will be the same sort of thing every month.

Interviewer: That seems reasonable .... Those things are necessities. What do you think you can do to pay for them?

Client: Well, it would be nice if I had a job, but I doubt that I'll find one right away. I could go on unemployment, but that's like going on welfare. I could get a loan, but I've no idea when I could pay it back.
Choose an appropriate response.

Interviewer: There's nothing wrong with going on unemployment. You just have to go down to the office and apply for it.   Go to 11.55

Interviewer: Even though your financial situation is desperate, you're reluctant to apply for unemployment benefits. It seems that applying for them runs contrary to your values.   Go to 11.56

Interviewer: You say that you could get a loan. Do you have a good credit rating?   Go to 11.57

11.50

Client: Well, it would be nice if I had a job, but I doubt that I'll find one right away. I could go on unemployment, but that's like going on welfare. I could get a loan, but I've no idea when I could pay it back.
Choose an appropriate response.

Interviewer: Even though your financial situation is desperate, you're reluctant to apply for unemployment benefits. It seems that applying for them runs contrary to your values.   Go to 11.58

Interviewer: Maybe you should get a small loan for a month and then try really hard during that month to find a job.
Go to 11.59

Interviewer: Have you ever had a loan?   Go to 11.60

11.51

Client: I don't know that it's a problem really. I just can't go on unemployment benefits. It's like going on welfare.
Choose an appropriate response.

Interviewer: Since you have such strong feelings about this, we'll have to search for another alternative.   Go to 11.61

Interviewer: In your situation, you should have been on unemployment months ago.   Go to 11.62

Interviewer: Even though your financial situation is desperate, you're reluctant to apply for unemployment benefits.

It seems that applying for them runs contrary to your values. Go to 11.63

11.52

Client: Well, that's not really my concern. I know you can help me. I just don't want to talk about going on unemployment. It's just like going on welfare.
Choose an appropriate response.

Interviewer: Since you have such confidence in me, I'm sure you'll follow my advice and apply for unemployment benefits as soon as possible. Go to 11.64

Interviewer: Even though your financial situation is desperate, you're reluctant to apply for unemployment benefits. It seems that applying for them runs contrary to your values. Go to 11.65

Interviewer: I have to stress that you have a right to unemployment benefits and that it's not like going on welfare.
Go to 11.66

11.53

Client: But I don't want just any job. I've had this uncertainty. What I want is a secure job, and that means that I'll have to retrain. I just don't know what area to enter or what I could do.

Interviewer: What I hear you saying is that you feel you've reached a turning point with respect to your work situation, and that, before you make any decisions, you need to examine your skills and your possibilities very seriously. It's not part of my job to become involved in career planning, but I can refer you to a vocational counselor. The appointment would be for tomorrow.

Client: I've avoided doing that for a long time, but I know I should. I have to begin somewhere. I'll be there whenever you say.
Choose an appropriate response.

Interviewer: Let's just review. You've decided to explore your career possibilities with our vocational counselor, and you'll see him in the morning. I wonder if there's anything else you'd like to discuss before we conclude.
Go to 11.67

Interviewer: Let's just review. You've decided to explore your career possibilities with our vocational counselor, and you'll see him in the morning. I guess we've covered everything. I'm sure that your problems will be sorted out now. Go to 11.68

Interviewer: Let's just review. You've decided to explore your career possibilities with our vocational counselor, and you'll see him in the morning. Perhaps we should discuss the kinds of jobs you might be interested in.

Go to 11.69

11.54

Client: I'm beginning to feel that way more and more. My biggest problem is that I don't know how to go about it.

Interviewer: So you need some help in organizing a retraining program. It seems essential that you see a vocational counselor as soon as possible. If you agree, I can arrange an appointment for tomorrow morning.

Client: That sounds fine to me.

Choose an appropriate response.

Interviewer: Well, I think that we've dealt with all your problems. Make sure that you show up for your appointment in the morning. Go to 11.70

Interviewer: Let's just review. You've decided to explore your career possibilities with our vocational counselor, and you'll see him in the morning. I wonder if there's anything else you'd like to discuss before we conclude.

Go to 11.71

Interviewer: You've been out of work for some time, and you can't find a job in your former occupation. Your wife has told you that you should try something new. You want to hold your marriage together, so you're going along with this. I think everything is under control now. We can conclude at this point. Go to 11.72

11.55

Your Answer: There's nothing wrong with going on unemployment. You just have to go down to the office and apply for it.

At this point, the client needs help in confronting his feelings about using the one financial resource available to him, not advice and instructions. Return to 11.49 and try again.

11.56

Your Answer: Even though your financial situation is desperate, you're reluctant to apply for unemployment benefits. It seems that applying for them runs contrary to your values.

Correct. By confronting the client with his financial need and the resources that are available to him, you help him to examine his feelings about applying for unemployment benefits. Proceed to 11.74.

11.57

Your Answer: You say that you could get a loan. Do you have a good credit rating?

Your closed inquiry doesn't initiate a very extensive discussion of this option. In order to explore this possibility, you need to respond in a way that leads to an open discussion. However, the discrepancy between the client's financial situation and his reluctance to apply for unemployment benefits requires confrontation at this point. Return to 11.49 and try again.

11.58

Your Answer: Even though your financial situation is desperate, you're reluctant to apply for unemployment benefits. It seems that applying for them runs contrary to your values.

Correct. By confronting the client with his financial need and the resources that are available to him, you help him to examine his feelings about applying for unemployment benefits. Proceed to 11.74.

11.59

Your Answer: Maybe you should get a small loan for a month and then try really hard during that month to find a job.

The client has generated a number of alternative courses of action. You need to confront him with any discrepancies in his statements and then discuss the relative merits of each course of action. Return to 11.50 and try again.

11.60

Your Answer: Have you ever had a loan?

This closed inquiry calls for a simple "yes" or "no" answer and places the responsibility for the discussion on you. The client is working toward a solution of his financial problems; your response should encourage him to continue this problem solving. Return to 11.50 and try again.

11.61

Your Answer: Since you have such strong feelings about this, we'll have to search for another alternative.

Because the client's strong feelings may be based on a misunderstanding or a false assumption, you should confront him with his feelings so that he can explore and resolve them. Return to 11.51 and try again.

11.62

Your Answer: In your situation, you should have been on unemployment months ago.

This confrontation is much too direct. It will either put the client on the defensive or cause him to avoid the topic altogether. Confrontations should be tentative, not aggressive. When you confront tentatively, the client is more likely to explore feelings and behavior and arrive at a resolution. Return to 11.51 and try again.

11.63

Your Answer: Even though your financial situation is desperate, you're reluctant to apply for unemployment benefits. It seems that applying for them runs contrary to your values.

Correct. By confronting the client with his financial need and the resources that are available to him, you help him to examine his feelings about applying for unemployment benefits. Proceed to 11.74.

11.64

Your Answer: Since you have such confidence in me, I'm sure you'll follow my advice and apply for unemployment benefits as soon as possible.

It's inappropriate for you to use your authority and your position to influence the client. Instead, you should facilitate discussion of his feelings about unemployment benefits. Return to 11.52 and try again.

11.65

Your Answer: Even though your financial situation is desperate, you're reluctant to apply for unemployment benefits. It seems that applying for them runs contrary to your values.

Correct. By confronting the client with his financial need and the resources that are available to him, you help him to examine his feelings about applying for unemployment benefits. Proceed to 11.74.

11.66

Your Answer: I have to stress that you have a right to unemployment benefits and that it's not like going on welfare.

By emphasizing your own views, you've denied the client the right to his own feelings. He is unlikely to change his views until you help him to explore his feelings and the assumptions that underlie them. Return to 11.52 and try again.

11.67

Your Answer: Let's just review. You've decided to explore your career possibilities with our vocational counselor, and you'll see him in the morning. I wonder if there's anything else you'd like to discuss before we conclude.

Correct. Your restatement of the decision that you and the client have made provides him with structure for his upcoming appointment. Also, you've given him an opportunity to discuss other problems. Proceed to 11.73.

11.68

Your Answer: Let's just review. You've decided to explore your career possibilities with our vocational counselor, and you'll see him in the morning. I guess we've covered everything. I'm sure that your problems will be sorted out now.

Your restatement is appropriate, but you've attempted to terminate the interview prematurely. In his initial statement, the client said that he has financial problems; your final statement assumes that these problems were resolved when the referral to the vocational counselor was made. This may be the case, but you need to check this out with the client before terminating the interview. Return to 11.53 and try again.

11.69

Your Answer: Let's just review. You've decided to explore your career possibilities with our vocational counselor, and you'll see him in the morning. Perhaps we should discuss the kinds of jobs you might be interested in.

Since you've referred the client to a vocational counselor, your restatement is appropriate, but your attempt to discuss his job situation is not. You might invite him to explore other problem areas with you if he wishes. If he declines this invitation, you should terminate the interview. Return to 11.53 and try again.

11.70

Your Answer: Well, I think that we've dealt with all your problems. Make sure that you show up for your appointment in the morning.

This response is premature and abrupt. Before you terminate the interview, you should give the client a chance to discuss any other problems he may have. If the client doesn't have any other problems to discuss, you should terminate the interview. Return to 11.54 and try again.

11.71

Your Answer: Let's just review. You've decided to explore your career possibilities with our vocational counselor, and you'll see him in the morning. I wonder if there's anything else you'd like to discuss before we conclude.

Correct. Your restatement of the decision that you and the client have made provides him with structure for his upcoming appointment. Also, you've given him an opportunity to discuss other problems. Proceed to 11.73.

11.72

Your Answer: You've been out of work for some time, and you can't find a job in your former occupation. Your wife has told you that you should try something new. You want to hold your marriage together, so you're going along with this. I think everything is under control now. We can conclude at this point.

The client has told you that the decision to retrain was his. Your inaccurate summarization deflects him from focusing on the career plan he is attempting to formulate. Moreover, both you and the client must decide when to conclude the interview. Return to 11.54 and try again.

11.73

Client: Well . . . there is one problem. How are we going to pay our bills next week? There just isn't any money left.

Choose an appropriate response.

Interviewer: Your financial situation is quite critical, and you don't know what to do about it. Go to 11.75

Interviewer: Couldn't you secure a loan to cover you until you find a job? Go to 11.76

Interviewer: That must be making things very difficult for you. Go to 11.77

11.74

Client: When you put it that way, I guess I can see why I should apply. It's just that, in my family, that sort of thing was looked down on. But then, nobody in my family was ever in this position. My father always had a good job, so how could he know? I guess I'd better apply. My wife will be pleased. But if I do that, it's even more important that I find a job as soon as possible.

Choose an appropriate response.

Interviewer: I get the feeling that there's some friction between you and your wife. Is that right? Go to 11.78

Interviewer: Your decision to apply for unemployment solves your immediate financial crisis but makes your desire to find work even stronger. Go to 11.79

Interviewer: I'm glad to hear you say that you'll apply. That's one problem under control. Let's move on now to discuss the job issue. How are you going to go about finding a job? Go to 11.80

11.75

Your Answer: Your financial situation is quite critical, and you don't know what to do about it.

Correct. By restating the content of the client's message, you verify that you've understood him and facilitate further discussion of his problem. Proceed to 11.83.

11.76

Your Answer: Couldn't you secure a loan to cover you until you find a job?

This closed inquiry is inappropriate at this point in the interview. As the client begins to talk about a problem, you need to make a response that will facilitate discussion. An open inquiry or a reflective response is an appropriate stimulus for such a discussion. Return to 11.73 and try again.

11.77

Your Answer: That must be making things very difficult for you.

Correct. By reflecting feeling, you encourage the client to tell you about his difficulty and provide him with support. Proceed to 11.84.

11.78

Your Answer: I get the feeling that there's some friction between you and your wife. Is that right?

There may be friction between the client and his wife; however, he hasn't raised this as a major problem. This response distracts him from his present line of concern and thus demonstrates poor focusing and following. Also, your closed inquiry will require you to direct the discussion once he has answered "yes" or "no." Return to 11.74 and try again.

11.79

Your Answer: Your decision to apply for unemployment solves your immediate financial crisis but makes your desire to find work even stronger.

    Correct. This accurate restatement of the client's feelings about his situation shows him that you are interested in what he is saying. Proceed to 11.81.

11.80

Your Answer: I'm glad to hear you say that you'll apply. That's one problem under control. Let's move on now to discuss the job issue. How are you going to go about finding a job?

    Correct. Your expression of feeling is appropriate, and you've structured the interview in such a way that the client's other concern—finding a job—becomes the focus of discussion. Proceed to 11.82.

11.81

Client: I just have to find work now. When I called you, I thought that you might be able to help me make some plans. One of the things that I had thought about was retraining to work in another field, but I don't know how to go about it or how I would live if I did that. Can you help me?

    Choose an appropriate response.

Interviewer: I wonder if retraining is really appropriate, given your age and responsibilities. It might be better to look for a job for which you are already trained.   Go to 11.85

Interviewer: Do you think you should enter retraining? What does your wife think about it?   Go to 11.86

Interviewer: You really have given this some thought. Maybe we should set up an appointment for you to come in tomorrow and speak with a vocational counselor. How does that idea sound to you?   Go to 11.87

11.82

Client: Well, it's really a problem. I thought that, when I contacted you, you'd give me some ideas. I've exhausted the list of jobs that I'm trained for. There's just nothing in real estate. There's no heavy industry here, not that I want to get into that again. Do you think I would be able to find work in another field altogether if I retrained? I've tried to look at what I might do.

Choose an appropriate response.

Interviewer: You say that you've exhausted the list of jobs that you're trained for. I don't really think that's possible. There must be jobs you don't even know about. I know it's difficult, but you have to keep trying.

Go to 11.88

Interviewer: I believe that your chances of finding work in another area are very poor. There are thousands of people looking for work, and, as a result, employers have many applicants to choose from. You can be sure that a person who has experience will be preferred.

Go to 11.89

Interviewer: It seems as though you've been giving this serious consideration. I think that you should see a vocational counselor. How do you feel about that?   Go to 11.90

11.83

Client: It *is* critical. As far as I can see, there's only one thing to do. I'll go on unemployment. But, up until now, I've refused to do that. I suppose that, as long as I'm doing something about retraining for a job, it will be all right.

Choose an appropriate response.

Interviewer: Now that you've decided to take some steps to find a job, you feel a little more comfortable about applying for unemployment benefits. It's important for you to earn the money you receive.   Go to 11.91

Interviewer: I don't understand why you feel that way. We all pay unemployment insurance, and we're all entitled to it, including you. I don't know why you aren't on unemployment already.   Go to 11.92

Interviewer: I think that you've been unduly harsh on your family by refusing to go on unemployment. They have to be considered, too.   Go to 11.93

11.84

Client: Yes. It's making things very difficult. I guess some of it is due to my stubbornness about applying for unemployment benefits. I've always looked down on people who were on unemployment. I thought that they were lazy. But, now that it's me, it's hard to admit that I've been wrong all this time . . . . I do need the money.

Choose an appropriate response.

Interviewer: I once thought that people on unemployment were a little lazy.   Go to 11.94

Interviewer: Where did you get that idea? Everyone is entitled to unemployment benefits.   Go to 11.95

Interviewer: Until now, you've associated receiving unemployment benefits with being lazy. It's hard to change your views, even when you're involved.   Go to 11.96

11.85

Your Answer: I wonder if retraining is really appropriate, given your age and responsibilities. It might be better to look for a job for which you are already trained.

If this decision is made, it should follow from a careful exploration of the client's abilities and work potential. It shouldn't result from an opinion based on limited information. Return to 11.81 and try again.

11.86

Your Answer: Do you think you should enter retraining? What does your wife think about it?

You've asked the client one question after another without giving him an opportunity to respond. Moreover, you've changed topics. If this information is important to the client, he will bring it up when he feels that it is relevant. Return to 11.81 and try again.

11.87

Your Answer: You really have given this some thought. Maybe we should set up an appointment for you to come in tomorrow and speak with a vocational counselor. How does that idea sound to you?

Correct. In your summary sentence, you've indicated that you realize how much effort the client has expended. You then structured the situation so that the client was made aware of an appropriate action plan. Finally, you've invited him to discuss his reaction. Proceed to 11.100.

11.88

Your Answer: You say that you've exhausted the list of jobs that you're trained for. I don't really think that's possible. There must be jobs you don't even know about. I know it's difficult, but you have to keep trying.

Since the client feels that he has exhausted his possibilities, your statement will give him the impression that you don't understand his situation. This could cause him to withdraw from his relationship with you. In order to help him, you need to explore his problem with him so that you understand his situation. Return to 11.82 and try again.

11.89

Your Answer: I believe that your chances of finding work in another area are very poor. There are thousands of people looking for work, and, as a result, employers have many applicants to choose from. You can be sure that a person who has experience will be preferred.

This pessimistic response is not appropriate at this point in the interview. If you feel that it's important to discuss the consequences of the client's action plan, you should ask him to explore those consequences. An open inquiry would be appropriate in that case. However, because of the complexity of the job situation, this discussion is best left to another time. Return to 11.82 and try again.

11.90

Your Answer: It seems as though you've been giving this serious consideration. I think that you should see a vocational counselor. How do you feel about that?

Correct. Your brief restatement of what the client has said, followed by a proposed action plan, will help him to deal with his problem. Also, you've invited him to respond to your suggestion. Proceed to 11.99.

11.91

Your Answer: Now that you've decided to take some steps to find a
job, you feel a little more comfortable about applying
for unemployment benefits. It's important for you to
earn the money you receive.

Correct. This reflection of feeling and content identifies the important aspects of the client's problem. You've encouraged him to explore his problem further. Proceed to 11.98.

11.92

Your Answer: I don't understand why you feel that way. We all pay
unemployment insurance, and we're all entitled to it,
including you. I don't know why you aren't on unemployment already.

It's inappropriate for you to impose your biases on the client. You should stimulate discussion of this issue so that he can reach his own conclusions. Return to 11.83 and try again.

11.93

Your Answer: I think that you've been unduly harsh on your family
by refusing to go on unemployment. They have to be
considered, too.

This dogmatic, biased statement could destroy the rapport that exists between you and the client. It will not help him to explore his feelings or resolve his problems. Return to 11.83 and try again.

11.94

Your Answer: I once thought that people on unemployment were a
little lazy.

This inappropriate self-disclosure might reinforce the client's bias. Self-disclosure should facilitate rather than inhibit action on the part of the client. Return to 11.84 and try again.

11.95

Your Answer: Where did you get that idea? Everyone is entitled to
unemployment benefits.

Considering the client's views about unemployment benefits, it is inappropriate to abruptly terminate discussion of this topic. Your response should demonstrate that you are aware of the difficulties the client is experiencing and encourage him to continue discussion of this topic. Return to 11.84 and try again.

11.96

Your Answer: Until now, you've associated receiving unemployment benefits with being lazy. It's hard to change your views, even when you're involved.

Correct. Your accurate reflection of the client's concern identifies the source of his difficulties and encourages him to try to resolve them. Proceed to 11.97.

11.97

Client: It's hard to change your views. I don't like being wrong. I guess I was wrong, and it's time to admit it. Then I can go down and apply for my benefits. When I do that, I'll solve my immediate problems. And I'll see the vocational counselor tomorrow.

Choose an appropriate response.

Interviewer: It sounds as though you maintain very fixed views. Could you tell me about any other instances in which your beliefs created problems for you? Go to 11.101

Interviewer: You're comfortable with the decisions you've made, and you feel that you can go on from here. Now that things are under control, I think that this is a good time to close. Go to 11.102

Interviewer: It's good to see you taking some action. Before we close, I want to stress the importance of following through with those plans. We won't be able to do this sort of thing again, so *do* follow through.

Go to 11.103

11.98

Client: Yes. I'm more comfortable when I earn my money. But I guess there are other things that are more important, like taking care of my family and paying the bills. I'll apply for unemployment right away, and then it will be done.

Choose an appropriate response.

Interviewer: Before you do that, maybe we should talk about your family some more. Go to 11.104

Interviewer: That's a good idea. As soon as you've applied, you'll feel great. I'm sure you'll realize then that you've made a great deal of fuss about nothing.

Go to 11.105

Interviewer: It will be difficult, but it will be over. Now, just to review your plans. You're coming to see the vocational counselor in the morning, and you're going to apply for unemployment benefits right away. Perhaps this would be an appropriate time for us to conclude the interview. If anything comes up, feel free to get back to me. Go to 11.106

11.99

Client: I think I'd prefer to talk it through with you, but, if you feel that I should see the vocational counselor, I will.

Choose an appropriate response.

Interviewer: I get the feeling that you find it difficult to meet people. You really shouldn't let your problems get you down like that. Go to 11.107

Interviewer: It's difficult to start all over again. I'd be hesitant, just as you are. But a vocational counselor will be able to help you more than I can. I'll set up an appointment for you, and, if you have any concerns in the meantime, please feel free to get back to me. Go to 11.108

Interviewer: Please don't misunderstand me. I would like to discuss your problem with you, but you should see the vocational counselor. I have to meet with another client now. Go to 11.109

11.100

Client: Well . . . if I'm going to sort this out, I suppose I need to do it properly this time. I don't ever want to be mixed up like this again. You set it up, and I'll be there.

Choose an appropriate response.

Interviewer: Let's just briefly review your plans. You're going to apply for unemployment benefits as soon as possible, and you're coming in tomorrow to discuss your job situation with the vocational counselor. If you have any further difficulties, feel free to get back to me.

Go to 11.110

Interviewer: Mixed up. What do you mean by "mixed up"? I thought that your problem was settled now. Is there something else? Go to 11.111

Interviewer: You must be relieved to have made these decisions. How do you think you should behave in the future if a situation like this develops? Go to 11.112

11.101

Your Answer: It sounds as though you maintain very fixed views. Could you tell me about any other instances in which your beliefs created problems for you?

The client has told you that he has the situation under control and is comfortable with the action plans the two of you have formulated. It's inappropriate to initiate a discussion of his past experiences at this time. You should focus on the relevant issue the client has brought to your attention—the termination of the interview. Return to 11.97 and try again.

11.102

Your Answer: You're comfortable with the decisions you've made, and you feel that you can go on from here. Now that things are under control, I think that this is a good time to close.

Correct. Your restatement accurately reflects the client's message, and your structuring response shows that you agree that it is appropriate to close the interview.

In reaching this point, you've used a variety of interviewing skills. Now return to 11.1 and choose another appropriate response. You've already chosen 11.4, so don't choose that response. If you've already completed your second sequence of responses, proceed to 11.113.

11.103

Your Answer: It's good to see you taking some action. Before we close, I want to stress the importance of following through with those plans. We won't be able to do this sort of thing again, so *do* follow through.

    The client hasn't indicated that he won't follow through with the decisions he has made. In any case, it's inappropriate for you to lecture him about this. At this point, your response should merely close the interview. Return to 11.97 and try again.

11.104

Your Answer: Before you do that, maybe we should talk about your family some more.

    This response gives the client no structure within which to reply; therefore, it will probably confuse him. In responding to a client, you need to focus and follow within a coherent structure. Return to 11.98 and try again.

11.105

Your Answer: That's a good idea. As soon as you've applied, you'll feel great. I'm sure you'll realize then that you've made a great deal of fuss about nothing.

    It's more likely that the client will continue to feel discomfort until he has found suitable work. You need to identify and reflect feelings accurately. Return to 11.98 and try again.

11.106

Your Answer: It will be difficult, but it will be over. Now, just to review your plans. You're coming to see the vocational counselor in the morning, and you're going to apply for unemployment benefits right away. Perhaps this would be an appropriate time for us to conclude the interview. If anything comes up, feel free to get back to me.

    Correct. Following a brief reflective statement, you've summarized the decisions that you and the client have made and provided a support system for him.

In reaching this point, you've used a variety of interviewing skills. Now return to 11.1 and choose another appropriate response. You've already chosen 11.4, so don't choose that response. If you've already completed your second sequence of responses, proceed to 11.113.

11.107

Your Answer: I get the feeling that you find it difficult to meet people. You really shouldn't let your problems get you down like that.

You should follow the client carefully and focus only on relevant information, not on assumptions or interpretations. The client hasn't indicated that his difficulty in changing interviewers is associated with problems in meeting people. It's more likely that he finds it difficult to discuss his problem and is reacting to the necessity of explaining his situation again. Return to 11.99 and try again.

11.108

Your Answer: It's difficult to start all over again. I'd be hesitant, just as you are. But a vocational counselor will be able to help you more than I can. I'll set up an appointment for you, and, if you have any concerns in the meantime, please feel free to get back to me.

Correct. By accurately reflecting feeling, and by self-disclosing, you help the client to cope with the difficulty of changing interviewers. Your structuring response provides an explanation for this change. You've also provided a support system for the client.

In reaching this point, you've used a variety of interviewing skills. Now return to 11.1 and choose another appropriate response. You've already chosen 11.3, so don't choose that response. If you've already completed your second sequence of responses, proceed to 11.113.

11.109

Your Answer: Please don't misunderstand me. I would like to discuss your problem with you, but you should see the vocational counselor. I have to meet with another client now.

This abrupt response suggests that the client has been an imposition. You should leave the relationship open so that the client will feel free to contact you if he requires your help in the future. This response is more likely to make him think twice about contacting you again. Return to 11.99 and try again.

11.110

Your Answer: Let's just briefly review your plans. You're going to apply for unemployment benefits as soon as possible, and you're coming in tomorrow to discuss your job situation with the vocational counselor. If you have any further difficulties, feel free to get back to me.

Correct. This structuring response briefly reviews what has occurred during the interview and offers the client the option of returning to see you.

In reaching this point, you've used a variety of interviewing skills. Now return to 11.1 and choose another appropriate response. You've already chosen 11.3, so don't choose that response. If you've already completed your second sequence of responses, proceed to 11.113.

11.111

Your Answer: Mixed up. What do you mean by "mixed up"? I thought that your problem was settled now. Is there something else?

It's inappropriate to make assumptions based on insufficient information. Instead, you should help the client to explore a problem during the interview so that more information is made available. However, since you are moving toward the termination of the interview, this strategy is not appropriate at this time. If the client is concerned about another issue, you should arrange to meet with him again. Return to 11.100 and try again.

11.112

Your Answer: You must be relieved to have made these decisions. How do you think you should behave in the future if a situation like this develops?

This open-ended question will initiate discussion at a time when the interview is moving toward its conclusion. At this point, your response should summarize the interview and bring it to a close. Return to 11.100 and try again.

11.113

The material in this chapter is intended to help you integrate the skills covered in this book. As you will have observed, a variety of skills can be used in any one situation. The manner in which you adapt and develop these skills will reflect your own personal interviewing style. In order to acquire a relaxed, natural, and facilitative style, you need to practice these skills. And in order to maintain your competence, you need to review your interviews periodically. One way of doing this is to tape an interview and then identify the types of responses you use and their effects. As you gain experience, you will develop skills to complement those you've learned here, thereby establishing your own effective style.

POINTS TO REMEMBER ABOUT INTEGRATING SKILLS

1. **WHEN USING SKILLS IN AN INTERVIEW:**
   a. Use each skill to a high level of expertise.
   b. Structure the interview appropriately.
   c. Respond in a way that is both facilitative and comfortable.
   d. Combine the skills as required.
   e. Don't overuse a single skill.
   f. Don't use a limited range of skills.

MULTIPLE-CHOICE TEST

In order to evaluate your mastery of the material presented in this chapter, you should answer the following multiple-choice questions. In each case, choose an appropriate response. The correct answers are presented in the Appendix.

Begin here ↓

1. Client (voice unsure, looking at the floor): Well, I guess this is our last session.

   a. Interviewer: Yes, it is our last session. I feel good about what we've accomplished. I'm wondering how you feel.
   b. Interviewer: Yes, it is our last session. What are your feelings about the future?
   c. Interviewer: Yes, it is. And I'm wondering if you have any feelings about the fact that this is our last session.

2. Client: I'd like to kill that old man of mine because of the way he has treated my mother all these years.

    a.   Interviewer: You're really angry with your father.

    b.   Interviewer: You're perturbed because your father has treated your mother badly over the years.

    c.   Interviewer: You've built up a great deal of anger toward your dad over the years.

3.   Client: I felt alone, but I just sat there by myself.

    a.   Interviewer: Could you tell me more about how you felt as you sat there by yourself?

    b.   Interviewer: Uh . . . hum.

    c.   Interviewer: How long did you sit there?

4.   Client: My wife and I have decided to have a family. We think that it would be fun to be parents and watch the children grow and develop. But when I think of how it will change things for us, I'm not so sure.

    a.   Interviewer: It doesn't sound as though you're very sure that you want to have children. There are some real advantages to having children, but they do bring about drastic changes as well.

    b.   Interviewer: You talk about some of the positive aspects of family life, but you also foresee changes in your life that you aren't comfortable with. Your feelings about having children seem ambivalent.

    c.   Interviewer: Have you talked with your wife about the concerns you have?

5.   The client is experiencing difficulty in implementing an action plan for a specified goal.

    a.   Interviewer: It seems that there is a discrepancy between your desire to become more assertive and your achievement of that goal. Could you help me to understand this discrepancy?

    b.   Interviewer: Are you uncomfortable when you try to be assertive in the situations we defined?

    c.   Interviewer: Sometimes it's difficult to succeed in reaching a specific goal. However, it seems worthwhile for you to keep working at this goal. Do you agree?

6.   Client: I've never been in trouble like this before. My parents don't have any idea that I smoke.

    a.   Interviewer: What do you think your parents will say?

    b.   Interviewer: Do your parents smoke?

    c.   Interviewer: How will you tell your parents what has happened?

7. Client: I just feel so alone. I don't have anybody who cares if I'm alive or dead. It seems as though everyone else has somebody who cares for them, but I'm all by myself.

   a. Interviewer: I've had some pretty low times myself, but I've never really felt as though there was nobody who cared. That must hurt.
   b. Interviewer: When I feel that no one cares for me, I feel really alone, too. It's really a heavy feeling. I think I have some idea of how you feel.
   c. Interviewer: When I feel that no one cares for me, I feel really alone, too. What do you do with your time when you feel this low?

8. Client (a parent who has been approached by a teacher about psychological testing for his child): My child doesn't need to be tested. What he needs is competent teachers who understand him. He's not dumb or crazy.

   a. Interviewer: You feel that we think your child is dumb or crazy.
   b. Interviewer: You feel strongly that your child doesn't need to be tested.
   c. Interviewer: It sounds as though you feel that the teachers here don't understand your son.

9. Client: Now that I've gone back to school, my husband is beginning to complain about the fact that I don't have any free time to spend with him and the kids. We both decided that it would be good for me to go back to school, but now I'm not so sure it's worth the hassle.

   a. Interviewer: Not long ago, I was completing school and dealing with the same kinds of problems at home. It was really frustrating for both my husband and I until we got things settled.
   b. Interviewer: My husband and I are struggling with the same issue. Since he's in school and spends a lot of time studying, I feel that the kids and I don't get to see him enough.
   c. Interviewer: You're finding that, since you've returned to school, a number of unforeseen problems have developed. What attempts have you made to solve these?

10. Client: They're going to be disappointed and hurt by what I did.

    a. Interviewer: Do they know that you drink?
    b. Interviewer: Why do you think they'll be hurt?
    c. Interviewer: Uh . . . huh. Go on.

11. Client (an elderly widower): I seem to be managing. (Looking off with no inflection in his voice): I take care of the house and the dog. And I get out some with my friends. (Hands folded and body slightly stooped): I'm managing pretty well, generally.

   a. Interviewer: I'm pleased to hear that you're managing. But right now you seem to be anxious. Could it be something that has happened recently?
   b. Interviewer: You say that you're managing, but your voice and your actions suggest that things might not be going so well. Could it be that you're still feeling sad or depressed?
   c. Interviewer: It's hard to believe that you're managing when you sit there looking away and speaking in a flat tone of voice. I wonder if you're feeling upset about something we talked about today.

12. The client is finding it difficult to define an obtainable goal.

   a. Interviewer: Sometimes it's difficult to define a concrete goal. Could you give me some examples of how you would like to behave in that situation?
   b. Interviewer: You're really finding it difficult to set a specific goal. Maybe we need to go back and start over. Does that seem appropriate to you?
   c. Interviewer: Sometimes it's difficult to define a concrete goal. First, I suggest that we consider the way in which you relate to your wife.

13. Client: We took your advice and set aside some time to talk with each other. At first, it was hard to find anything to talk about, but now it's a lot easier.

   a. Interviewer: It sounds as though you feel better with each other now.
   b. Interviewer: I suspect that it was difficult for you to start talking with each other again.
   c. Interviewer: It must be satisfying to find that you can talk with each other again.

14. Client: If I were still at home, maybe I could talk my parents into staying together.

   a. Interviewer: Have you thought about quitting school so that you could be there?
   b. Interviewer: You feel that, if you were home, you might be able to change things.
   c. Interviewer: Why would your presence make any difference?

15. Client: I get so frustrated. My mother feels hurt if I don't do what she wants. Doesn't she realize that I have my own life?

a.   Interviewer: That must be aggravating. My mother used to do that to me, too.
b.   Interviewer: My mother used to do that, too. I'm not sure that I've ever forgiven her for that.
c.   Interviewer: You must feel angry about that. I can remember when I felt that my mother wouldn't let me make my own decisions.

16.   Client: I really don't know whether I've been making any progress since we started. I've been working on my problems for a long time, but nothing has changed much . . . despite all the time and money.

a.   Interviewer: Although you feel as though you haven't made any progress, I've seen some. Let's look at that.
b.   Interviewer: You sound irritated with me because you don't think you've made any progress.
c.   Interviewer: It sounds as though you've become frustrated. Maybe you're wondering whether you should continue to see me.

17.   Client (looking out the window, speaking with no inflection in her voice):   My husband got a promotion, and we're moving next month. I'm really happy about that.

a.   Interviewer: You sound pleased with his promotion but apprehensive about moving.
b.   Interviewer: You must be excited about that. Where are you going to live?
c.   Interviewer: Are you unhappy about moving?

18.   Client (a student who studies very little):   I really want to get into medical school, but I'm not getting the grades. I don't know what I'm going to do.

a.   Interviewer: How do you expect to get into medical school, which requires a lot of studying, when you don't study now?
b.   Interviewer: Although you study very little, you say that you want to get into medical school. This is difficult for me to understand.
c.   Interviewer: You say that you want to get into medical school but that you don't have the grades because you don't study enough. With your study habits, do you really expect to be able to enter medical school?

19.   Client (a woman talking about her husband): When he's home, he doesn't pay much attention to what's happening there. He's always thinking about work. I'd really like him to be more interested in what's going on at home.

    a.   Interviewer: You realize that your husband is quite involved with his work right now, but, when he's home, you would like him to really be there.

    b.   Interviewer: It sounds as though you're perturbed because he's preoccupied with his work.

    c.   Interviewer: You'd like him to be more interested in you when he's home.

20. Choose the response that will initiate the termination phase of an interview.

    a.   Interviewer: We've attained the goals you set for yourself. I wonder whether it's time for us to terminate our interviews.

    b.   Interviewer: In the past several months, you've made considerable progress toward your goals. At this point, I wonder whether there are any other areas of concern that you would like to explore.

    c.   Interviewer: We seem to have been successful in reaching the goals you initially set for yourself. I've been thinking that perhaps we should terminate our contact after this interview. Do you agree?

Appendix:
ANSWERS TO
MULTIPLE-CHOICE TESTS

Chapter 2

1. b   2. c   3. a   4. b   5. a   6. a

Chapter 3

1. a   2. b   3. c   4. a   5. b   6. c

Chapter 4

1. b   2. c   3. a   4. b   5. a   6. c

Chapter 5

1. c   2. a   3. b   4. a   5. c   6. a

Chapter 6

1. a   2. c   3. c   4. a   5. b   6. a   7. c   8. c   9. a   10. a

Chapter 7

1. b   2. a   3. c   4. c   5. a   6. b

Chapter 8

1. a   2. b   3. b   4. a   5. a   6. c

Chapter 9

1. a   2. a   3. b   4. c   5. b   6. a

Chapter 10

1. b   2. a   3. c   4. b   5. c   6. a

Chapter 11

1. c   2. c   3. a   4. a   5. a   6. c   7. b   8. c   9. b   10. c   11. b
12. a   13. c   14. b   15. c   16. c   17. b   18. b   19. a   20. b

Interviewing involves a delicate interplay between a knowledge of "why" you are doing what you are doing and "how" to do it. The primary focus of this book is on "how" to interview. Instructors may wish to use this book in conjunction with one or more of the following books, which focus on the theoretical aspects of interviewing. Readers may wish to supplement the information they obtain here by consulting some of these books.

Benjamin, A. *The helping interview* (2nd ed.). Boston: Houghton Mifflin, 1974.

Brammer, L. M. *The helping relationship: Process and skills.* Englewood Cliffs, N.J.: Prentice-Hall, 1973.

Brammer, L. M., & Shostrom, E. L. *Therapeutic psychology: Fundamentals of counseling and psychotherapy* (3rd ed.). Englewood Cliffs, N.J.: Prentice-Hall, 1977.

Corey, G. *Theory and practice of counseling and psychotherapy.* Monterey, Calif.: Brooks/Cole, 1977.

Cormier, W. H., & Cormier, L. S. *Interviewing strategies for helpers: A guide to assessment, treatment, and evaluation.* Monterey, Calif.: Brooks/Cole, 1979.

Dugger, J. G. *The new professional: Introduction for the human services/mental health worker.* Monterey, Calif.: Brooks/Cole, 1975.

Egan, G. *The skilled helper: A model for systematic helping and interpersonal relating.* Monterey, Calif.: Brooks/Cole, 1975.

Eisenberg, S., & Delaney, D. J. *The counseling process* (2nd ed.). Chicago: Rand McNally, 1977.

Goldfried, M. R., & Davison, G. C. *Clinical behavior therapy.* New York: Holt Rinehart & Winston, 1976.

Ivey, A. E., & Authier, J. *Microcounseling: Innovations in interviewing, counseling, psychotherapy, and psychoeducation* (2nd ed.). Springfield, Ill.: C C Thomas, 1978.

Mueller, W. J. *Avenues to understanding the dynamics of therapeutic interactions.* New York: Appleton-Century-Crofts, 1973.

Okun, B. F. *Effective helping interviewing and counseling techniques.* North Scituate, Mass.: Duxbury Press, 1976.

Pietrofesa, J. J., Hoffman, A., Splete, H. H., & Pinto, D. V. *Counseling: Theory research, and practice.* Chicago: Rand McNally, 1978.

Pietrofesa, J. J., Leonard, G. E., & Van Hoose, W. *The authentic counselor* (2nd ed.). Chicago: Rand McNally, 1978.

Schulman, E. D. *Intervention in human services.* Saint Louis: Mosby, 1974.

Truax, C. B., & Carkhuff, R. R. *Toward effective counseling and psychotherapy: Training and practice.* Chicago: Aldine, 1967.